STACK STEVENS

STACK STEVENS

CORNWALL'S RUGBY LEGEND

STEVE TOMLIN
Foreword by John Inverdale

AMBERLEY

First published 2016

Amberley Publishing
The Hill, Stroud
Gloucestershire, GL5 4EP

www.amberley-books.com

British Library Cataloguing in Publication Data.
A catalogue record for this book is available from the British Library.

ISBN 978 1 4456 5291 7 (paperback)
ISBN 978 1 4456 5292 4 (ebook)

Typeset in 10pt on 13.5pt Sabon.
Typesetting and Origination by Amberley Publishing.
Printed in the UK.

Contents

Foreword

Rugby is special to Cornwall and Stack Stevens was a very special player.

This book recalls rugby's previous life with its strange mix of the amateur, the Corinthian and the serious that made it such a unique sport, many elements of which have been lost in the modern professional world.

It is evocative of the people, places and matches that Stack was an integral part of, and if you loved that era of the game, or think you would have done, then this book will take you there.

John Inverdale
2016

Introduction

Prop forwards are a hardy breed – they have to be. And perhaps they're just a little bit crazy as well. After all, what sort of person willingly spends his free afternoons with his face squashed up against the unshaven jowls of an equally fearsome-looking specimen while gasping and grunting into a steaming tunnel which is invariably dark, wet and smelly?

Only an infinitesimally tiny proportion of the human race will have ever placed themselves into that seemingly masochistic situation. So just for a moment imagine that you are in the front row and packing down at Pretoria's Loftus Versfeld stadium against the mighty Blue Bulls of the Northern Transvaal. The enormous stands are packed with over 60,000 screaming spectators and stretch up into the cloudless sky. You could almost be at some ancient Roman coliseum where the citizens are all baying for blood. Preferably yours.

The referee blows for a scrum and you instinctively wrap your arm around your mate who, like you, has travelled thousands of miles just to be there. You both know what's coming. It's what they picked you for. Facing you is over 130 kilos of raw Afrikaner beef comprising one of the ugliest looking bastards you have ever set eyes upon and he is glowering and cursing at you in a strange language that you don't even begin to understand. You couldn't give a toss anyway.

You stare coldly back into his eyes, not daring to blink or reveal even the tiniest chink of fear, rather like a poker player in an old Hollywood movie. You nevertheless have a deep inner conviction within you to draw upon. After all, you are a big strong lad yourself, you are as fit as you have ever been in your life and you have already been through something like this so many times back at home. Indeed you have met some pretty tough old hombres along the way and bounced back for more, so why should this be any different? But for all that your pulse rate is still going berserk.

Thud! With an unstoppable surge of power coming in from behind, you are launched forward to lock shoulders with this unlovable-looking lump in a massive jolt. A little cloud of choking dust swirls up from the parched pitch and sticks itself like cement to the little rivulets of sweat that are running into your eyes and mouth. An overpowering stench fills your slightly bloodied nose – a mixture of sweat, body odour, liniment and bad breath – as you try to ease your feet into that ideal scrummaging position you have practiced a thousand times before.

Some home town referee, who probably stopped playing at the age of eighteen and has never been in a scrum in his life, is shouting incomprehensible instructions and threats at you in that same weird foreign tongue. You just ignore the silly sod and concentrate everything upon what's coming next.

You take in a huge gulp of the fetid air, clamp your teeth into your gum-shield and then the ball comes in. A second surge of power comes on. It is simply huge and you feel it is going to crush you – rather like having a wall fall in on top of you or perhaps undergoing the G-force experienced by diving supersonic jetfighter pilots. Your eyes are shut tight by now but you can still see little swirls spinning around under your eyelids and hear a strange swishing noise in your ears as though somebody is running a bath next door. Your ribs feel they are about to collapse and then – suddenly – it's all over.

As the power comes off you stagger upright. Somebody gives you gratuitous clout but, already numb, you are barely aware of it. You have won the ball, your mouthy little scrum-half is hurling it out and then some silly bugger in the backs knocks it on and you are going to have to do it all over again. Alternatively the play takes off at a breakneck speed and it is your job to run forty yards to the breakdown. Forty yards – that doesn't sound very far but the sun is blisteringly hot and the air is thin up on the veldt so that every breath seems to be short-changing you. Suddenly the ball comes flying at your knees as a body crashes simultaneously into your chest and somehow you just fail to hold it. Those backs immediately all moan at you – stupid donkey prop!

That kind of situation has helped to give rise to the wicked myth that props are intrinsically not very bright and, in the tongue-in-cheek words of that entertaining TV rugby pundit Austin Healey, 'only good for pushing, eating, drinking and falling over'. Really? What does he know? How could he possibly understand when he has only ever stood out there calling the next move, numbering off the opposing backline and adjusting his shorts? As a former prop forward myself, I naturally reject this vile assertion totally. A bit crazy? Obviously. But stupid? Bollocks!

There are of course props who have been research scientists, poets, computer nerds, philosophy dons and brain surgeons. More typically, many of the very best of the breed have come out of equally dark tunnels down a Welsh coal pit or a Cornish tin mine where the virtues of sweat, toil and looking out for your mates are bred from the cradle. Such men frequently displayed an abiding love of music and a deep Christian – often Nonconformist – faith. Rugby and singing have been wedded for generations and go a lot deeper than just those rude ones so favoured by Old Boys' teams and medical students.

Another rich source of the propping species is farming. From tough sheep farmers in the hills of New Zealand to those sturdy Boers on the Transvaal or the wool producers of the Scottish borders, hundreds of these largely unsung heroes have been nurtured and flourished. They may have been unsung in that they rarely – if ever – hit the newspaper headlines with dazzling tries or last-ditch tackles but were nevertheless deeply appreciated by their glossier teammates in the backs – even if they never quite understood what the hell they were actually doing in there and had at last stopped moaning at them.

Such a man is Brian 'Stack' Stevens. He is quintessentially both a farmer and a proud Cornishman but one upon whom God bestowed a very special talent. This meant that he could surmount all that toil and stress and still have bags of energy and ball-handling skills to match each and every one of those other men, who were just standing around while he was pouring out his soul in all those scrums. The fact that he was able to capitalise upon it and overcome seemingly unsurmountable financial and geographical odds to represent his country no fewer than twenty-five times, travel the world and be hailed for the rest of his life as a local hero in the county of his birth, all with an infectious smile on his face, is the essence of his story.

I was also born and raised on a farm no more than a couple of miles as the crow flies from where he grew up and worked for his living. I am nearly seven years younger than Stack, which is quite a lot in one's formative years and, as such, could never have been counted as one of his close friends. However, we knew many of the same people, drank our beer in the same pubs and, more importantly, both played rugby for Penzance & Newlyn, which was our local club. The 'Pirates', as they are still known, are tucked away in the far-flung south-west tip of England and this was just one of the many steep hurdles he had to overcome in his quest for international recognition.

I was privileged to have played alongside him in the same front row on numerous occasions, but there the similarity ended. Whilst Stack worked away for long hours on his father's farm doing heavy manual labour, I never really had to do so. This had the result that, although we were both born with the same number of arms and legs, and were of roughly the same weight, he was exponentially stronger, fitter, faster and more accomplished than I could ever possibly have laid claim to be.

Amateur rugby in the 1960s and 1970s often provided the opportunity for reasonable club players like myself to rub shoulders in a very literal sense with some of the top performers of the day. However, the competing calls of career, family life and other interests generally precluded most of us from truly maximising whatever talent we did actually possess. It took a certain type of man to sacrifice nearly all of this – at least until his rugby career was behind him. In other words, whereas I and most of my club colleagues merely *played* rugby football, Stack Stevens truly *lived* it.

His international rugby career stretched to just over five years from December 1969 to March 1975 and was thus set against a background of some very turbulent times. First-class sportsmen and women inevitably live and play in something of a self-obsessed 'bubble' but external events repeatedly impacted upon the lives of the England rugby team of that era.

Northern Ireland was in flames, militant trade unions dominated the industrial scene, the war still raged in Vietnam and President Nixon was soon mired in the Watergate scandal. Meanwhile, the international spotlight on civil rights was switching from the burning crosses in Alabama and Mississippi to the plight of the non-white population suffering the indignities and miseries of apartheid in South Africa. In addition, terrorists murdered innocent hostages in the middle of an Olympic Games, while urban guerrillas threatened visiting sportsmen in Latin America. Men facing a top-level rugby match might be able to ignore much of this – but certainly not all.

When attempting to tell the story of someone's life it would be normal to sit down with a recording machine and talk for many hours with the man himself. Tragically, this has been impossible in this instance as for approximately the past ten years, Stack has been afflicted by a rare condition known as Progressive Supranuclear Palsy, which, among other things, renders normal speech virtually impossible. He is nevertheless extremely alert and has taken a very close interest in every aspect of this book as it has been developed.

Indeed, the idea of it ever being produced sprang from his devoted wife Jane who, during a conversation in their kitchen one afternoon, pointed out that whereas many of his England and British Lions colleagues from that era had seen their lives appear in print, her husband never had. This is therefore a belated attempt to address that imbalance.

Thus the opportunity arose for a friend and someone of his own generation to tell his life story. In the light of his debilitating illness, it was important that somebody put pen to paper and recorded an extraordinary life and one that could never happen in today's environment. It was a sporting life that took place a million miles away from the drug-tested, diet-fuelled, iron-pumped, DVD-analysed world of the modern professional rugby player. He was able to live in his home village, remain part and parcel of his local community, keep the same loyal friends, but through sheer bloody-mindedness still reach the summit of his sport.

Fortunately I have enjoyed fantastic support and encouragement not only from his family and friends but from so many of his old playing colleagues at club, county and international level, all of whom have generously given me both their time and reminiscences. Professional rugby football is now such a serious business. Since Stack's era the standards of fitness, preparation, coaching, medical support, tactics and refereeing have progressed beyond all recognition – as indeed have the physical size of the players themselves – but one is forced to question whether they ever derive even a fraction of the friendships and fun enjoyed by the players and officials of that time.

With this in mind I have deliberately and liberally sprinkled his story with some tall tales and hoary old anecdotes from his career just to try to capture a tiny flavour of the sheer joy of rugby at the time. Some may sound familiar and a few will inevitably have grown a bit in the telling – but then who cares?

Given the circumstances, this book could not have even been attempted without the help of so many people, and these include John Inverdale for kindly writing the foreword to this book, to Stack's immediate family – Jane, John and Sam Stevens – who have provided me with so much encouragement and endured my ceaseless requests for photos, press cuttings and phone numbers, as well as providing numerous delicious meals.

I am also greatly indebted to so many of his family, friends and past players who shared his rugby journey and generously gave me both their time and memories. These include Bill Beaumont, Mike Burton, Fran Cotton, John Dawes, David Duckham, Treve Dunstan, Gareth Edwards, Geoff Evans, Keith Fairbrother, Mike Gibson, Willie Goldsworthy, Paul Greaves, the late Roger Harris, Peter Hendy, Bob Hiller, Tony Horton, Roger Hosken, Ian King, Jason Leonard, Mike Luke, Peter Luke, Terry Luke, Anne May, Charlie May, John May, Willie John McBride, Ian McLauchlan, Ray McLoughlin, Peter Michell, David Muirhead, Tony Neary, Kenny Plummer, David Powell, Peter Preece, Terry Pryor, John Pullin, Chris Ralston, Graeme Roberts, Roger Roberts, Peter Rossborough, Derek Rowe, Geoff Rowe (Jethro), Ivan Rowe, Don Rutherford, Mary Sargeant, Juliet Shore, John Skewes, John Spencer, Tony Stephens, John Tellam, Delme Thomas, Roger Uttley, Geoff Vingoe, Jim Walton, Jan Webster, Lionel Weston, Phil Westren, John White, Pippa Wiegersma, Alvin Williams and Tinky Youngson, plus my wife Micky for all her diligent proofreading and support as well as Alan Murphy of Amberley Publishing for his help and encouragement.

I would also wish to thank David Norrie and Coloursport, *Western Morning News*, Tom Roskrow (Truro), Mirror Group, *Cornish Times*, Penzance & Newlyn RFC and the Stevens family for the use of their photographs.

To each and every one of these I would like to express my grateful thanks.

Growing Up in Cornwall

In an exploration of West Cornwall, the traveller might stumble upon the little granite village of Godolphin, tucked away down the narrow twisting lanes. Perhaps his satnav would eventually lead the family to the large Tudor National Trust manor house which has dominated the area for centuries, but, without it, he would probably become completely lost.

For many years that great house had been the country seat of the dukes of Leeds, who owned all the mining rights in the area since those distant times (and indeed right up until the mid-nineteenth century) and nearly all the locals had once risked their lives and health in the back-breaking and often dangerous pursuit of tin. One of the local mines, named Wheal Reeth, might have sounded vaguely familiar, as it was used as the name of the tin mine in the popular TV series *Poldark*. The Duke's own Great Work Mine had employed hundreds of people but all of that had long since died out by the time young Cecil Bailey Stevens – always to be known as 'CB' – returned to Cornwall from serving with what we now term the Fleet Air Arm in France during the First World War.

CB was the only son of a house builder named Thomas Stevens, who had also gained a reputation as a stained-glass expert in nearby Penzance and whose skills had taken him out to work on a new clock tower at Durban in South Africa. His work had been so well received that he had tried but failed to persuade his wife to come out to join him and settle there. Her bags were packed and, had she not somehow won the marital tug of war, perhaps her famous grandson might one day have grown up to have been a Springbok.

Before his war service, CB had trained as a miller in Camborne and, upon his return to Cornwall his father Thomas purchased a mill for him just outside of Godolphin, where he married and settled down. He was a man steeped in the virtues of hard work. The business did well so he began to expand into farming and bought one of the village's local shops, which his wife Beatrice then ran for many years. She bore him six children in all, by which time the family had moved into a house in the village next door to the shop.

The first three sons were christened Cecil junior, who left behind the farming life to run a garage in Plymouth, then Roy who followed his father to run the local mill and Owen who, although also a farmer, did so at the other end of Cornwall at St Neot near Liskeard. These were followed by two sisters: Mary, who went into the teaching profession, and Anne, who married a rugby-playing auctioneer but one who played for local rivals Redruth.

The youngest was a bouncing boy who came into the world on 2 January 1940, just four months into the Second World War. They gave the little baby the same initials of C. B. but, with a second Cecil already in the family, this time it was to be Claude Brian and, despite being known around the world of rugby as 'Stack', back in Godolphin he remains Brian to this day. If the name Claude seems unusual for a Cornish farmer, he was apparently named after a Frenchman who had befriended CB during the First World War.

Children were usually born at home in those days and, despite the devoted care of the local midwife, Nurse Penrose, Beatrice went down with double pneumonia and, with penicillin not yet readily available to most people in those pre-NHS days, that was then a very serious situation. She soon recovered but her new baby was lovingly cared for by a cherished daily help called Muriel Andrews, and as such Muriel must gain some of the credit for the early nurturing of one of the strongest prop-forwards of his generation.

Since the closure of the mines the local villagers had adapted to working the land in smallholdings – tiny farms of a few acres supporting perhaps some cows and pigs, vegetables and perhaps spring flowers. There was little money to spare but it was a healthy outdoor life; nobody ran short of food and conditions in Cornwall during the 1930s had been undoubtedly less cruel than in the industrial areas of Britain during the Depression. The village had three shops, tennis courts, a pub, an Anglican church plus a Methodist chapel with a Sunday school attached. The 500 or so villagers all knew each other well, and undoubtedly had their petty squabbles, but invariably helped each other along in times of need. However, CB was far more ambitious. He bought two good-sized farms and for a short while he owned the then-derelict Godolphin Manor along with all its attendant land as well.

At the time of Brian's entry into the world, village life received a big shock with the appearance of dozens of evacuees. The school doubled in size, rationing was beginning to bite and many young men were once again enlisting in the forces. As the war progressed, local farm labour was supplemented by many Italian and a few German prisoners of war, and little Brian grew up with them all around him. Living in the centre of a peaceful village, his childhood was blissfully happy with lots of friends, a dog and five older brothers and sisters to look out for him.

With hardly any traffic it was easy to play with a ball in the road and running and catching one came to him just as easily as kicking it. Kids could play perfectly safely on bikes and they also built contraptions which were known as 'butts'. These were little self-propelled chariots mounted upon old pram wheels and steered from the front with heavy string called binder-twine which could readily be found on any farm at the time. These butts could be raced down a slope and, with practice, could act like fairground dodgem cars.

At the end of the war, and just as Brian began at Godolphin School, CB suffered a serious accident when he was crushed by part of a wall falling on top of him. Indeed, for a while he was on the danger list and spent weeks in Redruth hospital. As the oldest of the Stevens children, Roy stepped up to run the farm as well as the mill, and perhaps this persuaded Brian to take an initial interest in farming – a point not lost upon his recuperating father. To add to their woes, before long Roy then also had a nasty motorbike accident and was laid up in Truro Hospital for a period.

His two elder sisters had been to a private school in Penzance and, at the age of seven, Brian might well have followed them to another one, St Erbyn's, which was a local preparatory school in the town. This was run by a rugby-mad headmaster named Rex Carr, who not only introduced young boys to rugby by the age of eight or nine, but prepared them to go on to the various public schools around the country, something that inevitably entailed becoming a boarder. It is believed that St Erbyn's had been full at the time and thus could not take Brian immediately. Furthermore, the seven-year-old made it very clear that he had no intention of ever going away to a boarding school, despite the fact that an older brother was already there, and would run away if anyone dared to send him to one. Had things worked out differently he would have almost certainly begun his rugby career very much earlier.

Although he never particularly enjoyed swimming, his sister Anne would take him to nearby Marazion to learn and CB had a motor boat on the Helford River and so he splashed about down there as well. But, perhaps unusually for his time in West Cornwall, he always remained very much a land animal. One of his earliest mates was a lad in the village called Willie Goldsworthy, who remains a firm friend to this day. Willie recalled:

We were kids always looking for a bit of mischief but Brian had those older brothers and sisters and had learned very early on how to look after himself. Even then he could be pretty crafty too and usually managed to keep out of trouble.

Around three miles away from Godolphin lay another ex-mining village named Leedstown, which had a school enjoying a much better reputation than Godolphin's at the time. Accordingly, Brian used to cycle there through the lanes, which continued right up to when he left school at fifteen to concentrate upon the farm. The headmaster was a Mr Pelleymounter who, like many others with large classes to teach, preferred to concentrate upon those who appeared academically ambitious and left the others more or less to their own devices.

Brian was a bright, quick-witted and fun-loving lad but was far more interested in the open air and tractors than Pythagoras or the convoluted goings-on of the Tudors and Stuarts. Woodwork, on the other hand, provided much more opportunity for fun. They were taught by a poor man, Mr Beam, in Godolphin where there was an available workshop. This meant that Brian could effectively miss most of a day of school without getting himself into trouble. All kids like woodwork for the God-given chance to bang things about and hit one another with pieces of wood, although one apparently bounced off his head and smashed a window.

In later life Brian occasionally reflected on the fact that his parents had not compelled him to take his schooling a little more seriously and so in due course he made certain that his own two sons took maximum advantage of a full and varied education. However, despite any lack of formal qualifications, Brian was undoubtedly a quick learner and could be described as very savvy, or 'schemey' as they say in Cornwall. He also had an innate Cornish cunning, which served him well on the rugby field with both awkward opponents and gullible referees. He once told his sister that he might have liked to have been a teacher like herself but, whether consciously or subconsciously, the hard-working CB had somehow allowed him to drift through school as he clearly wanted him back to help with running the farm as soon as possible.

Sport, however, was a different matter, although once again facilities were spartan in the extreme. According to one of his old classmates, Roger Roberts, who later played rugby with the Pirates himself, there was just a small and extremely muddy field with only one set of (soccer) goalposts – hence they did kick a football about but there was no sign of rugby.

Roger recalled:

One of our teachers was a chap called Max Biddick who played on the wing for Camborne and Cornwall but there was no opportunity for him to teach us any rugby at all. We lads used to run around kicking an old football about and on a Monday Max would turn out without bothering to change. He would just roll up his socks over his suit and pull on some boots and strut around in the mud. Brian spent most of the afternoon trying to blast the mud-encrusted lump which passed as a ball straight at him followed by a loud 'Sorry sir' whenever he scored a hit ... Once an uncle of mine who worked at Truro School found us an old rugby ball case, my dad got hold of a bladder for it and we tied it up with a bootlace and so the school had its very first rugby ball.

The distinguished rugby career of Stack Stevens had thus made a very modest start.

Before his rugby-playing days had even begun he had already managed to lose his front teeth thanks to a misunderstanding with a tractor starting handle. In later years he rarely bothered with a gum shield, but would invariably hand his false teeth over to the Pirates' long-suffering first-aid man 'Bosun' James just as he was about to take the field and then just treat everyone to a distinctive gap-toothed grin.

Despite being something of a workaholic, CB enjoyed sport, having played a little cricket, and like most people in Cornwall he liked to follow rugby even though he had not actually played it himself. One evening he took his nine-year-old son along to see the great Cardiff team, packed with famous Welsh internationals, play against the Penzance and Newlyn Pirates. The noise, colour and excitement of thousands of people jammed like sardines around the touchlines must have touched a nerve and a few years later he was being taken up to Twickenham on the train by his father to see Pirates' legend John Kendall-Carpenter play for England against Ireland. Again it must have been a thrilling but exhausting trip as he apparently slept the whole way back to Camborne in the compartment's luggage rack.

By the time he left school in 1955 he had already been spending most of his spare time working on one of CB's two farms in the area, so the transition to full-time farm work was fairly seamless. He soon acquired a small BSA bantam bike – essentially a bicycle with a tiny 50cc motor to help you very slowly over hills – initially to get around the farms but it also enabled him to visit Helston and even Penzance if the weather was kind. He had also discovered beer and, as his house and mother's shop were right next door to the village pub, the underage drinker used to try to outwit his mother by clambering in through the back window.

Around this time he joined the Praze Young Farmers Club, which was actually based in Leedstown. These clubs played an important role in rural life at the time and, with some 25,000 current members in the UK, evidently still do so today. Farming can be a solitary life – working alone in a field all day or driving a tractor – and they provided a vital opportunity to put on a collar and tie, go to dances, meet girls and generally feel part of the wider world. Clubs from various villages would meet up and long-lasting friendships forged.

Terry Luke, another future Pirate player, was a YFC member at another village called St Hilary and they struck up one such enduring friendship. Terry is a couple of years older than Brian, had played rugby at school and, most importantly, had both a car and a driving licence. The YFC in Cornwall used to run an inter-area rugby competition and Terry lost no time in taking his new fit, strong young friend along to see what he could do. Brian had seen the Pirates play quite a few times, been to Twickenham and thus knew the basics of the game but, apart from those carefree kick-abouts with Max Biddick, had as yet never actually played in a proper match. Being big and strong, he immediately went into the forwards and soon two games were played at Newquay and Wadebridge.

If his talent was incredibly raw, it was nevertheless blindingly obvious. The touchline sages nodded in approval. This boy could play.

2

Rugby Then and Now

The lengthy rugby career of Stack Stevens spanned almost a quarter of a century between the mid-1950s and about 1980. Given that this is now many years distant, it may be helpful to be reminded of just what an enormous contrast exists between rugby as it was then played, administered and reported, with that of today. This is not to try to extol the virtues of the supposedly 'good old days' but simply to give some meaningful context to his extensive rugby career.

First and foremost, it was a passionately amateur sport at every level, from the famous international star right down to the portly little fellow with odd socks puffing around for the Extra B XV in front of no spectators and only twelve other men in his team. Many sports during that time were nominally amateur, including tennis, athletics, hockey and swimming. Others, such as football, cricket and boxing, had a rigid demarcation between amateurs and professionals within their umbrella organisations. One by one they blurred the differences but Rugby Union held on, with an almost religious fervour, to an amateur-only purity until the mid-1990s – long after Stack's career had come to an end.

Players were not only denied any remuneration whatsoever for playing the game (and only a very few at senior level were provided with any travelling expenses either) but players were generally obliged to fork out a match fee for the privilege of playing. Usually this was a fairly small amount to defray the cost of getting shirts washed and chipping in for a jug or two of beer but the principle was clear: you paid for your rugby – rugby did not pay you. Furthermore, you provided your own boots, shorts and training gear and, at junior club levels, often socks and shirts as well. Kit was generally heavy, hard-wearing and the very idea of any of it bearing a sponsor's logo would have been met by a gasp of horror. Boots were universally black and certainly anyone stepping out in any of those yellow or pink affairs we see today would have received some very strange looks and a few politically incorrect remarks.

The game was also administered on a purely honorary basis by elected ex-players who saw it as a matter of pride to 'give something back to the game'. Praiseworthy though that undoubtedly was, this tended to add to the innate climate of ultra-conservatism, reflecting a spirit of 'well it was good enough for me, so it is good enough for them'. Progressive new initiatives were generally viewed with suspicion at best and outright hostility at worst, all frequently based on the vague notion that it might somehow compromise the 'amateur ethos of the game', although nobody could ever clearly define what that actually was. While there was a very great deal to commend a major contact sport being played without any taint of money, it also led to much 'amateurishness' in matters of training, preparation, skills improvement, medical care and player safety which, with the benefit of hindsight, seems to have been a great pity.

The Union game's greatest bête noire was the sport of Rugby League, which could offer a talented player a substantial signing-on fee and then modest match fees and bonuses. 'Going North' was viewed as the ultimate sin and anyone who did so was immediately cut off from all contact with the Union game for the rest of his life. Players who could look forward to rewarding business careers rarely took much interest, although a few, mainly from Wales and the north of England, sometimes rose to the bait. As a man with a well-defined farming future, Stack was never seriously tempted and, of those among his contemporaries who did take the plunge, it was probably only John Bevan of Wales and Keith Fielding of England who made much of a success of the transition. It is perhaps no coincidence that they both played on the wing where the code differences were far less pronounced than in most other positions on the field.

With very few exceptions, all matches were nominally 'friendlies' in the sense that there were no formal leagues and few cup competitions. The County Championship was keenly fought and for Cornishmen like Stack Stevens it was something of an annual obsession. It was also one of the precious few occasions when a man playing outside the elite circle of senior clubs might be noticed by the national selectors. Without the meritocracy of a league structure, clubs arranged their own fixtures and often these continued on a reciprocal basis for decades. As a result there were occasionally some embarrassing mismatches but, as the best players tended to be drawn inexorably to the clubs with the most attractive fixture lists, the status quo was generally maintained. Only in the early 1970s did cup knockout competitions begin to appear both on a county and national basis in England and Wales with the RFU version ironically being sponsored by a cigarette company.

Some leading clubs might have their games reported in the national broadsheets but it was down to just local papers for the great majority. Metropolitan clubs like Wasps, Rosslyn Park and Richmond might field a dozen or more teams on a Saturday and a player's ability to rise through the ranks was largely at the mercy of the respective team captains who exchanged impressions at a Monday night selection meeting. Most clubs ran two or three teams with standards of fitness, refereeing and playing pitches deteriorating rapidly as one descended to the lower levels. Some clubs ran an Under-18 Colts team but mini-rugby only began to appear in the late 1970s. There were a few veterans' teams but women's rugby was still virtually unknown. Rugby club members were certainly not all unreconstructed male chauvinists but candidly quite a few still were, and the fate of many wives and girlfriends who loyally supported their menfolk was often to be asked to butter the sandwiches and help with the washing up.

Crowds, even at top-level matches, were generally numbered in hundreds rather than thousands and most clubs took far more money over the bar than they ever gleaned through the turnstiles. Some clubs had a grandstand and floodlights but many did not and when lights did appear they were often only suitable for midwinter training rather than for the playing of actual matches.

Even the most cursory look at a top-level match from that period on YouTube or on a DVD would illustrate a number of major differences in the way the game was played and refereed compared with today. The first thing one would notice would probably be the physical size of the players themselves. A player such as Stack, standing around six feet tall and weighing around 215 pounds, would then be considered a relatively big man, more than adequate to prop an international scrum. A lock-forward at six-foot-four would be considered tall and if he weighed 230 pounds he would be regarded as a bit of a giant. Today, this is about par for many professional centre threequarters.

Line-outs were often something of a mad scramble, with players usually pushing, elbowing and barging into one another. Jumpers were not supposed to be lifted when they took off but were expected to rely upon their own natural spring to outreach their opponents. An experienced prop like Stack could usually get away with a sly 'hoik' on his jumper's shorts to gain him an extra few inches but always risked being penalised by the referee for doing so.

The standard of tackling was usually significantly lower than today and all that defensive jargon like 'blitz', 'drift' and 'line-speed' were still far away into the future, although good defenders already did them naturally. Handling was far less sure than it usually is today, when it is probably helped by the better design of modern rugby balls. There were no goal-kicking tees and a man had to create a small mound in the turf on which to place the ball, which was frequently kicked on its point in what was then known popularly as the 'torpedo' style.

The referee was the sole man in charge and even at top level he had no technology or even referees' assistants to aid him. Touch-judges were appointed by the clubs themselves and were confined to waving a flag if the ball went over the touchline and to signal successful kicks at goal. There were no yellow cards or sin bins, and any foul or unfair play was invariably dealt with by a stern 'ticking off' from the referee and a penalty kick. It was extremely rare for a man to be sent off the field and referees tended to avoid doing so if they possibly could. Indeed many long-standing 'whistlers' would happily boast that they had never felt it had ever been necessary to do so.

Scrums were far less rigidly refereed but ironically almost never collapsed. The referee insisted the ball was put in more or less straight, and rival front rows fought out their own game-within-a-game with hookers living up to their name by being acknowledged experts at hooking back the ball. They were perforce smaller and more flexible than their modern counterparts but, apart from the very best ones, were not expected to contribute as much to general handling, tackling nor, until the early 1970s, throwing in to the line-outs.

Many people described Stack Stevens as having been a fine technical prop. At the time he was playing the skills and tactics involved were somewhat different from those employed today. Reference will be made repeatedly in this book to the 'loosehead' and the 'tighthead' propping positions. For the uninitiated, the loosehead packs onto the left shoulder of the hooker and, when his team has been awarded the scrum by the referee, the ball is put in on his side of the scrum. Stack's role was to help his hooker by ensuring, as far as possible, that the tunnel was high and clear enough for the hooker to have an uninterrupted view of the ball coming in and prevent the other team from either disrupting him or pushing his team backwards off the ball. As such it was an essentially defensive skill with a vested interest in keeping things as smooth as possible.

Conversely, the tighthead, packing onto his hooker's right arm, would try to keep a straight push on his team's own put-in and then outsmart the opposition on theirs. He might do this by either pushing the opponents off it, lowering the scrum to an uncomfortable position or, if sufficiently strong and adept to take all the weight on his left foot for a split second, to try to sweep the ball back with his outside right foot as the opposing scrum-half put the ball in.

As a consequence, scrums played a more important role in the game in those days with often thirty occurring in a game. Because of that, a dominant front row could make a massive contribution to the eventual outcome of a rugby match. As can be imagined, there were hundreds of tricks of the trade and, with minimal formal coaching, a young prop would generally have to learn them from his elders or by hard and sometimes painful experience.

Most props had a strong preference for one position or the other and their muscles developed accordingly. Stack Stevens could play happily on either side but at international level he predominantly worked as a loosehead, wearing the Number 1 shirt on his back. Today, packs of forwards are probably 20 per cent heavier and, with full-time professional coaching, the combined skills and weight distribution of sixteen huge men driving against one another in a closely coordinated shove presents a very different set of issues – including those of physical safety. Indeed, the pressure generated is so immense that a present-day 'hooker' often dare not lift his foot from the ground for fear of his team immediately being shoved off the ball and probably incurring a penalty kick. Rugby lawmakers and referees have struggled to deal with this and innumerable scrums have ended up either collapsing or resulting in the referee awarding yet another penalty to one or other team with perhaps only the sketchiest idea of what may or may not have actually happened. Such is progress.

The only television station to show rugby was the BBC, who generally restricted their coverage to international matches, a few games when touring teams such as the Springboks were in the UK and the annual Varsity match. Almost invariably the commentary would be heard in the rich Border tones of Hawick headmaster Bill McLaren, who could somehow remain irreproachably impartial even when the Scots were performing at Murrayfield. There was never any advertising on shirts, pitches or even pitchside hoardings, which of course suited the BBC admirably.

Then there was always the notorious rugby tour. Stack's club Penzance & Newlyn – and indeed all clubs in the West Country – hosted swarms of them almost non-stop during the September and April of each season. They were looked forward to eagerly both by the touring teams themselves and also by the spectators and players in Cornwall and Devon, who got the opportunity to watch and lock horns in action with many of the best men of the day. In time, and with the increased availability of cheaper flights, many senior clubs began to look more towards sunnier climes in Kenya and Bermuda, but for all that the practice still survived.

Stack's senior career was to take him to New Zealand (twice), South Africa, Fiji, the USA and Canada, but he only went on a single club trip with the Pirates and that was to south Wales when he was still a teenager. Those major overseas tours were unquestionably life-enhancing experiences and lasting friendships were forged between men from very different backgrounds. The rugby might vary, the refereeing might be infuriating, the standards of accommodation might not be of the best, but they were invariably enormous fun. This held equally true whether it was a Lions tour to face the All Blacks or just a boozy college team celebrating their Easter vacation in Newquay.

The period around 1970 was the time in rock music of people like Jim Morrison and Janis Joplin, and touring bands lived a frenetic life of sex, drugs and rock 'n' roll. For rugby tours you would have to substitute gallons of beer for any notion of drugs and the singing might be a bit variable but fit young men away from home were going to have a good time, come what may. There would be endless pranks, things would get 'acquired' or broken, food fights were par for the course and many a group of errant medical students would find themselves kicked out of a seaside hotel in the middle of the night by an infuriated landlady.

There was always an extra unwritten rule of rugby that you would never have found in the IRB Law Book but one which was virtually never broken: the mantra that 'what goes on tour stays on tour'. In other words, once players returned to their homes and families, an *omerta*, which would have done credit to the Sicilian mafia, would descend, and there matters would lie untroubled, often to the grave. There are many anecdotes to relate about quirky incidents on Stack's various trips abroad but in principle that unwritten law will remain inviolate.

In fact, most of what occurred would just be high-spirited, if sometimes embarrassing, pranks. One of these was the time-honoured tradition of a 'Fire Brigade'. These guys always had a penchant for invading other players' rooms, rearranging things and, if possible, supplementing their deeds with the use of hotel fire extinguishers and water hoses. Woe betide the smooth talker who had convinced a young lady to join him up in his room for a 'coffee', as he was likely to have his door burst open and both his and her ardour rudely dampened by a jet of freezing water. Old tour hands would often try to minimise this risk by pinching someone else's keys for their illicit trysts, but even this could backfire spectacularly, one example being when, during one particular Lions tour, a double bluff had been called and the unlucky recipients of a high-pressure hose had been an elderly pastor and his wife who were staying in town for a church convention.

International rugby tours were of course much more newsworthy than a humble club excursion but the reporters who accompanied the players abroad at that time were true rugby men and not nosey newshounds. Thus they restricted their accounts rigidly to the actual matches, training and injury reports and loyally left it at that. There were also no social media, smartphones or red top newspapers snooping around for lurid stories. Sadly, this is no longer the case, as the England World Cup players in 2011 found to their cost.

When the rugby supporter in the early 1970s went along to Twickenham to watch the Stacks, Duckhams and Ripleys strutting their stuff, they would have entered a cavernous old stadium which looked almost exactly as it had done in the early 1930s when George V used to visit it. There were three tall, dark, double-decker stands and a huge propped bank at the south end of the ground where a spectator could still watch a match for a couple of quid. There were precious few facilities, no floodlights and sometimes spectators had to spend the last twenty minutes of a match peering through the gathering gloom. Nobody really seemed to mind as they had never known anything different.

The crowd itself was different as well. Corporate entertaining was still some time into the future and so the car parks were full of Rovers, Triumph Stags and a few shiny Bentleys, from which sumptuous picnics would emerge to be washed down with expensive bottles of wine. Old friends would meet up and most seemed to be 'ruggah buggahs' from the shires as opposed to the boozy bankers from Canary Wharf who appear to noisily dominate the place today.

There were as yet no tiers of replica shirts on display either. Hordes of singing Welshmen would appear in red scarves and sprouting leeks. Scots in kilts, Irish priests sporting shamrock and hidden bottles of potcheen, Frenchmen dancing around in berets with brass bands and cockerels – they were always there in abundance. Meanwhile, the poor old buttoned-up English had to contend themselves with an overpriced little white nylon rosette, which had usually fallen to bits by half-time. Programmes all looked the same with the front cover a diagonal of England's white with the team colour of the opponents of the day and would set you back 1s 6d, which jumped up to ten pence after decimalisation.

Pre-match entertainment, in so far as it existed, was invariably provided by an immaculately turned-out military band, who would lead up to the anthems by belting out a selection of tunes from West End stage shows plus a few old faithfuls like 'Loch Lomond' or 'Danny Boy', depending upon who was in opposition that day. As for pom-pom girls, fireworks, clouds of impenetrable smoke and laser shows? Not a chance.

International and top professional rugby today is as much a business as it is a sport. It is worth repeating that the standards of training, coaching, tactical appreciation, playing kit, refereeing, pitches, medical care, spectator amenities and media coverage, together with the sheer size and pace of the players, have all progressed massively since the time Stack was pounding the turf for England's cause.

Whether it is all as much fun is however a moot point.

3

The Young Pirate

As the Allies battered their way towards Germany, and the war at last appeared to be all but won, two fierce local rivals in Cornish rugby had sat down and agreed to amalgamate and form a club known as Penzance & Newlyn. With an obvious reference to Gilbert and Sullivan, they were to be popularly known throughout the land as the Pirates. By the mid-1950s they were already well established, enjoying an enviable reputation for playing exciting rugby and as very hospitable hosts to dozens of leading teams from England and Wales, who loved to tour Cornwall and Devon during September and also around Easter.

The club had also developed a number of fine players and had already produced two England internationals, although it was still to be some years before Stack eventually became their third. In the early post-war years they enjoyed huge local support at a time of austerity – no television, most things still on ration and very few motor cars.

When he first contemplated playing rugby back in the mid-1950s Redruth was, at least temporarily, the top club in the county and was situated almost as close to Godolphin. However, Penzance was very much the home town of the Stevens family. His grandfather had worked there; it was where his mother did her shopping and both his sisters went to school in the town, and while the bus service was infrequent and seemingly took forever, it could at least get you there and back again each day. For those reasons alone his destiny was always going to be with the Pirates.

The club were still riding high by the summer of 1956 when the sixteen-year-old young farmer, along with his pal Willie Goldsworthy, first turned up at training with the club's Colts Team known as Mounts Bay. Jim Laker had just taken his world-record nineteen wickets against Australia, Prime Minister Anthony Eden was struggling with mounting problems in Egypt and Cyprus, the press had cottoned on to the shenanigans of Dr Bodkin Adams allegedly bumping off wealthy widows in Eastbourne and Princess Margaret was finally giving up the chance of marrying Captain Peter Townsend. Meanwhile, kids of Brian's age were all going crazy over Elvis and his 'Heartbreak Hotel'. In his case, however, getting to grips with the rudiments of rugby seemed much more appealing.

Mounts Bay was an established nursery team for the main club and was coached by three former Pirate players named Des James, Ben Jelbert and Ben Perrin. It is perhaps more than a coincidence that the latter two had both been prop-forwards in their recent playing days and were thus not slow to recognise a potential propping diamond if ever they saw one. Although Brian had not played very much organised rugby to date, all that hard farm work under the demanding eye of his father now came to the fore. He was big for his age, could seemingly run for hours, had good hand and eye coordination and, to cap it all, was already unusually strong and physically hard.

Brian attributed Ben Perrin with being a major influence upon him at that early stage. Ben was a town character who had been a prop for Penzance both before and after the war and possessed the hairiest chest and arms that most people had ever set eyes upon. He could often be seen in the depths of winter pushing his bicycle around the town clad in just dungarees and his vest. Although a delightful fellow, he was not a man to trifle with, often filling in at weekends as the doorman at the local dance hall near the promenade, where even the local teddy boys of that era gave him a wide berth.

Ben's main job had been as a firefighter and the fire station was situated close to the rugby field. One day the siren went off in the middle of a match and he apparently excused himself to the referee and ran off in his rugby kit to leap onto the wailing fire engine, leaving the other twenty-nine players to get on with the game on their own. For all that, he had a heart of gold and struck a strong bond with his young protégé.

A teammate from the time was Derek Rowe, who recalled:

In those days Brian played in the back row and was always on the move – never far from the ball. We played against all the local clubs' Under Eighteen teams like St Ives, Redruth, Falmouth, some of the rugby-playing schools plus a home and away fixture with Kelly College from Tavistock and an annual visit by a team from Germany.

One evening at training we were practicing our tackling in pairs – head on and one against one. I went first and threw myself at him but it was like hitting a granite gatepost. I just bounced off him and landed on the turf gasping for breath. Remember he was then only sixteen, but he stooped down and with just one arm lifted me bodily into the air and popped me gently back onto my feet. All the time he was grinning at me like a Cheshire cat.

He also had a habit of playfully grabbing people by their tie or shirt front and lifting them off their toes. He would be laughing when he did it but he clearly wasn't someone you wanted to upset. However, much of the time he was very quiet and this just added to the effect. The Colts then had another forward who later developed into a very useful player in his own right. However, he was rather a loudmouth and actually a bit of a bully. He once tried it on with Brian who just stared soundlessly back at him and laughed in his face. He was left alone after that.

Another player in that team was Tony Stephens, who recalled:

In those days players under eighteen were not even allowed into the clubhouse – let alone to buy a drink – so we all used to go into a couple of the pubs in town. We were a close-knit group of friends and often got together during the week for a pint or to go swimming. Brian could only join us at weekends as he was always busy working on the farm ten miles away and although he never swam he loved to muck in and have fun with the rest of us whenever he could.

We used to have a few beers and then go down to the dance hall – where Perrin usually waved us in without paying – and it was our chance to meet a few girls. Brian was popular with them as he was a bit of a hunk but it was all very casual and innocent. He wasn't really bothered and just lived for his farming and rugby.

Already, though a young player, his biggest assets were his stamina and strength. He and his older brother Roy would have a regular contest, which involved standing on the back of a lorry and hurling hundredweight sacks of grain back and forth to one other until one was exhausted and had to give up – sibling rivalry ensured that neither ever gave in easily. He was also blessed with the ability to run all over the park for eighty minutes seemingly without ever getting tired, which allowed him to be involved in the game more than anyone else. However, even with the bantam bike he was unable to join in as often as he would have liked with the training nights in Penzance (he hitched lifts whenever he could) but he would pound the lanes and beaches around Godolphin like Forrest Gump. Allied to his constant farm work, this soon made him both the strongest and fittest kid on the block.

In his second and final season with the Colts, rugby in Cornwall received a big boost when the county team reached its first Championship final since the 1920s. Along with thousands of excited Cornishmen, Brian and some of his mates made the long trip by train up to Coventry to see their heroes battle it out with a Warwickshire team that included most of the current England team. A photograph duly appeared in the press of the seven of them, with Brian in a smart new duffle coat, parading an enormous replica Cornish pasty to the delight of the crowds packed onto the terraces. The excitement and the opportunity struck a deep chord in his mind, but little did he imagine that a mere four years later he himself would be back out on that same pitch battling it out with Warwickshire once again. The game itself was played in a partial snowstorm and in the bitter cold he somehow caught a severe chill.

It was now the moment to embark upon adult rugby. It was also around this time that he acquired the name 'Stack', which is how he has been universally known in the rugby world ever since; however, as mentioned, he is still called Brian by his family and neighbours. There are two stories as to its origin. One is that he was playing cards with some of the older players and, having run a bit short of money, continued to stack rather than place a bet until an exasperated teammate named Tony Stevenson duly christened him as 'Stack'. Another version insists he acquired the nickname when he gave the excuse that he was busy stacking corn for being late for pre-season scrummaging practice and was promptly told by a senior teammate, Peter Michell, 'Well now go and stack that bloody scrum.' Whichever version you prefer, 'Stack' certainly stuck and will be the name applied to him henceforward.

Stack began in the reserves, still playing in the back row, but immediately it became apparent that his was a very special talent. The reserves' captain was Geoff Vingoe, an ex-Loughborough winger who had returned to Cornwall to teach and was combining a final year of playing with serving as a club selector. Vingoe takes up the story:

> This lad was not only strong beyond his years but was incredibly mobile and seemed to have an innate instinct on how to cut corners and anticipate events so that he would invariably arrive at the breakdown at precisely the right moment. Many good players develop this skill by the time they are nearing thirty and saving their legs but here was a young man bursting with energy who could somehow do it instinctively. He also had pace, good handling skills and could seemingly run all day. After a storming performance in a match at a little place called St Day, I told the selectors he was already far too good for second team rugby and should be given a shot in the first team.

What Geoff could never have contemplated in his wildest dreams was that Stack would one day become his son-in-law.

At 3 p.m. on Saturday 8 November 1958, a young Glaswegian boy stepped out onto the football pitch to make his senior Scottish League debut for Queen's Park at Stranraer. His name was Alex Ferguson. At precisely the same moment, over 500 miles to the south, Stack ran onto the Mennaye Field in Penzance to face a team representing the Coastal Command Division of the RAF. He was at Number 8 and acquitted himself well in a 17-0 victory.

A few days later it was back into the reserves but this time he was moved up to the second row of the scrum, from where he scored the only Pirates try in a 3-6 loss to St Ives Reserves under the Mennaye floodlights. This was hardly a game likely to live on in memory but is notable as, from this match onwards,

Stack was destined to play virtually all of his rugby in the front two rows of the scrum. He was clearly too short to ever be a top-rated lock forward, but if he could become a prop like his old Mounts Bay mentors Perrin and Jelbert, he would not only be a tough competitor up front but he would surely be the fittest and fastest gun in town.

Being a prop forward in the late 1950s was usually reserved for rather tubby individuals whose main tasks in life often seemed limited to justifying Austin Healey's taunt of 'eating, drinking, pushing and falling over'. If ever asked to indulge in things like tackling, handling, passing and – God forbid – actually sprinting they would probably have gone a funny colour. To be fair, many of them were immensely strong and relished their own personal man-to-man battles with their opposite numbers with very little protection or interference from referees who generally just left them to sort it out among themselves. Not to put too fine a point on it, some of them were very hard cases indeed.

Stack was something completely different. He relished all those things that props were not generally expected to do and he was already strong way beyond his years. His was not the strength of modern-day muscle-man professional props with their endless hours pumping weights in a gym and special diets. It was that natural hardness derived from day after day of physical toil on a farm, much the same way that Welsh props developed their strength in the coal mines and steelworks of the valleys, or acquired by tough sheep farmers in the wilds of New Zealand. Getting to grips with all the dark arts of scrummaging was, however, now going to be the challenge.

After a few games back in the reserves, he was briefly recalled to First Team duty after Christmas – again in the second row. The Pirates had just received a seismic shock when two of their star players had signed for Hull Kingston Rovers in the Rugby League. Rumours abounded about other players potentially 'going north' and certainly a few had received clandestine approaches, although fortunately nothing more came of it. It was nevertheless an unsettling atmosphere for a young man about to break into the team.

His big breakthrough came at the end of February when the current county leading lights Redruth rolled into town. The Pirates then had an experienced and solid prop named Harvey Jose who had been forced to withdraw from the match due to illness – which in time turned out to be diabetes, sadly bringing his rugby career to a premature close. Harvey's misfortune gave Stack his first opportunity to prop at senior level and he grabbed it with both hands. The Pirates had not beaten Redruth for three long years but this time their faithful supporters had something to cheer with a 6-0 victory, along with the capture of their captain Harold Stevens' shirt as a trophy. Cornwall had only used three props over the past three years, including the redoubtable Bonzo Johns, and they had all featured for the Reds in that match. Despite all this the young tyro had not been found wanting.

Indeed he was to cement his place in the team to such an extent that he was an automatic selection whenever he was available for virtually the next two decades. His learning curve in the demanding and sometimes brutal world of the front row was then to take a sharp upward swing. Games followed thick and fast. A week later he got his first try in a win over Newton Abbot and the next one saw his first overnight away trip to claim a draw at Torquay.

His early development was probably helped considerably by playing alongside a veteran hooker named Jimmy Hosking. Known to all affectionately as 'Ock', he was a small, wiry, almost Fagin-like plumber who weighed barely eleven stone and only stubbed out his cigarette when the match was due to start. However, what he didn't know about winning a ball in a set scrum was frankly not worth knowing and for the next eighteen months or so he would have demonstrated dozens of tricks of the trade to his ambitious young prop.

On Easter Saturday he faced his biggest challenge to date when the Wasps visited Penzance on one of those popular late-season West Country tours. Today, the Wasps are a highly professional organisation playing at Coventry, but even in those days they were nobody's mugs. The England team that year included two Wasps forwards in flanker Alan Herbert and tighthead prop Gordon Bendon, and it would be the vastly experienced Bendon who would pack down against a nineteen-year-old Stack. The Wasps had several other future and ex-England players but, despite this, the Pirates won an exciting and occasionally bad-tempered match by 14-5. Stack not only survived the experience but bounced cheerfully out to play two more matches over the Easter weekend.

If that wasn't enough the next weekend saw mighty Cardiff come to town. Many considered Cardiff in those days to be *the* biggest club in rugby football and their presence invariably drew large crowds. This time the Pirates couldn't overcome their famous opponents but lost only narrowly, and again Stack came out with flying colours.

He had no time to sit and contemplate his progress as first thing the following morning the Pirates were all on a bus and heading for south Wales. There was no M5 in those days, or even a Severn Bridge, so it was a long, tedious journey before they made it to Port Talbot to face Aberavon, which was another of the leading clubs in Wales. The 'Wizards' team and raucous supporters were mostly made up of tough steelworkers and could call upon several members of the current Welsh team.

One of those Welsh international players was a rock-hard, crew-cut prop called Les Cunningham and it was he who would present Stack with his next major hurdle. This turned out to be a fairly torrid evening as, unlike Bendon, who was winding down his season on an Easter tour, Cunningham was on his home turf and performing in front of his own critical fans; he was not likely to hold anything back. But, once again, the challenge was accepted, the lessons learned and the young man from Godolphin was certainly learning them fast.

If he was acquiring the arts of propping in some fairly exalted company he also had to take in the usual camaraderie and banter of an amateur rugby team away on tour. He was still very much the new kid on the block and so after one fairly heavy drinking session was despatched by the old hands to 'find us some more bloody food'. Twenty minutes later he returned triumphantly clutching a small tin of biscuits.

One of his most experienced teammates and another mentor was a fine lock forward named Alvin Williams, who recalled:

> Four of us decided to hire a small Morris Minor and go into Cardiff to look for a bit of mischief but also to go swimming in the large indoor pool which had been used the year before for the Empire Games. We didn't realise Stack could only just about swim and having already had a couple of pints he started to sink in a flurry of bubbles. We only just managed to pull him out.
>
> On the way back we were mucking about in that little car and someone put their foot through one of the back windows and smashed it. Stack was only a kid but he was already a crafty sod and as it had wind-down windows with handles he wound them all down and we then returned it innocently back to the depot. The bloke carefully checked all the doors and wings for scratches but never looked at the windows and so we all just belted off around the corner and disappeared.

The city obviously impressed him as many years later Stack was back in Cardiff with some of the lads while on a Barbarians tour and he had somehow smooth-talked them all into a fairly swish nightclub in the city centre. The glamorous receptionist rather hesitatingly let them in on the strict understanding that they would all behave themselves. They had been joined for the evening by the Pontypool and Wales flanker Terry Cobner, and Stack had been quietly topping up Cobner's pints of Guinness with quite a few other things. No sooner had he given the young lady his smiling assurances as to what entirely sober and sensible chaps they all were than poor old Cobner threw up all over her front desk. Stack laughed so much he could hardly stand up either.

It hardly seems credible today but the Pirates travelled with only twenty players and took part in four hard matches, including not only Aberavon but also Cross Keys and Treorchy followed by a brief stopover at Bridgwater on the way home. This was all crammed into a mere five days and Stack propped in the whole lot. Indeed, during the month of April he took part in no fewer than twelve hard matches. Today, everyone talks about burnout if modern players appear in just four or five and they have a revolving door of substitutes so that props rarely play a full eighty minutes. By the time the last fixture had been fulfilled with a home win over Cheltenham, he had already made twenty first-team appearances, his first being in the back row, five as a lock and fourteen as a prop. He had cemented his place in the first team in his very first year of adult rugby and the future looked rosy.

He had by then acquired a car, Austin A40 pickup, and, as with most farmers, was very adept with changing engines and fixing gearboxes and he much later progressed to doing up a racy little Triumph TR4. He had a driving licence of course, but by some strange fluke he never had to actually pass a driving test. This was allegedly something to do with testing being temporarily suspended during the Suez Crisis and perhaps the paperwork never quite sorted itself out. Either way, Stack was not one to worry about trivial details like that.

Both on and off the pitch he was undeniably on his way onwards and upwards.

4

Onwards and Upwards

The Pirates opened their new season with an intriguing fixture against AS Milano of Italy to celebrate the opening of a new covered stand at one end of the ground and a large crowd gathered on a warm September evening to welcome them. Stack was selected in the second row alongside Alvin Williams and at that early stage of his career the selectors did not appear to have made their minds up quite where to put him. Whether this flexibility helped or hindered his cause, at least in the short term, is debatable.

To complicate matters further, the club had been joined by a strong aggressive Irish prop called Tony Byrne who, though lacking Stack's mobility and ball skills, was bigger and more experienced, and the two were destined to be rivals not only for the club but soon for Cornwall as well.

He was given his first opportunity to represent Cornwall in an early season 'friendly' against a United Hospitals team at Camborne. After that heroic but ultimately unsuccessful final at Coventry, the Cornish had experienced a disappointing campaign the following year but could still boast a powerful team, which included the blond fly-half Richard Sharp, who was soon to become the darling of English rugby and was himself only a few months older than Stack. The two appeared together in that match but beyond that seemed to have little in common.

Sharp was an ex-public schoolboy who had already been commissioned as a Second-Lieutenant while doing his National Service in the Navy and was about to study at Oxford. With long legs that appeared to mask a devastating change of pace allied to a bewildering dummy, he was one of those rare rugby players who had 'star' written all over them. Furthermore, he was a Cornishman based in Redruth and within four months he was to be setting Twickenham alight in the white shirt of England. Stack's road to the top was going to be very much longer and a hell of a lot harder, but ultimately just as successful.

That first Cornwall appearance was followed by a second three weeks later when Surrey brought a strong team down for another non-championship match in Penzance. The game took place in a thick fog and it was Sharp with a brilliant solo try and a raking drop goal who was the standout performer as Cornwall pulled away to win. Cornwall scored four tries, one of them Stack's as he crashed over early in the second half.

Several years later, when he was asked about some of the props he had faced and whom he particularly admired he mentioned Karl Wronski. That name never hit the headlines but he was a bullet-headed muscleman of Polish descent who played for Rosslyn Park and appeared several times against Stack and the Pirates over the next few years. Wronski was in that Surrey team and gave his still-teenaged opponent an uncomfortable evening. More valuable experience could now be stored in the memory bank.

He was not selected for the opening two Championship matches against Devon and Gloucestershire but, following the withdrawal of one of Cornwall's more notable hard nuts named Gary Harris, he found himself brought into the side as a lock forward to face Somerset at Taunton. Fortunately, Stack was again to have his club colleague Alvin Williams packing down beside him but he was clearly stepping up a level. His father had dropped him off at Camborne and he caused plenty of amusement to his teammates when he shouted out of the window to CB as to where he had just remembered leaving some bullocks as the train pulled slowly out of the station.

The old Priorybridge Road ground in Taunton was packed to the rafters as referee Denis Thatcher of Kent got the game underway. His days of gin and tonic, golf and walking dutifully a few paces behind his Prime Minister wife still lay many years ahead – for the time being he could concentrate his spare time on being one of the RFU's senior referees.

This was a match Cornwall had to win to stay in the competition and waiting to greet him in the Somerset second row was John Currie, who was one half of the celebrated Marques and Currie partnership, which was a permanent feature of the England team at the time. At the first line-out Currie towered over Stack and looked down at him in that half-mocking, half-genuine way that experienced men used to greet youngsters in those days. 'Have a good game sonny,' was his patronising welcome to the County Championship. Cornwall won the match by a single point in a breathless finale and so qualified for a play off against Devon at Redruth.

Ironically, Byrne had also been drafted into the Cornwall team for the match at Taunton but in his case was the one to get the nod as a prop. Harris returned for the Devon match to leave Stack on the sidelines. Following an unfortunate off-the-field incident, Harris was then suspended for the semi-final which took place at Twickenham, but the committee plumped for a Royal Navy man called Dick Hollick while Byrne kept the propping job throughout the rest of the campaign. It was a first career disappointment for

Stack, whose Twickenham debut was thus to be delayed for almost ten years. But his time would surely come.

Meanwhile the Pirates were gradually emerging as the major force in Cornish rugby, slowly toppling Redruth from their lofty perch. Back in those days, there were no official leagues – nor indeed cup competitions – and all club matches were nominally friendlies but it was always apparent who was ahead of the rest. Nevertheless, 'friendly' was not a term that sprang readily to mind when the Pirates and the Reds packs squared up to one another. You could almost pick up the smell of cordite mixed in with the liniment and sweat as they each went at it like hungry dogs, and Stack simply loved it.

The Pirates claimed two memorable scalps when they defeated first Saracens and then Cardiff, the latter for only the second time in the club's history. In truth, Saracens bore no resemblance to the ultra-professional corporation that they have become in recent years, but Cardiff was the club that Stack had been taken along to see by CB when he was only nine, and still considered to be the UK's glamour team, setting the standard for everyone else to follow. It was a glorious victory in the context of the time.

Before the season drew to a close, Ebbw Vale had also only just managed to force a 6-6 draw despite including future Welsh internationals David Nash and Denzil Williams in their pack. Stack faced a veteran gnome-like prop called Les Dimmick, who was about as broad as he was high and had the reputation as being probably the hardest man to scrum against in Wales. Once again, he had come up smiling and his front-row education was gathering pace.

He had trained hard throughout the summer of 1960 and was looking forward to nailing down his place in the Cornwall team. Furthermore, the Springboks were due to visit Britain and their itinerary was to include a match against a combined Cornwall and Devon team at Camborne, so there was much to play for.

Up until then, he had been reasonably lucky with respect to injuries but fate was soon to deal him his first cruel blow. The Pirates' last player to be selected for England was a man named Ginger Williams, and each September he brought a guest team of International players down to Cornwall for a match with the Pirates. This time they included the current glamour boy of British rugby, Tony O'Reilly, and a large crowd turned out to watch the big Irish star with flaming locks and glistening thighs go through his paces. He rewarded them with three spectacular tries of his own as Williams's team gave the Pirates a bit of a walloping.

However, for most of the match they were facing only fourteen men. Not long into the match Stack was seen to be sitting disconsolately in the middle of the pitch as the game carried on nearly fifty yards away. His right ankle was badly broken and all those thoughts of Cornwall and even the Springboks had disappeared in a searing flash of pain.

He was never one to dwell on his misfortunes and kept nurses and patients in stitches of laughter with his antics at the West Cornwall Hospital, which apparently involved placing bedside flowers into the hands of dozing patients. After a few days he was allowed home but it was found that the ankle had to be reset, which delayed his recovery. He was soon back driving his pickup with his foot encased in plaster, instead using his National Health crutch to work the accelerator, and putting that untested driving licence into mortal peril. Nevertheless, it made life difficult on the farm and he had already celebrated his twenty-first birthday by the time he pulled a rugby shirt back on again.

The club finished the season as the unofficial Cornish champions based upon a complicated percentage system worked out by the local newspapers. There were of course no medals, trophies or anything quite so 'vulgar' in those days of puritanical amateurism but there were still plenty of bragging rights to be had, and so if you managed to get one over Redruth or St Ives the beer certainly tasted pretty good. Stack was back in time to help defeat Redruth and Pontypool as well as taking part in defeats by Cardiff, Ebbw Vale and the Wasps.

However it had been a frustrating season. He had only managed twenty matches for the club, his Cornwall place had gone elsewhere and the Pirates' selectors still kept bouncing him around between the front and second rows. His only consolation had been helping to win the Cornwall sevens title at Camborne, but this seemed scant reward. Things, however, were about to improve significantly.

The next season the Pirates were probably at the height of their powers and were playing consistently at a level which was not to be matched again during the rest of Stack's long career – and arguably not until the onset of professional rugby in the new millennium. They were led by a twinkle-toed fly-half with a quick wit and even quicker feet named Johnny Thomas, and the following year by the fast, hard-tackling and spectacular centre Gerald Luke. Both Thomas and Luke insisted upon the team playing fast and expansive rugby whenever there was a possible chance of doing so and this suited Stack perfectly.

The lynchpin of the side was a tough and resourceful scrum-half with a deadly left foot called Peter Michell, who conveniently happened to be the established captain of Cornwall. Michell was the man whose job it was to move on all that possession gained by Stack and his colleagues to those formidable backs for them to gorge themselves with spectacular tries. One of these was Tony Stevenson, who was not only the man alleged to have given Stack his nickname but was a flying and somewhat unorthodox winger who helped himself to twenty-seven tries during that single season.

The previous year Stack had suffered that ankle injury against Ginger Williams's XV. They were back again at the start of September for what was an intriguing fixture against a team that combined the Pirates and Redruth in a composite side which included the Reds' winger John May, who would in time marry Stack's sister. They lined up with those usual county compatriots Abrahams and Johns but could make little impression on the celebrated visitors. O'Reilly was back again but the real damage was done by Scotland's Arthur Smith, who ran in several tries and ended the season captaining the British Lions in South Africa.

Although he was primarily a loosehead prop, and indeed played all his international rugby with that Number 1 on his back, he could perform perfectly well as a tighthead if ever asked to do so. The selectors finally got used to the idea of both he and Byrne propping together and by then if either was to drop back into the second row it was usually Byrne who was asked to do so. At the end of September he had claimed his Cornwall place back in a hard-fought draw with Lancashire at Redruth followed by a victory over Sussex and then a clean sweep of the south-western group, culminating in a stirring win over Gloucestershire.

As stated, his colleagues in the Cornwall front row were Redruth's Bonzo Johns and hooker Ken Abrahams. Both were selected for the first England trial, which was held for the first and only time in Penzance but, not for the last time, Stack was to be the Cinderella left on the sidelines. To be fair it was probably much too early at that stage for him to be considered seriously for an England trial and he certainly admired the huge and ebullient Johns, who was very much the local folk hero. He also missed the quarter-final at Oxford, but in early February the Cornwall team was back at Coventry to face another extremely powerful Warwickshire team.

Four years earlier Stack had been just another fan on the terraces parading a giant pasty before the game, but now he was out there and on the stage for real. Interestingly, he was the only change in the two front rows from the previous encounter in 1958. Johns and Abrahams had appeared at Coventry the last time and Warwickshire's trio comprising Phil Judd, Herbie Godwin and Mike McLean remained intact.

By the end of his career Stack had appeared in large numbers of high-profile matches on several different continents, but at that point this was without doubt his biggest test by far. It must be remembered that, because there were then no official club competitions, county rugby played a very important role in the annual rugby calendar. The County Championship served as a shop window for players with international aspirations and, in counties such as Gloucestershire, Yorkshire, Lancashire and indeed Warwickshire, it drew large attendances. In Cornwall passionate crowds of between 8,000 and 10,000 were par for the course.

Many of the faces in the Cornwall dressing room would have been very familiar to him. The Pirates comprised nearly half the team and included not only Michell, Williams and Luke but they also had centre Jimmy Glover and lock David Mann to run out beside them. They also featured the superstar Sharp who was soon to become a British Lion and Northampton's rangy full-back, Roger Hosen. Hosen had pulled a muscle in the 1958 final and had a major point to prove. He was another very fine player who would also soon star for England in his own right and was a deadly goal-kicker with a boot like a howitzer.

Warwickshire had a couple of established stars of their own in the brilliant Peter Jackson and the highly astute Peter Robbins but, when it came down to the crunch, it was their fearsome tight five which carried the day and left the Cornish fans bereft. Their two lofty England locks, Tom Pargetter and Colin Payne, virtually cleaned the Cornishmen out in the lineouts and it was indeed Payne who claimed the only try of the match.

Stack battled away and got stuck in with a will. On one occasion in the second half he ploughed into a ruck with boots flying when a massive uppercut from McLean whistled inches past his chin. Had it landed, his rugby story might well have ended then and there. That snapped-up try from Payne and a couple of successful kicks at goal from Coventry scrum-half George Cole finally quelled the Cornish fire and the match slipped inexorably away. In future years, there were to be several more maddeningly frustrating days to come for him while wearing a Cornwall shirt but he had again stepped up to the mark in front of 12,000 noisy fans, done his job and could face the future with ever-growing confidence.

The topsy-turvy nature of amateur rugby in those days was demonstrated graphically by the contrast a week after that showdown at Coventry. The Pirates took part in a jolly run out at Liskeard-Looe and Stack entered into the festive spirit by kicking a conversion as the team ran up a cricket score. The rest of the season followed much the same pattern as before and he appeared regularly, including taking part in good wins at Redruth and at home over Torquay. The eagerly awaited annual match with Cardiff followed but then his season was to finish early after taking a knock in a mid-April clash with Exeter.

He was now an established fixture for both his club and county. He still played in other positions but was increasingly featuring as the highly mobile prop forward. By now, this position was clearly going to be his rugby-playing destiny.

The question now was simply one of how far could he go.

5

The Son of the Father

Although another seven years were to pass before Stack was to eventually make it to the 'big time' and international rugby, the circumstances and pressures that affected both his character and his later rugby career were beginning to crystallise.

Having passed his twenty-first birthday, it was clear that the responsibility for the future of the two farms was going to fall increasingly upon his broad and willing shoulders. Although the youngest of a sizeable family, one of his sisters, Anne, had married and moved on; Mary was now a qualified teacher; his eldest brother Cecil was busy running his garage; and Roy was committed to his nearby mill and haulage business. Owen, his other brother, had already moved off to farm elsewhere.

The phenomenon of the young son toiling away without any regular salary in a family business on the basis of 'one day my son all this will be yours' is as old as the hills – it even echoes the position of the stay-at-home son from the parable of the Prodigal Son in the Bible. This situation was certainly common in farming communities and particularly so in the West Country, and CB's attitude as he neared the age of seventy seemed to mirror this principle.

CB had always been a man who had prized hard work, was careful with money and also tended to see the world very much upon his own terms. He was a meticulous diarist and from these it is obvious that he loved his youngest son and was very proud of his achievements, but that if he was going to inherit the fruits of his labours he was going to have to work bloody hard for it. Sport was a fine thing to let off a bit of steam on a Saturday afternoon and a good excuse to enjoy a pint with your friends afterwards but business always had to come first, and possibly second and third as well.

Stack had already become very adept at little dodges to avoid his father's incessant demands upon his time – sometimes by apparently vanishing into thin air. One particular stunt had involved lowering himself halfway down a mineshaft on the end of a rope, thus giving a whole new meaning to rugby players getting themselves suspended.

To begin with he had two people to mediate on his behalf once the needs of Cornwall and other matches began to involve a bit of travel, going to team practice sessions and occasionally staying away. The first was Beatrice his mother. Her life was centred very much around CB and the family, running the shop and taking a full part in the life of the village, including the local Women's Institute. She washed Stack's kit, tended his wounds and gave him encouragement when he most needed it, but as far as it is known never attended any actual rugby matches herself – that was very much the preserve of CB and his brother Roy.

In 1963 Beatrice was taken into hospital for an operation and tragically died while under anaesthetic. Stack had been working earlier that day and had planned to visit her the following morning. He felt devastated and utterly bereft but it somehow made him determined to redouble his efforts both as a farmer and a rugby player.

His second advocate was Roy, who frequently backed up and covered for him whenever necessary. However, Roy was also to die a mere five years later at the early age of only forty. These two heartbreaking events were to prove massive personal shocks to the young man who had suddenly lost two of the people who were not only the most precious in the world to him but, from a purely rugby standpoint, could also gain him a bit of leeway whenever he really needed it.

Stack, CB and his sister Mary continued to live in the house in the village next to Beatrice's shop, which was later leased out and was subsequently closed many years ago. In due course Mary was to build and live in a house in the village but continued to come in and cook at weekends after teaching all of the working week. This continued for several years until she also married and went to live in the nearby village of Porthleven.

This situation led to the other problem which bedevilled Stack's entire career: access to ready cash. In his meticulous diaries, CB recorded the wages paid out to his staff each Saturday and even when Stack first played for England he was only receiving £10 a week, which had merely risen to £15 by the time he had gained his final 'cap'. Even allowing for inflation, this would be close to a modern minimum wage. Admittedly he lived at home, had his food and transport provided and had no family or mortgage to worry about, but the expenses of travelling long distances and playing senior rugby were potentially crippling.

Were he an England prop of recent vintage from a farming background such as a Phil Vickery or a Julian White, he would be picking up over £200,000 a year from a Premiership rugby club, but in those days Rugby Union was fanatically amateur and made an absolute fetish about it. Cynical zealots in blazers would forensically scrutinise every expense claim in the minutest detail and frequently took the attitude that 'the chaps can afford it and are damned lucky to be playing at this level in the first place'.

Stack lived comfortably enough at home and his longer-term potential net worth was probably as good as anyone else, but when England came knocking and were making demands for matches, trials, training camps plus celebratory dinners (and of course he lived 300 miles away), the pressures on both ready spending money and his time would quickly become horrendous. All this largely lay in the future but if Stack acquired a reputation for being 'careful' with money and not always being readily available to play whenever required by his club, it is not too hard to understand why.

The farms were quite sizeable by local standards at over 115 acres of arable land with some 400 pigs, and in the 1960s they still had a dairy herd of thirty milking cows, which of course all had to be milked without fail twice a day. The family also grew potatoes, cauliflowers (which the Cornish confusingly always call 'broccoli'), spring greens, anemones and violets. CB loved to visit Helston market and do the buying and selling and meet up with old friends, but much of the workload back on the farm fell to Stack and a very small staff. An unlikely occasional helper was Frank Cousins who, as one of the leading lights of the post-war trade-union movement in Britain, had been a scourge to a succession of Tory governments. He had now retired to live quietly at Godolphin and had become a firm friend of CB.

Meanwhile the Pirates, under their new captain Gerald Luke, continued to carry all before them in Cornwall and Devon and completed some fifty matches. Stack appeared in no fewer than thirty-nine of these matches, mainly as a prop but occasionally reverting to the second row if required. Much to his frustration, he lost his Cornwall place after a disappointing loss to Devon at Camborne. The match took place at the very height of the Cuban missile crisis and, perhaps for those who allowed themselves to even contemplate the potential nightmare consequences, it somehow made a cross-Tamar rugby match perhaps seem just a bit of an irrelevance.

Whether the returning British Lion Richard Sharp and the goal-kicking wonder boy Roger Hosen had their thoughts so distracted is unclear, but they both played poorly and Cornwall sagged to an unexpected defeat. Sharp and Hosen kept their places but Stack and his Pirates teammate Alvin Williams were both unceremoniously dropped for the rest of the season.

After Christmas, the entire country was frozen up for weeks on end. The Cornish Riviera usually escapes the worst ravages of English winters, but not this time, with farmers like the Stevens family facing the gruelling task of looking after their livestock during this freak spell. Early in this period, the Pirates received unexpected visitors when the San Isidro club from Buenos Aires arrived in Penzance. They had saved up, travelled thousands of miles during their summer only to arrive in a freezing Britain with little prospect of any rugby. A trip down to Penzance gave them that heaven-sent chance. Stack played in the second row in the hastily arranged mid-week fixture, which was narrowly won by the tourists.

One of his best friends at the time was fellow Pirate and nearby farmer John Skewes who, though a few years younger, shared many of the same interests and also liked to run in the evenings. Those two, along with another local lad who was not a rugby player but a distance runner, would regularly pound the lanes together. 'The Pirates used to do quite a few road and beach runs as part of their pre-season routine,' said Skewes. 'Stack and I would be miles ahead of all the fat shopkeepers and schoolteachers puffing along behind. By the time they staggered back into the ground we would be coming out of the showers.' Stack, remembering how difficult it had been when he was a junior, would often drive John into Penzance to train and Stack was soon to be best man at John's wedding.

Two other close friends at the rugby club were each members of families which ran very successful – and uniquely Cornish – local businesses. One was winger Tony Stevenson, who worked for his father, who in turn owned a whole fleet of fishing boats based in Newlyn. There were still plenty of fish around the coast and as it was some years before the advent of Russian supertrawlers, British membership in the EU and rigid fishing quotas, it was still a thriving industry.

Another pal was Brian 'Oggie' Warren who, when not playing for the Pirates alongside Stack as a hooker, was part of a successful bakery business based out of St Just near to Land's End. The Warrens, and as his own nickname indicates, had already been making Cornish pasties in large quantities for generations. They were all of a similar age, had a shared sense of fun and between work and rugby had some good times together. In due course, Stack again would act as best man, this time at Warren's wedding.

By then, Stack had filled out and settled to a size which, by today's standards, would still seem very small indeed, but was considered about average for a senior prop forward in the 1960s. He stood a fraction under six feet tall, weighed a rock-solid fifteen stone plus a bit, and had a lean waist, abnormally strong arms and shoulders and muscles up and down his spine like a pair of steel girders. By the time he became an international player many props were already beginning to get considerably bigger, although still nowhere near to the twenty-stone-plus behemoths who trundle around for little more than sixty minutes of a match today.

He enjoyed a beer or two but during the week drank large quantities of milk and would have been the despair of modern-day sports dieticians by devouring a fair number of Cornish pasties, usually with a high fat content, and mountains of Hovis bread. None of this appeared to do him the slightest harm as he could apparently work off all the calories in just a few hours of heavy farm work.

He was never a great talker on a rugby field and would seldom get involved in tactical discussions, preferring just to concentrate on his job. However, when he did speak it was invariably worth listening to as it was either very incisive or extremely funny. The Pirates had a flank forward at the time by the name of Ray Burroughs, who was unfortunate enough to pick up a virus that left him for several months with severely impaired hearing. One freezing day at Camborne, poor Ray received a nasty stray boot right in his 'crown jewels' and lay in a crumpled heap on the icy turf groaning softly. The game was stopped, the stand fell silent and the players huddled together in a futile attempt to keep warm. Stack then sauntered casually over to the referee and said, 'Don't worry ref. He can't feel pain – he's deaf.'

The following autumn, the All Blacks came to tour the United Kingdom and another combined county opportunity arose – this time at Exeter. Stack was playing consistently well for his club and had regained his place in the Cornwall team and the thought of packing down against the likes of Meads and Whineray was a mouth-watering prospect. By accident or design, Cornwall met Devon the weekend prior at Devonport and this time Cornwall's pack won the day. Unlike three years earlier, when the Springboks had last come to Camborne, he was fit, far more experienced and really fancied his chances.

Whereas the previous year the fixture had been blighted by the Cuban missile crisis, this time the crowd stood in silence as President Kennedy had been shot dead the previous day. The entire world was stunned. Stack was probably equally stunned when the selectors mysteriously overlooked him in favour of a virtual unknown from Torquay called Roger Smerdon. Predictably, the All Blacks ran the combined counties team all over the park and one by one the West Country forwards failed to last the pace, with the unfortunate Smerdon one of those seen to be struggling. While Stack's presence would clearly never have altered the eventual outcome, he would certainly have still been flying about the field and giving his all until the final whistle.

To add to his frustration, he picked up a rib injury in March during a drawn match with local rivals St Ives and thus his season finished early. As a consequence, he missed all the plum touring sides that came down to Penzance every spring.

The next two years followed in much the same pattern with his farm responsibilities weighing down heavily upon him, and he was beginning to have to pull out of a few more club matches, which did not always endear him to the Pirates selectors and committee. Unfortunately, the team were just beginning a slow but inexorable decline, ceding their primacy in Cornwall not to Redruth but more surprisingly to Penryn. Fixtures that would have been won a couple of years before now became a struggle and the win to lose ratio began to deteriorate alarmingly. It is always difficult for a front-row forward to really shine in these circumstances and, although he invariably stood out in the company of lesser performers around him, his opportunities to be noticed by selectors when plying his trade in faraway Cornwall diminished accordingly.

He kept his Cornwall place for another year and somebody must have taken note as in November 1964 he was sent a card to be a 'Non-travelling Reserve' for a first England trial at Weston-super-Mare, but nothing more became of it. Future England wing Ken Plummer was brought into the Cornwall team at that time as a young seventeen-year-old and recalled that Stack was the one who immediately took him under his wing with a reassuring, 'Don't worry, we'll look after you boy,' which was greatly appreciated at the time.

At the end of the season he and Richard Sharp went as guests of the Truro club to Hanover in Germany, a city that had established links at several levels with Cornish rugby, and it will be recalled that they had sent a team of youngsters to Penzance when Stack was still in the Colts. The team also flew to the divided city of Berlin where they played against an army team as well as visiting the Brandenburg Gate and gazing at the grim and forbidding Berlin Wall, which had then not even been up for four years.

In September 1965 he played for Cornwall in an early season friendly against Crawshay's Welsh team, whose front row included a certain army officer called Bill Carling. If that name sounds slightly familiar, it will be because his son Will would go on to become the world-famous England centre. Carling senior, however, was a solid prop who played several times for Cardiff and had only limited connections with Cornwall. However, when the serious championship games got underway, Stack found to his chagrin that he had been omitted for the 'upcountry ringer'. Most players suffer that fate at some time or another but it was a new and not very welcome experience for the local man from Godolphin.

Furthermore, the club had experienced a further downturn in its results: his elder brother Roy had become unwell and farm and father were becoming increasingly insistent in their demands upon his time and attention. He was now twenty-six and physically approaching his peak, but his rugby career had reached something of a crossroads.

6

Losing a Brother and Looking From Cornwall Towards England

Throughout the long hot summer of 1966, the sporting public – and indeed almost the entire nation – were transfixed with England's World Cup-winning footballers. By contrast, the British Lions were getting slaughtered in New Zealand where all four Test matches against the All Blacks were lost comprehensively.

Meanwhile, Stack spent it toiling away on the farm as usual while religiously topping up his fitness with endless gruelling runs along Praa Sands, the nearest long beach, where he could usually still be seen most evenings threading his way up and down along the shoreline and over the soft and unforgiving dunes. Sometimes he would again be accompanied by the aforementioned local cross-country runner and they would chase each other over the loose sand. If he could keep up with a speedy athlete in that environment, then outlasting rugby players on a grass pitch would be relatively easy.

Extended solo beach running has of course long been practiced by athletes and sportsmen from Stanley Matthews to Red Rum, but that unremitting toil undoubtedly paid dividends. All those countless hours spent on this lonely vigil ensured that not only was he now nearing his peak with regard to raw strength but that he also had the stamina to last eighty minutes of rugby without any undue difficulty.

Another devotee of the seashore was the Cornwall hooker Roger Harris who was to follow a similar regime on the beaches at nearby Perranporth. Within three years they had both forced their way to the forefront of West Country rugby and indeed into the notebooks of the rugby writers and selectors of the London rugby establishment.

Over the next three years he and Harris were to play around thirty matches together for Cornwall, during which time the Duchy were to take part in four County semi-finals and once in the final itself, and this was to provide both of them with a convenient shop window for their skills. Indeed no fewer than ten Cornishmen were to get picked for international trials during that three-year spell with half actually getting selected at least once for England, demonstrating ably the value of County rugby at the time.

By now very single-minded about his priorities and acutely conscious of the demands of the farm, he had begun to pick his games for the Pirates so that he would not only have built up some credit with his family but to also come to each County match as fresh as a daisy. The first competitive match saw Cornwall overcome Gloucestershire at Bristol and Harris, Stack and Bill Carling shaded the up-front honours against John Pullin, Bev Dovey and Jack Fowke, of whom the first two were already England men. Somerset and Devon were both well beaten back in Cornwall to leave the Cornishmen sitting at the top of the south-west group and ready to face a home quarter-final with Oxfordshire.

Before that could take place, there was an eagerly awaited match at Camborne featuring a combined Devon and Cornwall team against the touring Australian Wallabies. Three years earlier Stack had missed out on the chance to face the All Blacks and now lightning was to strike a second time. Rather than simply choosing the best players available, the selectors followed a politically correct but selectorially insane policy of slavishly picking eight players from one county and seven from the other. Both Harris and Carling were included but Stack had the galling experience of once again being named only as a reserve on the day.

What must have made it even harder to stomach was that the man who took his place was a Devonian called Nick Southern who, although a highly competent rugby forward with a good reputation, was essentially a lock filling in as a loosehead prop. Furthermore, he was to be propping directly against Wallaby captain John Thornett, who had already amassed nearly forty caps for his country. The upshot was entirely predictable and Stack must have writhed in his seat in sheer frustration when the combined counties team were well beaten up front as the Aussies stole a narrow but ultimately decisive victory.

Ten days later, Oxfordshire arrived in Redruth to be turned over comfortably with both Carling and Stack getting tries for the Cornishmen. Thus the stage was set for a semi-final showdown with Surrey, although nobody could have predicted just what an epic struggle it would prove to be. Cornish patriotism is always stirred to the soul by the chorus of the Reverend Hawker's anthem about the imprisonment of Bishop Trelawney sparking a march upon London, which climaxes with the evocative line, 'Twenty thousand Cornishmen will know the reason why.' Somehow a number not far short of that mystical figure squeezed themselves into Redruth's famous old Recreation Ground, complete with its infamous Hell Fire Corner, to scream and yell – never mind any polite clapping and cheering – their boys to victory. For a long time they had plenty to yell about as both Stack and Ken Plummer scored tries for Cornwall. Sadly, Cornwall's normally dependable full-back Graham Bate had a rare off day with his goal-kicking and failed to convert both tries and indeed several kickable penalties into the bargain. Conversely, Surrey had the ice-cool Bob Hiller who popped over two penalties to take everyone back to Richmond for a replay a fortnight later.

When the time came, the Athletic Ground was a picture of good-natured chaos as thousands of wildly enthusiastic Cornishmen thronged the touchlines, climbed trees and perched on the top of buildings to catch a glimpse of their heroes. In a desperate climax, Cornwall snatched a second draw with a late try once again from Plummer topped off by an enormous touchline conversion by the restored England full-back Roger Hosen, who had by then replaced the luckless Bate. The Surrey and later England full-back Bob Hiller remembered:

> I was standing under the posts when Hosen's kick sailed over the bar and I caught it. I thought there might be a minute or two left but I was immediately engulfed by a mass of dancing black-and-gold-covered crazy Cornishmen and couldn't even move. The referee took one look, thought better of it and blew up for full time!

For his part Stack had another excellent match and found his photo adorning the front cover of *Rugby World* the following month.

A third match was therefore required back at Redruth. However, whatever the reason, this time the Cornwall team failed to do themselves justice and slipped somewhat ignominiously out of the competition to leave thousands of glum-faced locals nursing their inner pain as they shuffled silently out into the equally mournful streets.

For Stack, however, that twice-replayed semi-final presaged a big step forward in his career. Not only had the epic and raucous enthusiasm of the thousands of Cornish fans caught the imagination of Fleet Street, but he had thrice faced A. L. 'Tony' Horton, who was widely considered at the time to be just about the most forbidding tighthead prop in Europe. A Londoner who was some eighteen months older than Stack, he was a converted full-back with the upper body of a giant but surprisingly short legs. He had a barrel chest and a massive neck, which reputedly required a twenty-two-inch collar despite his being both under six feet tall and sixteen stone in weight. He thus constituted a nightmare to prop against, had already gained six England caps and was destined to be the cornerstone of the British Lions pack in South Africa a year later.

Despite all this, Stack had emerged from his potential ordeal of well over four hours of high-pressure combat not only unbowed but bouncing back for more and racing around in the last few minutes of each match as energetically as he had at the beginning. Horton was not only a fine sportsman but was suitably impressed by this virtually unknown Cornish prop who seemed to possess such physical strength, indomitable spirit and bucketloads of stamina. Moreover, when he got back to London, he said as much and this soon reached the ears of John Reason – then one of the most revered rugby journalists of the day who 'told it as it was' for the *Daily Telegraph*. Reason took a good look at Stack, readily agreed with Horton's assessment and soon began to promote his cause in his columns whenever a suitable opportunity arose.

Meanwhile, Stack himself continued to turn out spasmodically for the Pirates, and although he was their best player by some distance he showed no wish to become club captain. Indeed despite the fact that he was now a very experienced player he showed no real inclination to be a leader either on or indeed off the field. Time and again, playing colleagues of that era have remarked how he was generally quiet on the field (although he enjoyed a bit of cheerful banter with referees), got on with his job regardless of the opposition or the score and could certainly look after himself against the roughest and toughest around, but never once actively looked for any sort of trouble. He let his rugby do the talking.

Off the field he was nevertheless establishing himself as a character. He was inevitably seen as a bit of a non-conformist who only came to club training when he could squeeze it in with all his farming duties. These were simplified slightly in 1968 when it was decided to discontinue with the dairy herd and concentrate upon beef cattle, pigs and vegetables. CB was still very much in charge but the Stevens family only carried a very small staff largely made up of casual labour from the village and so his daily workload continued to be relentless.

Despite all this, whenever a game started, he was clearly fitter and quicker than any of his colleagues in the forwards who had turned up religiously to train twice a week throughout the season. He enjoyed a beer or two but was certainly not a heavy drinker and never smoked at a time when many players still did so. He was invariably good company on an away trip and loved a few harmless pranks. Indeed, for the rest of his career club officials at Penzance could never quite make up their minds about him. They knew he possessed exceptional talent, seemed a happy-go-lucky character and would be the first name on the team sheet – if he was available – but one or two of them made little secret of the fact that they did not think he made himself available anything like often enough.

It was in 1968 that he lost his elder brother Roy, who had always been his greatest supporter and advocate. As Roy was still a relatively young man this came as a shattering blow and for a while Stack was again grief-stricken. Up until then, he had been reasonably content to be an accomplished rugby player and a fixture for his club and county, but any ambitions beyond that were somewhat vague. He could have let himself be crushed by that cruel loss coming so soon after the death of his mother. Conversely he could perhaps somehow channel all that emotional pain and acute sense of loss into achieving something extra-special in his life that would have made his brother intensely proud. As he toiled away on the farm, and pounded the windswept beaches and country lanes, he became imbued with a renewed iron determination. Come hell or high water, he was going to do whatever it took to make it to the very pinnacle of the rugby tree.

All the difficulties were both immediate and obvious. It should be remembered that he was working over seventy hours a week on a farm alongside a demanding father who was now past his seventieth birthday. He was living over 300 miles away from London and playing for a club far removed from the fashionable teams where selectors concentrated all their attention.

On the other hand, at twenty-eight he was at the height of his physical powers, was as fit as anyone in the game and immensely strong. Now, buoyed up with Horton's recent testament, Stack knew he had the innate ability to make the grade if only he could somehow get the chance.

As his career was to progress, this situation was to intensify massively. Stack became increasingly single-minded in his pursuit of rugby fame and knew instinctively that a low-key friendly fixture against a Falmouth or a Barnstaple was never going to enhance his cause but might risk an injury. His relationship with his teammates at the Pirates was always first class, although certain of those committee men now began to actively resent what they saw as his lack of genuine commitment to their cause.

What his critics failed to appreciate was the intense pressure he was under to keep the farm going. His ageing father relied increasingly upon his youngest son. While he was working seven days a week, the calls came through for long journeys to and from representative matches, squad practices and, in due course, foreign tours, which were going to stretch his time and energies almost past breaking point. To his naturally sunny disposition was now added a steely determination which would carry him thousands of miles, into crushingly long hours, shortages of sleep and occasionally some difficult confrontations with his father. Cornishmen can usually be relied upon to be stubborn but now, if the situation truly demanded, he was going to be prepared to be sheer bloody-minded. Often he would leave a team hotel in Bristol or somewhere at two o'clock in the morning to drive back to Godolphin in time to be back running the farm by seven o'clock. Occasionally, something just had to give, and if that sometimes turned out to be his club team then 'que sera sera'.

Nothing much had changed for him during the season of 1967/68. He played regularly for both Cornwall and the Pirates but his overall career made little obvious progress. As a cattle farmer he worried about an outbreak of foot-and-mouth disease (a Cornwall match was postponed because of it), the All Blacks strode through the UK and France and the British Lions jetted off to South Africa with both Tony Horton and a future Pirate colleague in John O'Shea among the selected props. Stack still remained marooned well below the radar.

The following season, things at last began to happen. Cornwall won a rare victory at Kingsholm in Gloucester by 15-9, all through penalties by Graham Bate, who had happily rediscovered his kicking boots after his chastening experience two seasons previously. Back-row man Roger Hosken said about the occasion:

> This was the best display by any Cornwall pack with which it was my pleasure to be involved. They had a huge six-foot-six England lock named David Watt but our Penryn boy Colin 'Knocker' Kneebone - who seemed about half his size - took him apart. Stack was facing a future England prop called Barry Nelmes and had him up in the air half the time. It was terrific.

Once again, the Cornish topped the south-west group and at last Stack got selected for his first England trial. He had only been named as a reserve for one held a few weeks previously at handily placed Falmouth, but, true to form, when the England selectors did finally give him a chance, it was nearly 500 miles away in early January up at West Hartlepool on the north-east coast.

Despite this he was not without friends. Roger Harris was at his side in the front row of a side known as the 'Possibles' which was traditionally a mélange of genuine international contenders and a few hopeful 'wannabees' thrown together for the day to take on what the selectors had deemed as their putative England team for their Five Nations campaign in the new year. These in turn were termed the 'Probables' and, as can readily be imagined, led to some rather strange matches as players jockeyed frantically to catch the eye of the selectors rather like a line of aspiring out-of-work actors at a Broadway audition.

When the trial took place the loosehead prop for the Probables was another farmer who played for Northampton called David Powell. He had picked up a brace of caps three years earlier and had even been on a Lions tour to New Zealand. He had lost out for the past couple of years to the Midland policeman Mike Coulman, whose place was now up for grabs after he had recently signed to play rugby league for Salford. Powell had done well enough at Falmouth and hence held pole position. The man directly opposing Stack was the current England tighthead prop Brian Keen who had gained four caps the previous season while still at university and had, by coincidence, also trained with the Pirates back in Cornwall. Before long, Keen went off injured, to be replaced by a fast-talking fruit and vegetable merchant named Keith Fairbrother.

Fairbrother somehow stole all the headlines before returning to Coventry in his shiny new E-type Jaguar and made it all the way to the England team while Stack returned to Cornwall once again empty-handed. A month later, Powell and his England colleagues Bob Taylor and Budge Rogers came down to Redruth with the East Midlands for another county semi-final. Memories of Surrey were still painfully fresh but another huge and passionate crowd packed into the Recreation Ground. A wedding couple sat in the stand in full regalia having finished the service just in time for the kick-off before rushing back to their reception at the final whistle. This time Cornwall would make no mistake and swept to the final itself for the first time since a teenaged

Stack and that giant pasty had ventured up to watch at Coventry eleven years before.

Hosken again takes up the story:

> That semi-final was played on a glue pot of a pitch and having played downhill in the first half we turned to face both the slope and the elements in the second. The crowd were letting out a long intimidating roar but I never really seemed to notice it. Late in the game our fly-half Tommy Palmer thumped a high ball up the middle and, exhausted as I was, like any good back-row man, I tore after it. A second or two before I arrived to try to tackle the catcher I realised I wasn't quite going to make it. Then suddenly Stack appeared by my side like a runaway train, overtook me and charged down the attempted clearance kick from their full-back. It was sheer murder running up that bloody slope through all the mud with just minutes to go but how a prop who had been pushing his heart out all afternoon could ever manage that I still don't know to this day.

The county final of 1969 against Lancashire proved to be the only one in Stack's long and eventful career and once again provided him with both heartbreak and opportunity. It was early March and sometimes Cornwall's late winter mist and rain disappear as if by magic, and a warm spring day bursts forth upon the world, accompanied by a million golden daffodils. It was just such a day.

The Cornwall team had taken an early light lunch at Tyacks Hotel, which is in the centre of Camborne. When they emerged the streets were completely deserted – seemingly the entire town had disappeared three miles up the road into Redruth for the match. Somehow 22,000 perspiring black-and-gold-bedecked rugby fanatics were shoe-horned into the heaving Recreation Ground to hopefully cheer on their heroes to ultimate victory for the first time since 1908. At least two people were carried away having died of heart attacks among all the electric tension but sadly, even after all that, it was still not to be.

This time Cornwall played up the slope for the first half, went into a 9-0 lead but then, unaccountably, rather lost their heads with victory clearly in sight and were overhauled to once again break thousands of Cornish hearts. Stack however kept his head when others around him were rather losing the plot, did his job well and was arguably the best Cornish forward on the day. He finished the game ruefully swapping shirts with Broughton Park's Barry Jackson who a year later would temporarily displace him from the England team. Some players would have kept that shirt in a glass case but, true to form, Stack simply wore it to training until it finally fell to bits.

Despite all the frustration and bitter disappointment there were several England selectors attending the match and no doubt his name was underlined in a few little notebooks for the following season.

There was certainly plenty of reason to hope.

7

Breakthrough – Caps and Demos

The England team had finished the 1969 season on a desperately low note having been comprehensively thrashed by Wales in what was to all intents and purposes a temporary building site as the ramshackle old Cardiff Arms Park was at last being redeveloped. The Twickenham hierarchy were still completely wedded to the amateur ethos and indeed continued to be so for another quarter of a century, but at least the penny began to drop that amateurism did not necessarily require matters to be conducted in total chaos. That last England team had even attempted to hold an extra practice secretly on a field in the pitch dark, relieved only by the headlights of some parked cars, as they knew the bigwigs would frown upon any extra session as somehow smacking of 'professionalism'. Even the most dyed-in-the-wool traditionalist began to appreciate that all this was just a stupid farce.

Therefore they began to organise 'get-togethers' (they hardly yet warranted the term squad sessions) for prospective England players and even dipped their toes begrudgingly into embracing the dreaded 'c-word' – that is, having a coach. They actually went so far as appointing a technical director for the RFU. The first holder of that vaguely understood position was the ex-England full-back Don Rutherford, who coincidentally now lives in retirement as one of Stack's neighbours near Godolphin. Rutherford recalled:

> I wasn't allowed anywhere near the England team nor to have any say in selection matters but I was able to give things the odd nudge here and there and, as a former Gloucester player, I knew just how powerful and mobile a forward Stack really was.

The chosen 'coach' – although they initially shied away from that dreaded term – was the ex-Northampton and England flanker Don White with some, again unofficial, assistance from a famous old international centre colleague from the Saints, Jeff Butterfield. They had a long list of prospective players and those get-togethers began in August to then continue on a monthly basis. For Stack, this was both good and bad news. It was excellent in that his name was now firmly on the roster but he instinctively knew this would entail far more regular commuting to places like London and Coventry and thus place considerable extra pressure onto his farming duties.

The first such get-together was indeed miles away at Leicester. White gave a stirring little speech and then told the players to 'go and stand in their usual positions'. Some joker got them to all congregate behind the posts as if waiting for an opposition conversion to go over. That painful drubbing in Cardiff still provoked plenty of gallows humour.

Those initial meetings were quaintly haphazard by modern standards but they were a start. Roger Harris remembered:

> We once met up at the Lensbury club on the banks of the Thames. It was a somewhat old fashioned but luxuriously appointed place for the use of executives of the Shell oil company where you probably felt you had to be on your very best behaviour and turn up with your boots nicely polished. I had been in the squad for a little while and felt I sort of knew the ropes by then. I ran out onto the pitch and immediately saw this apparition in a dirty old torn rugby shirt and a pair of full-length and badly-ripped jeans trotting about the field. I did a double-take and realised it was Stack. Sure enough within five minutes some poor mug had taken pity on him and provided him with some pristine England training kit. Of course he just gave me a knowing wink and promptly took it all back home with him.

The players were all asked to give details of their professions, heights, weights, dates of birth and where they had been to school and university, which were all to be used later for programme notes. Stack was comfortable enough being a farmer but the other aspects perhaps needed some of his creative attention. He was acutely conscious that having a landmark thirtieth birthday only a few short months away might conceivably work to his disadvantage. Without blinking an eye he gave his year of birth as 1941 rather than 1940 and used his mother's birthday in June rather than his own, thus knocking eighteen months off his real age. Equally, old Max Biddick and Leedstown Primary School did not quite cut the mustard beside all the various famous old public schools and Oxbridge colleges so it miraculously became Leedstown High School and nobody was ever any the wiser. When this duly appeared in his first England programme and he was teased back at the Pirates as to quite what was 'high' about the little granite building perched on the edge of the village, he shot back that 'it's on top of a bloody hill isn't it?'

For all that he was a very good mixer who invariably got on famously with everyone and knew instinctively how to avoid ruffling the feathers of any of the assorted 'old farts' whose word continued to be law. This was later to stand him in good stead when he was able to get away with enforced absences and his little practical jokes, which might never have been tolerated had they come from some of the more truculent young men in the squad. His new colleagues inevitably tried to mimic his Cornish accent, which is difficult enough to get right for professional actors, as can be testified by anyone watching *Doc Martin* on television. For all that, it never bothered him in the least and with his quick wit he could usually get in the last word.

He was equally single-minded about preparing himself for the key England trials that were to be held in late autumn. He would train harder than ever and ration his appearances to Cornwall's games with just a handful of key fixtures for the Pirates to keep himself match fit. Potential players were all sent typewritten sheets of all the exercises they were supposed to do at home and fitness tests were instituted whenever they reassembled. Stack simply put his into a drawer, stuck to his usual routine of running and farm work and was still always one of the fittest forwards in the squad.

That autumn, the South African Springboks were returning to tour Britain and England's first match was due to be against them at Twickenham. The Basil d'Oliviera affair in cricket had done much to bring that country's highly controversial apartheid policies into public consciousness and widespread condemnation. Several of Harold Wilson's Labour ministers clearly felt unhappy about the tour even taking place but were unwilling to step in and prevent it. Church leaders widely denounced it and predictably university students saw demonstrations and pitch invasions as the appropriate response, some even chaining themselves to gates and goal posts.

The British rugby establishment took a contrary view, feeling that continued sporting contact was far preferable to isolation and stuck to the well-worn old mantra that 'politics should never impinge upon sport'. Rugby players of that generation were caught uncomfortably in the middle. Most felt distinctly uneasy about what they had heard and read about the apartheid regime and several returning British Lions from the 1968 tour had been visibly horrified by it. However, the majority, as single-minded and focused competitors, just wanted to get out there and play. Stack kept his own views to himself but must have dreaded the prospect of potentially being denied his big chance.

By unhappy coincidence the Boks' first fixture was to be against Oxford University, which has always been a hotbed of radical politics, and indeed the game only took place when it was switched at the very last minute from Oxford to Twickenham. Even then there was plenty of trouble. The first few matches followed a similar course and newspapers and television were filled with frightening scenes of violent confrontations involving protestors clashing with police and often overly aggressive stewards. One match was actually due to be held in Belfast but was switched to a secret location which turned out to be New Brighton on the Wirral in front of not much more than the proverbial two men and a dog.

While all this mayhem was going on, England held its first official trial at Moseley's old ground in Birmingham. Stack was once again in the Possibles line-up and again faced Fairbrother, but also had his Cornish buddy Roger Harris alongside to oppose Bristol's John Pullin. The selectors had included Pullin's club prop Bev Dovey at loosehead, who had been capped several years previously and was now teaching at Millfield School. Stack played like a man possessed and by the time the second trial was held at Twickenham three weeks later, the positions were reversed and he and Pullin were in harness together for the very first time.

The two of them remain close friends to this day. Forty-five years after that first game, Pullin unhesitatingly declares Stack to be the very best loosehead prop he ever played with in his long and distinguished career:

> He was naturally so strong, was an ideal size for me to scrummage alongside and could be relied upon to set and maintain a scrum at an ideal height for me to hook the ball. He knew all the usual old tricks too plus a few more of his own and he could run and handle better than any of the others around at the time.

For good measure, Pullin rated Horton, the man who had sung Stack's praises in the press only a year or so before, as the best tighthead in his long experience. Sadly England never managed to get all three onto the pitch together at the same time.

Suddenly it all seemed to be happening at once, but playing for England was the clear priority. He had only managed to play in three matches for the Pirates and a few for Cornwall but now he was to turn down a trip to Clermont with Cornwall to play a France B team and also a first invitation to join the Barbarians for a match against Oxford University. A couple of years before, he would have jumped at either chance, but now everything became secondary to finally nailing down that precious England place.

A second trial match was survived without mishap and, to his intense relief, he was named in the team to face the Springboks at Twickenham on 20 December 1969, so becoming the first man to be so honoured directly from a Cornish club since John Collins of Camborne had done so back in 1952. His front-row colleagues would naturally be Pullin and Fairbrother, while his friend Roger Harris was selected as a bench reserve – another recent innovation on the international rugby scene. Fairbrother has spent his life as a businessman and at the time had a flourishing wholesale vegetable concern in the Midlands:

> Stack used to come up to my place with a lorry load of broccoli and spuds. We were good friends and he could bring me good quality stuff from the warmth of Cornwall when it was not yet readily available from elsewhere. He was a tough old negotiator when it came to price though. Business was business.

The South Africans' tour had not gone particularly well to date. With all the constant hounding from demonstrators and sections of the media, they must have felt unloved, if not distinctly unwelcome. They had just been beaten by Scotland having already lost a few provincial matches that a touring team of their calibre would normally have been expected to win comfortably. Nevertheless, they had quite a number of superb players, including one or two of genuine world class at the time.

'World class' is an overused term but this could indeed be applied to J. F. K. Marais, the Springbok tighthead prop known by his nickname of 'Hannes'. The Springboks party included a couple of near-twenty-stone gorillas in the front-row in Myburgh and Potgeiter but Marais was a different proposition altogether. Both Pullin and Stack himself name Marais as the best opponent they ever faced, and yet surprisingly Tony Horton took a rather different view.

Horton and Pullin had faced them all the year before while with the British Lions and the ever-supportive Tony dropped Stack a helpful letter a few days before the match. It read:

Dear Stack,
Many congratulations, I am delighted that you've made it. I am sure you must be as well!!

Of the Springbok props Hannes Marais is no great shakes, Mof Myburgh will of course not affect you but he is very strong and solid. Potgeiter is perhaps your only worry as he is the old type of South African forward i.e. he scrummages very hard but you'll more than manage.

Best wishes on the day
Tony Horton

Perhaps this was just a bit of encouraging psychology from Horton but most would contend that Marais was indeed very great shakes and had given quite a few opponents around the world plenty of shakes of their own. He was far from huge by South African standards but possessed enormous power allied to a superb technique. That old black-and-white movie *High Noon*, which seems to be shown on television every Christmas, springs to mind regarding any new prop going out to face the opposition for his very first scrum in an international match. In those circumstances, Marais might well be the very last one on his preferred shoot-out list.

Hooker Roger Harris recalled:

I was a reserve that afternoon and in those days was covering all three front row positions. I was sitting there obviously hoping for a chance to get on but I certainly didn't fancy being a makeshift replacement prop against that lot. I had my eyes glued upon the first scrum and to my horror saw Marais twisting Stack all over the place. The referee penalised England and then I saw Stack get up and shake himself like a wet labrador. Welcome to international rugby! Then a little light must have come on in his head because after that he settled down, played superbly and handled Marias without any obvious problem.

Indeed, Pullin was to confirm that he had felt perfectly comfortable the whole afternoon; England recorded a historic victory and the Bristol hooker claimed the final winning try. The two countries had met five times before but, after an initial draw, England had lost every time ever since, so there was much to celebrate. Stack had shown up well with his ball skills around the park and had been up in close handling support when lock Peter Larter went over for England's opening try.

He had little time to relax as just a week later he met the Springboks again – this time playing for the South West Counties at Exeter. Despite the freezing wind, the old County Ground was well filled and on this occasion Mr Potgeiter did indeed put in a brief appearance. He was certainly a big lump of a forward but Stack and Harris got underneath him and after only a few minutes he was taken off with what seemed to be damaged ribs. It was never going to be a classic and the Springboks just scraped a win partly due to some wayward goal-kicking from the home side.

England wins were few and far between in the mid and late 1960s but they immediately secured a second one over the Irish thanks to a late drop goal from skipper Bob Hiller. That match is chiefly remembered for the fact that Tony O'Reilly, by then a highly paid executive with the Heinz food company, was dramatically recalled into the Irish team and arrived at training in a chauffeur-driven Rolls Royce. He apparently did little in the match but was hurled violently into touch by a couple of unappreciative and less affluent England forwards. This, according to well-worn legend, provoked a gravel-voiced cry from the crowd of 'Well done Stack – now kick his bloody chauffeur'.

They nearly made it three wins in a row for the first time in twelve years when Wales looked to be heading towards an unexpected defeat at Twickenham. The afternoon before the game, Stack and Roger Harris were strolling around one of the many prosperous parts of Richmond when they passed a middle-aged man in working clothes furiously polishing another gleaming Rolls Royce. 'Hope they're paying you alright for all that boy,' remarked Stack casually as they sauntered past. The man looked up, slightly taken aback, and Roger immediately saw that it was the famous film actor Sir John Mills.

On the day, Stack had another good game and was opposed by the hugely experienced Denzil Williams whom he had met a couple of times before when Ebbw Vale had made their annual Easter pilgrimage to Penzance. England led into the final quarter and seemed set fair. Gareth Edwards had retired hurt but Maesteg's Chico Hopkins hungrily grabbed his one and only chance in a Welsh shirt to spark a dramatic turnaround and Wales finally won the day.

It was now time to leave Twickenham and England's penultimate match was to be at Edinburgh's Murrayfield stadium. Sadly, England's pack were outplayed by the boisterous Scots and against the home trio of Suddon, Laidlaw and Carmichael, the England front row came out a poor second best. Fairbrother complained, 'The problem was we guys up front were getting nowhere near enough shove from behind and we got pushed around.' The selectors clearly had much to think about before the April trip to Paris.

The merry-go-round nevertheless kept spinning and it was now off to south Wales to take up a second invitation from the Barbarians. The historic old club were a hallowed institution and their blazer and tie then ranked only marginally below an international cap in terms of rugby kudos. They traditionally assembled on the Thursday before Easter at the now demolished Esplanade Hotel in Penarth before playing four matches in five days with the Sunday religiously set aside for compulsory golf. New arrivals were apparently greeted by the old Scotland man Herbert Waddell not with any rugby-related question but rather 'What is your wee handicap laddie?' Stack could have replied that his chief handicap was that he had never played golf before in his life.

Their president was an elderly brigadier-surgeon named Hughie Glyn-Hughes and he headed a heavyweight set of distinguished but equally elderly committee men with an abiding love of entertaining rugby for its own sake, plenty of gin and, of course, golf. It is easy to scoff at that 'olde-worlde' environment with its party games, concerts, jolly songs and little rituals but it was a kindly and supportive atmosphere, and generations of rugby men cherish their memories of those Easter tours as among the very best experiences of their entire playing careers. With both Pullin and Harris also along for the ride, Stack was fun, respectful and could certainly play rugby if not golf, and so fitted in very well. He appeared against Penarth on the Good Friday and at St Helens in Swansea on the Easter Monday and thoroughly enjoyed himself.

Another committee man on the tour was the former Cornwall and England forward Vic Roberts. Having been posted to London with the Customs and Excise, Roberts had enjoyed a distinguished rugby career with the Harlequins and was now a senior figure on their committee. Like Stack, he had forced his way into England recognition some twenty years earlier while still based in Cornwall with Penryn but only cemented his position in the England team once he got regular first-class rugby with the Harlequins. Stack's England colleagues had included no less than four Quins in the current team in the captain Hiller, future England coach Mike Davis, BBC commentator Nigel Starmer-Smith and a long-striding winger and medical student named John Novak.

The logic was crystal clear and Roberts's advice was unequivocal. If Stack really wanted to have an extended career in the big time, he was somehow going to have to follow his star and leave Cornwall and the Pirates behind him.

8

The Long Road Back
With the Quins

The England team for Paris was finally announced and the selectors had clearly decided that they needed to be seen to be making significant changes. The main headline featured not only the dropping of captain Bob Hiller, but Stack, along with the experienced Mike Davis and Bryan West, was also summarily axed – in the latter two cases never to return. Stack was replaced at loosehead prop by Lancashire's Barry Jackson, who had come on as a second-row replacement at Murrayfield and had played much of his rugby as a lock. They also brought in two further debutants into the pack, giving it a decidedly inexperienced appearance. Unless, as a visiting team, you keep the French on a very close leash from the start, they are liable to cut loose in the Parisian spring sunshine and run you ragged. That is precisely what happened and all the new men turned out to be 'one-cap-wonders' as the French centres Lux and Trillo tore a struggling England to shreds as France ran in six spectacular tries.

Meanwhile, back at the Pirates, Stack was joined briefly in the front row by Welsh international prop John O'Shea, whose company had posted him to manage a brewery depot near Penzance. 'Tess' O'Shea was an extrovert, hard-scrummaging tighthead prop and the current captain of Cardiff, who had gained a certain folk notoriety by becoming the first British Lion ever to have been sent off following a free-for-all during a provincial midweek match in South Africa. If the two were to play in tandem for a year or two they would potentially pose a formidable unit in West Country rugby and so aid Stack's own cause. This all seemed distinctly possible, especially when O'Shea was immediately elected club captain for the following season.

On the very same afternoon that England were being butchered at the old Stade Colombes, the two of them packed down together against France's B team, which had come over for a return match with Cornwall. The Cornish, without Stack in the team, had forced a creditable draw in Clermont Ferrand earlier in the season and now only just missed out by a single point back at

Redruth. This was in stark contrast with England's undignified drubbing across the Channel.

With the exception of his brief trip to Germany, Stack had never before undertaken an overseas rugby tour and livestock farmers were not in the habit of going on foreign holidays, particularly when they lived hundreds of miles away from any of the major airports. This was now all about to change as he was about to embark upon a sequence of five long-haul tours over the following six years.

Whenever his son was away, CB was able to enlist the help of three brothers named King who lived next door to Treweeth Farm. The youngest brother, Ian, recalled:

It was hard work with lots of pigs to be fed, spuds to be lifted, straw to be carried and quite a few beef cattle to be looked after. CB was always a very fair man to work for though. He always had high standards and saw that his workers were looked after okay. Nobody was ever asked to do anything which was unsafe, which was not always the case in Cornwall in those days.

CB loved to go to all the various markets. It was Helston on Mondays, Penzance on Tuesdays, Truro on a Wednesday and Camborne on a Friday. He used to meet his old friends and have a chat, although he would often not buy or sell anything if the prices were not to his liking. It was always the same routine and was as regular as clockwork. Meanwhile Stack, or whoever was filling in for him, got on with the job at home.

Not surprisingly, any opportunity to exchange all this for a bit of rugby touring seemed especially welcome. The Penguins are a globetrotting invitation rugby club that emanated from Sidcup in Kent in the early 1960s and for half a century have pioneered the game from the steppes of Russia to Thailand, Africa and Latin America as well as to every established rugby nation on the planet. In 1970 they had accepted an invitation to tour California and a strong team under former British Lion centre Colin McFadyean was assembled to make the trip. Stack was one of a number of current and recent international players in the party, and another was Brian Keen, whom he had met the previous year at West Hartlepool. Coincidentally, Keen had lived temporarily at Praa Sands, had trained with the Pirates and had run on the same beach prior to winning his four caps two years before.

After all the shenanigans with demonstrations on the recent Springboks' visit, Stack and the rest of the party landed bang in the middle of even more trouble. UCLA was a seething centre of student protest and violent opposition to the Vietnam War raged across all the campus sites throughout the summer. A combined Californian colleges rugby team was preparing to tour Australia and this game was billed to be their final 'tune-up' match prior to departure. Of course, any meaningful link between a few random British rugby players and the carnage being waged in South East Asia was non-existent but that did not apparently preclude threats of violent protest.

Indeed protests in the USA at the time were often much more violent than the rather more genteel sit-downs, arm-linking and banner-waving as was the norm in Britain. Looting, shooting and burning could sometimes break out on seemingly the flimsiest of pretexts. No doubt with painful recent memories of the shocking riots in the Watts area of Los Angeles concentrating their minds, the match was abruptly cancelled by the authorities. Fortunately, the rest of the tour, which took in both San Francisco and Santa Clara, passed off without disruption. Despite picking up a nagging injury, Stack had a great time, saw an entirely new part of the world and made a host of new friends.

During the summer he pondered long and hard upon how he might somehow regain his England place as he ran along the beaches and toiled away back on the farm. As a result of that injury in the USA, he played no rugby whatsoever until mid-November, when he and O'Shea played together for a final time in a minor floodlit match in Penzance. Furthermore, O'Shea's employers had dropped a bombshell upon the Pirates by suddenly relocating their man to Australia, thereby eliminating any prospect of the two ever forging any ongoing partnership.

He only returned to the Cornwall team against Pullin and company at Bristol for the last Championship match of the year against Gloucestershire, no doubt hoping against hope that the selectors would seize the chance to reinstate him. To his intense disappointment, the first trial at Wilmslow featured two young, and as yet virtually unknown, props in Nick Hinton and Fran Cotton, who were confronting Fairbrother and the recalled David Powell while Stack was named only as a travelling reserve. To have to journey all the way from Cornwall to the outskirts of Manchester just to sit on a bench was not his idea of fun weekend.

Sure enough, the England team emerged in the New Year for the visit to Cardiff with the same front row as had featured in that debacle two years before and with precisely the same result. By now, Stack had reluctantly reached the conclusion that Vic Roberts had indeed been right – if he was ever going to break back into the big time he would have to bite the bullet and commute to play for the Harlequins.

Needless to say this did not go down at all well with people at the Pirates, many of whom by now felt somewhat abandoned by their star player. Obviously in those days no money was involved, but it was nevertheless only confirming what everyone had known for several years – even if they did not wish to admit it – which was that the heyday of Penzance & Newlyn RFC was now largely a thing of the past. However well a man performed in Cornwall, it was almost certainly going to be ignored by selectors.

The logistics were extremely daunting. It had been difficult enough getting to the various trials, squad sessions and other functions from Godolphin for

England commitments but this new venture was going to involve a weekly commute with a round trip of 650 miles for every match. The M4 was still under construction, the M5 from Exeter to Bristol only existed on Ministry of Transport wall charts and the winding West Country roads in midwinter could be sheer misery. CB still wanted his son working flat out on the farm seven days a week and almost certainly did not view his lad going off to London just to play club rugby in the same light as representing his country. Furthermore, there were absolutely no guarantees that this major gamble would ever pay off.

The Harlequins themselves were not having an easy time of it. Captained by ex-England centre Bob Lloyd, they still included Hiller, Starmer-Smith and Davis, and had also recruited the services of the recent All Blacks fly-half Earle Kirton (the lead writer at the *Evening Standard* just could not resist the toe-curling headline 'Kirton's for the Quins'). However, his very presence also signified something else. The Quins had acquired a controversial reputation for giving immediate first-team places to outsiders. These were often from Oxford and Cambridge but also included overseas star players temporarily residing in London and club spirit inevitably suffered as a result. Bringing in a 'ringer' such as Stack was therefore rather par for their particular course.

However, Hiller was emphatic on one point:

> The idea that the Quins were somehow a snooty club was a silly myth. We had guys from every walk of life and we all mucked happily in together. When I first joined the club, our scrum-half used to weave some of his own clothes and lived in an old bus and by the way he once got a cap for England. An easy-going chap like Stack fitted in easily.

London's top club at the time was London Welsh, who were soon to supply a quarter of the entire British Lions team to New Zealand, including club skipper John Dawes. Furthermore Wasps, London Scottish, Blackheath, Richmond and Rosslyn Park were all at least on a par with the Quins at the time and frequently defeated them in fact.

He made his debut in the famous multicoloured shirt in late January against the Royal Air Force at Twickenham and contrived to appear each week for the next month taking in the London Scots at Richmond, Northampton at Franklins Gardens, US Portsmouth and finally a visit to Stradey Park at Llanelli. Each Friday night he travelled up to London, either driving or as a passenger in a lorry taking a load of broccoli or something similar to sell at Covent Garden market, and then played in a first-class match, hoping desperately to impress the England selection panel. Those long tedious hours of uncomfortable travel and lack of any proper sleep would make a modern rugby coach wince.

He sometimes stayed as a guest with a lady from Penzance named Tinky Youngson and her husband, who were living near Twickenham at the time. Tinky recalled:

He would occasionally come and then just disappear again but he was great fun to have around and we were always delighted to see him. He once absent-mindedly left his England blazer hanging in a wardrobe. My husband thought that for a laugh he would wear it to our local pub but when he tried it on the shoulders were so broad it hung off him like a shroud. I don't think Stack had even realised he had lost it when we handed it back to him.

International rugby players were supposed to cherish their England blazers almost like sacred relics, although the equally scatty Andy Ripley once swapped his with an All Black forward in New Zealand only to discover when he sobered up that he had handed over his wallet and passport as well! This all began to pay off when, in early March, he was invited once more to represent the Barbarians in their annual Edgar Mobbs Memorial match against a strong East Midlands team at Northampton. David Powell had taken back Stack's England loosehead propping slot and would be featuring in the opposing team. Selectors could therefore once again see them both operating in the same match. The Barbarians duly won a close encounter and he showed up to advantage over the solid but less mobile Powell, who nevertheless still retained his England place for the time being.

That match was followed a week later with a trip to France with the Cornwall team, where they lost to a regional team named Comite-du-Lyonnais at the small town of Vienne on the River Rhone, just south of Lyons itself. He was returned to the England squad as a bench reserve when England went down twice to Scotland both in the Five Nations championship and also in a special centenary match at Murrayfield, which turned out to be Powell's last hurrah as an England prop.

There were plans to further celebrate the centenary of that historic day back in 1871 when twenty Scots had opposed a similar number from England at Raeburn Place in Edinburgh in what was the first-ever recognised international rugby match. The RFU President had assembled what was essentially a World XV to play a short series of matches against three English provincial regions to then culminate with a full international against England at Twickenham.

Stack learned to his delight he was back in the team alongside his buddy Pullin and the beefy young prop who had done well in the trial at Wilmslow and made his debut in the Calcutta Cup match, Fran Cotton. He was a big muscular lad with a lantern jaw and bore an uncanny resemblance to Desperate Dan from the *Dandy* comic. Fran hailed from a Rugby League background in Wigan but had recently come to the fore at the famous Loughborough College. He also boasted a big, bull-like neck with hands like shovels and could reputedly play happily on either side of the scrum. He had shone brightly in a match for an England Under-25 team against the touring Fijians in the autumn, was years younger than Stack and, while he obviously lacked experience, it was confidently felt that his time would come. The two were soon destined to play effectively together on many occasions

The president's World XV included a host of stars, although some like All Black legends Colin Meads and Brian Lochore were on the last laps of their distinguished careers. Stack's immediate opponent was once again to be none other than his old adversary Hannes Marais, who conversely was still at the very peak of his powers.

The Queen came along to help celebrate the occasion and was introduced to all the players. Then she and some 60,000 spectators were treated to a feast of running rugby in the spring sunshine, which suited Stack's style admirably. The combined team had benefitted from a couple of weeks together and had a little too much class for a hastily reassembled England. It was, however, just the sort of fast open match ideally suited to Stack's superior fitness and, as he had not played a huge amount of rugby during the season, he was as fresh and lively as one of his newborn calves back in Cornwall.

As a result, he was soon nominated to go on England's ground-breaking tour of Japan, Hong Kong, Singapore and Sri Lanka, scheduled for the early autumn. In the meantime, he had gone back and had a couple of games for the Pirates, including one against Gloucester that saw him packing down against the formidable Mike Burton who, together with Cotton, was very soon to play a significant role in the next chapters of Stack's newly resurrected career.

He settled down for a summer on the farm and was keeping very fit in anticipation of an exciting trip to the Far East and contemplating how he might retain his place for the next Five Nations championship. Just for good measure, Dr Doug Smith, who was managing the forthcoming British Lions tour to New Zealand, had also asked him to attend the pre-tour training camp at Eastbourne and to keep himself trim … just in case.

9

A Call From the Lions

Doug Smith was a large, avuncular Scot who had already toured Australia and New Zealand as a British Lion winger twenty-one years previously, although he had been plagued with injuries for most of the trip. He was now an extrovert GP in Essex and undoubtedly the man to deal with the rugby powers that be, both in New Zealand and back at home, unlike his chosen assistant manager – and very much the coach – Carwyn James.

James had been a highly talented fly-half for Llanelli but had been limited to a single Welsh cap mainly due to the sustained brilliance of his contemporary Cliff Morgan. However, his playing talents had since been completely overshadowed by his creative thinking and brilliant coaching skills, honed first as a schoolmaster and then working at the Llanelli club. He and Smith epitomised the term 'the odd couple'. In stark contrast with Smith, James was a chain-smoking, intellectual Welsh Nationalist with a great love for the Welsh language, its music and poetry, coupled with very clear opinions on just how rugby teams should be selected and sent out to play. This did not seem to endear him to the current great and the good in the Welsh Rugby Union and he was hence condemned to be treated repeatedly in his homeland as something of a prophet who cried in the wilderness.

The two nevertheless complemented one another and worked together admirably. David Duckham was one of the tourists and a great admirer of both of them.

Dr Doug was like a father figure to us all. We were all young men away from our families and girlfriends for three long months and some of the lads inevitably got a bit homesick. Of course he was useful to help with tending the injured but he also fulfilled countless social engagements which could get pretty tedious. In doing so he took much of the weight off the shoulders of the players and also allowed James the space to get on with developing and running the team and its tactics and Carwyn was brilliant in that regard.

They were also fortunate that, despite both being former backs, they had a highly intelligent and technically gifted prop forward named Ray McLoughlin in the party. McLoughlin had already been to New Zealand on a disastrous Lions tour five years previously and, as a former captain of Ireland, had done much to turn his country's team into a tactically astute outfit from what had candidly often been something of a disorganised, if individually talented, group of perennial underachievers. Smith and James were astute enough to let McLoughlin lay down in precise terms the approach the Lions pack should take. Even after he had been forced to drop out from playing due to a broken thumb (received while belting a particularly nasty opponent in a running punch-up of a match in Christchurch), he could still be spotted with his 'Bob Dylan' cap and binoculars spying on opponents' practice sessions.

James was blessed with a dazzling array of talent at his disposal in his backs. A list of Barry John, Gareth Edwards, Mike Gibson, Gerald Davies, J. P. R. Williams, Duckham and the powerful John Bevan reads like a pantheon of twentieth-century rugby immortals. He also had the astute and vastly experienced London Welsh centre John Dawes as his captain, who shared much of the same rugby philosophy as himself. Dawes acted very much as the ringmaster with superb handling skills and a beautifully timed pass that could release the pyrotechnics of the stars lined up alongside him. Furthermore, they all remained mercifully free from injury, although sadly this was not going to be the case with the forwards.

After a shaky start in Australia, partially due to jet lag, the 1971 Lions had torn through the provincial teams of New Zealand like a forest fire and the press and public did not like it one little bit. The ninth match against Canterbury was a shameful affair as the locals had apparently decided to rough up and potentially injure as a many Lions as possible a week before the First Test.

John Pullin related:

> Whilst I had experienced an even dirtier match a few months before when the Fijians came to Gloucester this was still a thoroughly nasty affair. My tighthead prop Sandy Carmichael was a good scrummager but steadfastly refused on principle ever to retaliate when hit. His opposite number Hopkinson punched him in the face time and again and long before the game finished Sandy was a pitiful sight. He also refused to go off and let one of his less inhibited colleagues take over and sort out his tormentor.

While Carmichael stoically endured his martyrdom, the other twenty-nine players stood toe to toe and fought it out, with the Lions finally coming out on top. Nevertheless, the cost was high. Not only was Carmichael clearly out for the rest of the trip with both fractured cheek bones and eye sockets but McLoughlin, in landing his poorly timed left hook on that Canterbury forward, had managed to break that thumb. Suddenly the Lions were left with only two fit props.

It was a sunny Monday morning in the middle of June when the phone rang from Twickenham to summon Stack to the Lions colours. His sister Mary took the call and went out to find him in the process of castrating a set of bull calves, which on reflection was probably as good a preparation as any if he was due to meet up with many more characters like Mr Hopkinson. CB was visibly perturbed at the prospect of losing his son at short notice for weeks on end and it took a while to sink in. 'Does this mean he has to go all the way out there?' he asked plaintively to nobody in particular.

His call up, along with London Welsh lock Geoff Evans, was national news and several reporters, TV crews and cameramen found their way to Godolphin. Packing suitcases, as opposed to scrums, had never been Stack's strong point but, within a couple of days and now complete with a smart new Lions blazer, tie and training gear, he and Evans were on a twenty-six-hour flight to New Zealand. The replacement of two injured props by only one prop and a lock-forward seemed slightly bizarre but as yet no final decision had been taken on McLoughlin's prospects of returning to fitness. Additionally, many rugby coaches still laboured under the blithe assumption that lock-forwards could somehow perform equally well as props – often with disastrous consequences.

Of the two remaining props one was a pocket-Hercules Scot named John McLauchlan, whom everybody called 'Ian'. At a mere five-feet-nine and weighing under fifteen stone, he was a bit of a midget even by the standards of the time. One All Black who should have known better had referred to him disparagingly in a newspaper interview as a 'mouse'. Ian accepted this as a badge of honour and he began to make life a misery for a succession of bulky opponents and was dubbed 'Mighty Mouse' by Doug Smith. The other was a bouncing broth of a boy from Dublin known as Sean Lynch whose profession was described as being a 'vintner'. Lynch was a tremendous tighthead scrummager who would stand no nonsense but it is debatable whether he could have quite matched Stack either as a ball handler or for stamina.

Indeed, both were perhaps a little fortunate to have been chosen in the first place. Barry Llewellyn of Wales could not get release from his job and Fairbrother was also ruled out due to a combination of work commitments, imminent parenthood and injury. It was known that Stack could play on either side of the scrum, was renowned for his strength and stamina and, while never a dirty player, had none of the inhibitions of Carmichael if a bit of retaliation was ever called for. Indeed, if either Lynch or McLauchlan were to be injured or found wanting his chances of Test rugby suddenly seemed quite rosy.

He and Geoff Evans arrived in New Zealand just before the First Test was due to take place in Dunedin. Geoff remembered:

We had flown all the way in one hop with just a short changeover in the USA but when we arrived there was nobody there to meet us. Somebody told us the Lions were staying at the Southern Cross Hotel so I got us a taxi. I am still waiting for Stack to pay me back for his share of the fare.

Carisbrook, the local stadium, was forbiddingly nicknamed the 'House of Pain' and many previous Lions teams had come badly unstuck there at the hands of both the local Otago team and the full All Blacks as well. It was equally famous as the home of severe rucking. As if just to crank the tension up a few more notches, Ivan Vodanovich, the national coach, had inflamed resentment by accusing the Lions of repeatedly lying on the ball and warned of the Test match potentially becoming a 'Passchendaele'.

Fortunately, the match was nothing of the sort and the Lions pulled off a nail-biting victory despite being under enormous pressure in the latter stages of the match. McLauchlan got underneath the huge, near-twenty-stone All Black prop Brian 'Jazz' Muller and gave him a thoroughly torrid afternoon. To cap it all off, the indestructible little Scot charged down an attempted clearance kick to score the only try of the match. If Stack wanted that loosehead Test spot he was going to have a heck of a fight on his hands to stand any chance of wresting it away from the 'Mouse'.

He had arrived in South Island remarkably fresh and, after a long sleep, appeared to suffer less over the next few days from what Dr Doug Smith had referred to as 'circadian dysrhythmia' than many of his colleagues a few weeks earlier. Gareth Edwards, who was already acknowledged as one of the true stars of world rugby, was suitably impressed:

It was never easy to step in half way into a tour but he was so naturally fit he took it in his stride. Immediately you shook his hand you realised why – he was obviously a farmer who knew all about hard work.

Accordingly he was pitched straight into the team to meet Southland in the small town of Invercargill at the extreme tip of the country. Placed on the map, it looks to be somewhere like Penzance but perhaps due to everything 'down under' being upside down, it is very Scottish in character. Either way, it was about as far away from Cornwall to play a game of rugby as you could ever find.

The 1966 Lions had lost their opening match there and, despite the Test having been only four days earlier, eight of that victorious team again took to the field. Significantly, Stack was selected at loosehead with the big Welsh lock Mike Roberts to be tried on the tighthead alongside the established first-choice hooker John Pullin. At the last minute, Roberts pulled out and was replaced by Lynch.

It was a fast game on a rare sunny winter's afternoon and, having felt his way into the match with his new colleagues and strange surroundings, Stack finished strongly and would have felt pleased with his first performance. Off the field, he soon became an integral member of the Front Row Club, a clique of like-minded and broad-shouldered warriors that tends to develop on any extended rugby tour. Of course he already had a firm friend in Pullin, but soon struck up a great rapport with the two Scots – McLauchlan and the Melrose hooker Frank Laidlaw – plus, of course, Sean Lynch.

Lynch was an aggressive forward in contrast with the departing Carmichael and feared no man on the rugby pitch. However, for some reason he lived in mortal terror of creepy-crawly things. Stack soon made the poor lad's life a misery with an assortment of plastic hairy spiders and lizards, which invariably found their way into Lynch's bed, training kit or occasionally down the back of his bull-like neck. Lynch did not enjoy flying much either and, as internal travel frequently involved short flights in small chartered planes, it often required a few stiff drinks just to coax him into his seat.

Ian McLauchlan spoke of Stack's easy manner which, coupled with his natural strength and fitness, soon won him a host of new friends, not least among the Lions' extensive 'Celtic Fringe'. In fact, Stack enjoyed the tour enormously. Away from the everyday pressures of running the farm, his natural cheerful and fun-loving instincts were there for all to see and he became a popular addition to the touring party. Over the years, British Lions tours had often placed enjoyment and 'missionary' responsibilities as an even higher priority than winning, while in the present day victory is everything and the opportunity for actually spending time with local people, visiting schools and proper rugby clubs is now virtually non-existent. In 1971 Dr Smith, thanks in part to his devoted presence on behalf of the rest of the party at so many of the more tiresome dinners and cocktail parties, appeared to have got the balance just about right. As a result, not only did those Lions secure what is still their only series victory in New Zealand to date but they had a wonderful time and made a host of friends into the bargain.

Along with his farming pal John Pullin, Stack visited a number of sheep and cattle farms and enjoyed their generous hospitality. There are numerous photographs taken in the kitchens and gardens of private houses where they were obviously received as honoured guests. Furthermore, with a serious-minded man like Carwyn James in charge the wilder extravagances of the 1968 South African tour were not repeated. Pullin, who had been on both tours, enjoyed the 1971 trip much more and stated that, as the oppressive regime in South Africa was always hanging there like a lingering elephant in the room, he felt instinctively at home in New Zealand among its rugby folk and the population in general.

That friendliness of the people was not always mirrored by the local press, who seemed to look for any excuse to take umbrage at the slightest provocation or indeed where there had been none at all. They were no doubt keenly aware that, for once, their favourite sons were not getting things all their own way.

Stack's second match was against a New Zealand universities team in front of 35,000 spectators at windy Wellington in what turned out be another royal command performance from 'King' Barry John. Just how windy it was indeed going to be was brought home forcibly to him and the other Lions when, emerging from their plane onto the Wellington tarmac, an air hostess's wig blew off and wafted away down the runway with several gallant Lions in hot pursuit. When at last it was returned to its blushing owner, the doubtless expensive fashion accessory looked more like a rain-sodden squashed cat.

On match day Stack was paired with McLauchlan and this time propped Laidlaw for the first time, himself significantly selected as a tighthead. In a flowing match he distinguished himself by flying up alongside a searing break from John to take his off-load and send Duckham sailing over the line with a classic centre's pass. Props were not expected to be able to do things like that.

Four days later the Lions were decisively beaten for the first and only time in the Second Test at Christchurch, having fielded the same forwards as at Dunedin. Both McLauchlan and Lynch had only average games. Was there now an opportunity opening up for Stack in the final two Tests?

His first chance to stake his claim came in the next match against a combined Wairarapa and Bush team at Masterton, played out in pouring rain and a biting wind. This time, however, the management again decided to try the six-foot-four-inch Mike Roberts as a prop. Roberts was an excellent combative lock and a genuine hardman around the field but throwing him into the front row without any meaningful prior experience of the job was like asking a fine steeplechaser to run in the Derby – it was never likely to work.

The Lions won the match comfortably and there was a nice cameo to Stack's performance recounted in the late John Reason's book of the tour:

> In one of their rare moments of attack in the second half, the combined team actually forced the ball across the Lions' line but Stack Stevens saw that the referee was peering round the ruck and hesitating. 'A moment of indecision' said Stevens sagaciously, so he fell back on his Cornish cunning and promptly drove the referee into the ruck and bound him there with his feet waving in the air. Bob Hiller, the Lions' captain for the day, felt that it was the kind of thinking the Harlequins could adopt more often.

Little did Hiller know that back in Cornwall he had been craftily clamping unsuspecting opposing scrum-halves and anyone else he could lay his hands upon into rucks and mauls for years.

He was also highly regarded by the Welsh lads, who no doubt admired the strength and easy-going manner of a fellow Celt. Rugby tourists have always had a penchant for acquiring nicknames and, although he already lived permanently with one, it was somehow felt that the term 'Stack' sounded a trifle rustic for such an esteemed Harlequin. The chirpy scrum-half Ray Hopkins, always known himself as 'Chico', noticed his initials as being C. B. and so he and his bosom companion 'Boss' Hiller promptly christened him as 'Cyril', which he was then stuck with for the rest of the trip.

That match at Masterton had taken place on a Wednesday and everyone knew that selection for the Saturday team was – notwithstanding injuries – the usual route into the Test team. Sean Lynch had put on a bit of weight, had not done particularly well in the Second Test and so for a brief moment it seemed as though a real opportunity might present itself – perhaps on the tighthead side of the scrum. Sadly, it proved to be something of a mirage. Ray McLoughlin, who understood these things, had by then just departed back to Ireland and the all-threequarter selection trio of Smith, James and skipper John Dawes opted to persevere with the size and additional line-out presence of Roberts. Test hooker John Pullin was not consulted and nor was he impressed.

The Saturday game was held at Napier against Hawkes Bay and, although it never descended to the murky depths of the Canterbury debacle, it was nevertheless another mean-spirited encounter and the Lions pack predictably struggled in the scrums. Despite this, Stack had to be content with again being a midweek forward in the match at Gisborne against Poverty Bay, and then had to sit kicking his heels in the stand while the unfortunate Roberts was shoved all over the place in the next big game– almost a Fifth Test match – against Auckland. The Auckland pack drove the Lions off the ball on several occasions, including once with only seven forwards on the park at the time. Fortunately, there was sufficient firepower behind the scrum to still win the game by a seven-point margin.

Meanwhile, Lynch had made a major effort to improve his fitness levels and, with no midweek game, and the Roberts experiment at last abandoned, it was another disappointment for Stack when the same front row of McLauchlan, Pullin and Lynch was announced for the key Third Test in Wellington. That match resulted in a glorious victory for the Lions to go 2-1 up in the series thanks once again to some inspired back play coupled with a strangely out of sorts display from the All Blacks' pack.

However, Stack was not going to become downhearted and had two more midweek matches, firstly at Palmerston North and then against the Bay of Plenty at Tauranga. Indeed, he soon became an honoured member of Bob Hiller's 'T&W Club' (standing for Tuesdays and Wednesdays) and was accepted as a smiling, happy and witty addition to the party who took full part in the regular Sunday lunchtime drinking sessions and was a demon at arm-wrestling, when all those countless bags of spuds being manhandled on the farm must have helped his cause.

One of the achievements of the tour was that the midweek team won every single match. Gareth Edwards recalled:

Stack's regular hooker in that side was Frank Laidlaw, who was a man from the Scottish borders with an accent to match, so that whenever he spoke to his prop it sounded a bit like 'Stork'. When you were ready to put the ball in he would be jabbering away 'More weight Stork – more weight' and Stack would be grumbling away back at him with his Cornish burr. It was hilarious.

The Palmerston North fixture was a fine running display of the sort where Stack's mobility could excel, but the second against the Bay XV was a bit of a struggle and he was penalised for offside to concede the opening penalty of the match. The Lions nevertheless secured their victory to thus complete the first provincial 'clean sweep' since the 1937 Springboks. The crowning glory of a Test place had been denied him, but he had more than played his part.

History relates that the Lions closed out the series with a hard-fought draw in the Fourth Test at Auckland thanks in part to a fine late dropped-goal from J. P. R. Williams. The Lions were euphoric in their dressing room at the end and most were in tears as the almost unbearable tension flooded out of their exhausted bodies. Now the crazy partying could really begin. What was that like? What happens on tour stays on tour!

They broke the long weary journey back home with a four-hour stopover in San Francisco and some of the Lions fought back their weariness to visit the Golden Gate Bridge. Stack was now fast becoming something of a seasoned traveller and could boast that he had already seen it all before when with the Penguins the previous summer.

The bleary-eyed bunch of heroes arrived back in the UK to some rejoicing, although nowhere near to the extent enjoyed after the England 2003 World Cup win. Nevertheless, Barry John became probably the first rugby player ever to earn superstar status, which he unfortunately found difficult to cope with and retired prematurely from the sport only twelve months later. For his part, Stack came home to Godolphin to find the whole village decked out to welcome home their favourite son.

It had certainly been a summer to remember and he must have felt that his gamble of temporarily joining the Harlequins had at last paid a handsome dividend.

10

An England Fixture

Although he had not clinched selection for any of the Test matches, Stack returned home with his reputation sky-high. He was never going to be a national celebrity like Barry John or Gareth Edwards but, at a time when England teams seemed to struggle every year in the Five Nations tournament, he was one of the very few who could count on retaining his place, providing he kept himself fresh and match fit. Amateur players returning from extended tours overseas in those days were generally not expected to venture back onto the playing field much before mid-November and besides, there was much to do on the farm.

He had been scheduled to tour with the non-British Lions rump of the England squad on an early autumn trip to the Far East but understandably withdrew. None of the matches were deemed to be full internationals but the Japanese gave the English two quite stern examinations. Only three props travelled: the fast-emerging Fran Cotton, a perennial 'nearly man' in Coventry's Jim Broderick and a promising Bath youngster named Mike Hannell, who was to die tragically of cancer at a very early age. Broderick was injured early in the tour and a couple of matches were played with two hookers together in the front row, one of whom was a youthful Peter Wheeler. It also saw the introduction of Jan 'Sprat' Webster – a small and bouncy young scrum-half from Moseley who would grab quite a few headlines for himself over the next three years. All the matches were won but overall little else of much immediate value had emerged.

That tour had seen the introduction of another new coach in John Burgess. He was a passionate tub-thumping man who had made a name for himself coaching Broughton Park and Lancashire. Webster recalled:

Burgess would come bounding into the dressing room, slamming the door nearly off its hinges behind him. He would first throw off his England blazer, then his tie and finally rip his shirt off and hammer the table with his fists as he yelled at us. It scared the hell out of some players and gave the gee-up to a few more but as for some of the old hands like Stack - well they just let him get on with it.

Apart from one fairly gentle runout with the Pirates in an easy win over Newton Abbot, rugby took a backseat for a couple of months. November saw Stack return to London for a couple more matches with the Harlequins and also led the way as Cornwall defeated a strong Gloucestershire side, which still did not include Pullin, but had the beefy Mike Burton lined up directly against him. This was followed by two more matches against Somerset before all was set for another Probables v. Possibles trial at Bristol just before Christmas.

When the England team was announced to face a pre-eminent Wales at Twickenham, there were a lot of new faces, including yet another new coach in John Elders. A few of the established names like Hiller, Duckham, Pullin, Fielding and Neary remained along with Stack himself but no fewer than six new 'caps' were in a side being sent out to face what was arguably the best team in the world at that juncture. One of these was Webster, who felt the approach being demanded was defeatist from the outset:

> Clearly the selectors had taken a look at the Welsh backline with all its stars and decided that we should just adopt a damage limitation stance and kick the leather off the ball. I had expected to be really nervous but I just felt frustrated.

Stack's new propping partner was Gloucester's Mike Burton – a larger-than-life character and a typical product of Kingsholm and its noisy worshippers in the Shed. He was big, he was mean but, as a born comedian, he could also lift the spirits of those around him and was a nightmare to face in the scrum. Stack was to play his straight man to perfection.

By far the most interesting of all the debutants was the extraordinary Andy Ripley, who had only taken up rugby five short years earlier as a nineteen-year-old student at the University of East Anglia in Norwich, but had since emerged sensationally as a rip-roaring Number 8 at Rosslyn Park. Even that ridiculously short career had nearly come to an end with a broken kneecap that sidelined him for months. He stood at nearly six-feet-six with amazingly long legs and a huge stride that would see him hurtling up the field like a rampant giraffe; trying to stop him in full flight was not for the faint-hearted. Added to this, with his shoulder-length hair, bizarre taste in highly exotic t-shirts and rimless John Lennon-type spectacles perched on an aquiline nose, he was something refreshingly different. The Twickenham crowd could never get enough of him.

The Welsh coach at the time was a certain Clive Rowlands, who was another of the hellfire and brimstone school of motivation much like Burgess. He had no truck with the romantic notions of a Carwyn James and had acquired a certain notoriety a few years earlier when, captaining Wales at Murrayfield from the scrum-half position, he had booted every scrap of possession into the crowd to reportedly finish the match with 111 lineouts as the shivering 80,000 crowd probably lost all their remaining will to live.

His chosen captain was a big round slab of a Bridgend prop-forward by the name of John Lloyd, who was also slightly notorious but in his case for polishing off every scrap of food on his plate, and that of anyone else sitting anywhere nearby. He thus was known in the squad as Mr Greedy after the character in the Roger Hargreaves children's books. Rowlands would apparently yell at his players, stuff like 'Bevan – what are you going to do to that blond ponce David Duckham?' 'I'm gonna smash him, boss,' would come the stock reply and so it went on around the room. Finally he roared out 'Lloydy – what are you going to do to that bloody Stack Stevens?' 'Er – I – er – I'm gonna eat him, boss.' Collapse of team meeting.

On the day, the English underdogs tore into their illustrious opponents and the forwards, with new boys Ripley and Burton well to the fore, were on top for most of the first half but only had a single penalty from Bob Hiller to show for it. Nobody attempted any cannibalism on Stack and he, Pullin and Burton were giving as good as they got up front. Unfortunately, the Welsh tightened their grip in the second half and a Williams try settled the matter with England once again frustrated but having at least shown some very positive signs of improvement.

The Irish contingent had returned from the Lions tour full of ideas and, with McLoughlin restored to match fitness back alongside the vastly experienced McBride, Gibson and Tom Kiernan, they had assembled a formidable team. Tragically, the political situation in that beautiful country had been deteriorating rapidly and civil rights protests had become increasingly violent. On Saturday 29 January, Kiernan's team scored a notable victory over the French in Paris for the first time in twenty years. Back in Derry the following afternoon, all hell broke loose.

What has gone down in history as 'Bloody Sunday' was not only a disaster for Anglo-Irish relations but it soon became a potential hammer blow for rugby in the country as well. Since partition in the early 1920s, rugby had stood like a beacon of hope as one of the few – depressingly few – sporting activities where an All-Ireland team took the field and Protestants and Catholics had always played happily with and against one another for a couple of generations. All this would now be tested as never before.

By a twist of fate, Ireland's next match was scheduled for two weeks later at Twickenham and as the crowd of 60,000 gathered for the kick-off, things were understandably tense. A couple of middle-aged demonstrators had run onto the pitch before the start but, compared with the Springbok experiences of recent memory, it quickly passed. Once again, England flattered to deceive and took what looked to be a decisive lead after a snap try from Chris Ralston. Although it was pared back with penalties, they went into injury time still clinging on to a two-point lead. At the last gasp they were undone when centre Kevin Flynn sold a perfect dummy to slide through for the winning try. This was hard for the England lads to take.

Stack had been propping against his old spider victim Sean Lynch and soon found himself being penalised a few times at the scrum by Monsieur Austry, the French referee, and demanded to know why. Leedstown School never taught much French and Austry looked totally flummoxed by a Cornish accent. Andy Ripley, who was currently studying at the Sorbonne, tried to help but confessed afterwards that, although he could understand the referee perfectly, he hadn't the first clue as to what Stack was going on about.

The Irish celebrated their win as boisterously as ever but trouble lay ahead. Neither Wales nor Scotland were prepared to risk their players or their thousands of supporters going to Dublin while the atmosphere remained so tense, and accordingly both matches were reluctantly cancelled. Rugby in Ireland lagged behind soccer, hurling and Gaelic football in terms of public popularity and still does to this day. Thus they relied heavily upon income from the two home international matches that season and now this was to be snatched away. The Five Nations was consequently void for the season – ironically in a year when the Irish had a genuine and all-too-rare opportunity of actually winning it.

Stack had featured in another couple of matches for the Harlequins but, with his England place now as secure as it was ever going to be, he switched back to playing for the Pirates. Meanwhile, to their great credit, the French had generously intimated that they would play an extra international match in Dublin to help defray some of the revenue loss and indeed did so as the season drew to the end.

France was to be the next stop and for Stack it was his first visit to play in Paris. This was to be the last time that England would go to the rickety old Stade Colombes, tucked away in a staunchly communist suburb of the city and which had once hosted the 1924 Olympic Games, since recaptured in the 1980s movie *Chariots of Fire*. It had also marked the very last time that rugby had featured in the Olympics when the final was won – somewhat bizarrely – by the USA. If this did not seem strange enough, the match erupted into a massive brawl involving both players and spectators to the extent that the Olympic President Baron Coubertin had made it abundantly clear that, until they learned to behave, nasty rough rugby players were not going to be allowed anywhere near his precious Games. Over ninety years later, we are still making the first tenuous steps back by way of the Sevens tournament in Rio.

The England selectors had slightly lost their nerve after the Irish defeat and out went their charismatic captain and full-back Bob Hiller, who was never to regain his position, as well as the pocket-sized scrum-half Jan Webster. They were to be replaced by two relatively inexperienced young men in Peter Knight of Bristol and Lionel Weston, who was currently teaching in Glasgow.

Weston spoke of his first encounter with Stack:

> I was picked for the Possibles team for the Trial at Bristol and was understandably a bit nervous. At the very first lineout this big bloke with hardly any teeth grinned at me and said something like 'I'm coming to get yew, boy'. Of course he never did anything to me but it was all a bit spooky at the time and I still remember it.
>
> I was picked as a bench reserve for the first game with Wales and afterwards we were all booked into the Park Lane Hilton for the formal dinner and dance. It was my first time at one of these events and around midnight my wife and I slipped off quietly to our room for the night. At breakfast the following morning a bleary-eyed Stack and Burton rolled in together, still in their very crumpled and obviously slept-in dinner jackets and proceeded to tuck into vast amounts of sausage, egg and bacon. I really did feel like a little boy on his first day at school.

In fact the entire England team must have all felt rather like little boys when they trooped wearily off the pitch at Stade Colombes, having been taken to the cleaners by a rampant French team that had walloped them to the tune of six glorious tries to a single rather flukey one. The final score of 37-12 was the worst defeat England had ever suffered since 1905. Stack did his best, but once the French cut loose he was chasing shadows like the rest of them. There was nothing for it but to get that old dinner jacket back on and see what the delights of a night out in Paris might have in store.

Losing to an inspired French team in the Paris sunshine was one thing but getting thumped by a distinctly average Scotland one was quite another. Stack had shown his undoubted class in a derby win for the Pirates over their local rivals Redruth and then travelled up to Edinburgh later in the week. Lionel Weston again recalled:

> I was playing my weekly rugby for a team called West of Scotland in Glasgow. Two of my club mates, Sandy Carmichael and Gordon Brown, were in the opposing team so I knew what the bragging rights were going to be like.

The Scots scored in the first couple of minutes after a mistake in the England defence and were 14-0 up by half-time. Alan Old hauled England back with a couple of penalties but the Scots bagged three of their own to run out clear winners in a somewhat tepid finish. Stack battled away as only he knew how but to no great avail. He was now a fixture in the team but one that seemed to be going nowhere, having lost all four internationals in one season for the first time ever.

Back with the Pirates, he took part in a Cornwall cup semi-final when they were walloped by Penryn and then captained the club for one of only a handful of occasions in his entire career against the Saracens. That season he was joined in the club's front row by an interesting newcomer with a seemingly inexhaustible fund of hilarious stories named Geoff Rowe. In due course, as 'Jethro', he was to become the famous stand-up comic, who is still filling halls and theatres up and down the country with his zany Cornish stories that often involve his fictional mate Denzil. Life was certainly never dull with them both around and they were to play many times together during the mid-1970s. For his part, Stack finished the season with another meeting with that French team from Lyons making a return trip to take on Cornwall.

In the meantime, the Rugby Union had accepted an invitation to undertake a first-ever short tour to South Africa. This was an exciting prospect for Stack and all the others but would they merely face embarrassment? Time would tell.

11

Boots 'n' All

Despite becoming a well-known 'face' in English rugby, Stack continued to be perennially short of ready cash. Travelling to matches, squad sessions and Harlequins games, plus a few celebratory but virtually mandatory dinners, meant that the cost in financial terms began to weigh upon him almost as heavily as the time commitment. Whenever he was away from the farm other staff had to be brought in (and paid), and as he could generally be relied upon to do the work of any two – if not three – other men, this was a burden other players rarely had to deal with. For him, it was a constant worry.

Stack of course could always be relied upon to be something of the 'artful dodger' and his highly fertile mind usually conjured lots of ways of cutting his costs. Some were totally legitimate, but others occasionally strayed into the grey areas of the law, at least from the RFU's narrow-minded perspective. Taking rides to London via Covent Garden Market was not always feasible and many training sessions took place in the Midlands. Luckily, he had a number of willing rugby fans among the guards and other staff on British Rail and soon had his own particular version of a 'season ticket', which they cheerfully ignored. Sitting up all night, whether in a lorry or a train, was no preparation for a rugby match and so they frequently managed to find him an empty sleeping compartment as well.

Although he was undoubtedly the team member with the biggest logistical problem to wrestle with, he was far from being alone. Sport in the 1970s only attracted a tiny fraction of the revenue pouring in today from television contracts, corporate sponsorship and merchandising but the Rugby Union still earned hundreds of thousands of pounds each year from its England matches at a time when the pound was probably worth between ten and twelve times what it is today.

Meanwhile, the players got precisely nothing. The RFU did reimburse what they deemed to be 'legitimate' expenses, but their interpretation of what constituted legitimacy came straight out of Charles Dickens. Every claim for the tiniest amount had to be accompanied by detailed receipts and these were all scrutinised in minute detail by a scrooge-like zealot who took every possible opportunity to throw them back at the unhappy claimant. On one occasion Stack and an England colleague had a receipt for a steak sandwich turned down while an abstemious third got the thumbs up for a no doubt virtually inedible British Rail buffet cheese roll. This entire pantomime was all done lest something might, by some incomprehensible twist of tortured logic, define the player as being a 'professional'.

Occasionally, someone deliberately took the mickey out of the daft system, such as when Keith Fairbrother flew himself to a training session in his private light aeroplane and sent in a chit for 180 gallons of aircraft fuel. It was returned to him with the words 'Please re-submit' scrawled across it in blue pencil and without even a flicker of a smile.

The Scots and Welsh unions were equally parsimonious. In his entertaining book *Beyond the Fields of Play*, the late Cliff Morgan fondly recalled the occasion when he first queued up to reclaim his expenses from a Welsh RFU Secretary named Eric Evans, whom he already knew quite well:

'Name?' He asked aggressively.

'Morgan, Sir.' As if he didn't know already.

'Expenses?'

'Five shillings, Sir.'

Eric had in front of him a school exercise book with a black cover. He flicked over the pages as if he was reading a bad novel, suddenly slammed the book shut, banged the table, looked up and me and said 'You are a liar and a cheat. It is two shillings and four pence each way from Trebanog to Cardiff. That's four and eight!' With that he gave me a half-a-crown, a two shilling piece and two grubby pennies in an envelope.

By Stack's time nothing had changed very much.

Despite people like Mr Evans, it was widely rumoured that many clubs – especially those in France and to a lesser extent in Wales – paid small sums to attract and retain the best players with what was euphemistically called 'boot money'. This name came on the basis that a lucky player would somehow find a couple of £10 notes miraculously appearing like a sixpence from the tooth fairy in the toe of his boot when he went off to take a shower. Like all good stories they grew with the telling, but one thing was certain – there was no way that Penzance & Newlyn RFC was ever going down that particular road.

One or two of his England colleagues, such as Keith Fielding and Fairbrother, made the one-way transition to Rugby League but then the Union hierarchy would immediately pour forth its vengeance upon them by banning them for life, not only from playing the game but also from coaching or even entering a clubhouse. Furthermore, any other player found to have knowingly played alongside an ex-Rugby League man could also get himself into hot water with the authorities. If South Africa had its hateful apartheid laws then Rugby Union had some fairly brutal segregation rules of its own, which wouldn't last five minutes under the Human Rights Act today.

Stack's mobile style of play might have done particularly well had he elected to go 'Up North'. A £5,000 to 6,000 signing-on fee might have been initially attractive but, with a long-term commitment to a valuable farm and a deep love of Cornwall, it was never really going to prove very attractive.

A small chink in the RFU's armour appeared at this stage and once again it concerned boots. When Stack first came into rugby in the late 1950s, players had only just moved away from the old heavy leather horrors with nailed-in studs that had to be soaked in water for hours before you could even get them on properly. Ever after they required smothering with a greasy concoction called 'dubbin' before you tramped wearily around in them and through the mud like some unfortunate squaddie on the Somme.

The forwards' almost universal boot of choice in England throughout the 1960s, and indeed for a while afterwards, was the Cotton Oxford, which was much more malleable, only needed washing and polishing and had very practical screw-in aluminium studs. Fleet-footed wingers had already gone over to cut-away continental soccer boots. Cotton Oxfords gave good protection to the toes and ankles and were commendably long-lasting but still quite heavy and generally pretty boring, rather like running around a soggy field with your feet stuck in a couple of dependable black Morris Minors.

All this was to change dramatically when the products of the Dassler brothers from Germany came onto the UK market in the late 1960s. They each headed up their own large sportswear company and had since become deadly rivals. Initially, the more prominent was Adidas and their rugby boots were not only lighter with moulded soles but were readily identifiable by three vertical white stripes on either side of each boot. Moreover, they made different ones for beefy forwards and speedy threequarters. Unlike Cotton Oxfords, they were backed by aggressive marketing and, being readily identifiable and looking smart, soon became the fashion choice of many leading players.

Among Adidas' sales agents was the athlete John Cooper, who had won silver medals for the 400 metres at both the Tokyo and Mexico City Olympic Games. He had got to know David Duckham, who was probably England's most prominent star at the time. Cooper proposed that, through Duckham, he would supply free pairs of boots to each of the England players. This was hardly the stuff of revolutions but it had never been done before. The players accepted happily enough and before long were getting several pairs each and then tracksuits, sports bags and training tops all emblazoned with the prominent Adidas striped logo.

Stack naturally got hold of as much of this stuff as he decently could lay his hands upon and then took it all back to the Pirates to flog off to his club colleagues. One young forward took a pair of new boots one week and the following Saturday was sitting in the dressing room and ready to play but hadn't yet raised the money to pay for them. Stack grabbed them back and refused to hand them over until he got his money. Of course it was just another Stevens 'wind up' and the other players were all in on the joke. The poor lad was virtually in tears as kick-off time loomed nearer and nearer and he was still padding miserably around in his socks. At the last second he got his boots back to play in, but made sure he paid up on the nail at training the following Tuesday night.

The old boys in the RFU harrumphed at all this but largely chose to turn a blind eye. One of the committee men who didn't approve was an ex-England prop from the 1950s called Sandy Sanders, whose playing career had been prematurely curtailed by a motorcycle accident that left him with a pronounced limp for which he had to use a black walking stick. On a tour to New Zealand Stack 'borrowed' his stick when he wasn't looking and quietly taped three white Adidas stripes onto it.

However the other committee men might have been a bit more alarmed at what came next. The other Dassler brother had also entered the UK market with a company called Puma, which had its own scimitar-shaped white stripe emblazoned on the side of its boots and had become quite prominent when the star Portuguese footballer Eusebio had worn them in the 1966 World Cup. Puma had recruited their own prominent British athlete, Derek Ibbotson, who was keen to offer the England players a similar – and possibly better – deal if they wore their products when turning out for England games on television. These were soon followed by Gola who began to up the ante even more.

Accordingly, the players were all offered cash of initially £50, later rising to £100 for wearing their preferred boots. Initially Duckham hesitated. He did not actually need the cash himself and knew full well that if being supplied free kit was borderline, being paid cash under the counter was in rugby parlance 'way offside' and could potentially mean players getting banned – possibly even for life. Indeed, until rugby went 'open' in 1995 this was all kept very quiet, although it threatened to leak out at one point when the Welsh lads found out they were getting paid less than the English.

Duckham's colleagues also wavered but there was safety in numbers and most went ahead. As both Adidas and Puma were offering similar deals the players then faced a dilemma as to which one to choose. The ever-resourceful Andy Ripley solved the problem in one match by wearing a Gola boot on his left foot and an Adidas one on his right and actually succeeded in getting paid twice. A couple of others followed suit until a few weeks later one not very bright Welsh forward apparently turned up to play to find that having taken great care to ensure different stripes for each foot he had packed his bag with two left boots!

After Stack finished playing international rugby in 1975 the problem of expenses, interviewing fees, use of faces for advertising and book publishing proceeds rumbled on for another twenty years, becoming more and more of a farce as the years rolled by. Following his triumphant return from the British Lions tour, Barry John had retired after one more season and brought out a book. He was immediately declared a 'professional' although he had never played Rugby League, nor as far as anyone knew ever been paid for playing. Accordingly he could never coach the game nor hold any position in the Cardiff or Llanelli clubs where his genius had shone for a decade. As late as the early 1990s, England and Lions captain Bill Beaumont was still temporarily suffering the same fate. Now he is the head of World Rugby.

Meanwhile, back in Cornwall the old Cardiff and Wales winger and later Hunslet Rugby League professional Les Williams was employed as a county council sports organiser. In that role he had coached rugby to schoolboys every week for years and was apparently perfectly entitled to do so. The logic in all this escaped most people.

Such was the world that Stack inhabited throughout his career. Fortunately he had the attitude that all players seemed to display – he just loved playing rugby.

12

Into the Land of the Springboks

The England team had finished the 1971/72 season on a very low note and were stranded at the bottom of the Five Nations with the miserable record of four losses from four games and indeed had only emerged victorious in one solitary match out of the past twelve. Following the distinctly underwhelming performances in the Far East, coach John Burgess had been replaced by the ex-Leicester centre John Elders, but the losses had continued to mount alarmingly.

Against this sorry background, the prospect of a seven-match tour of South Africa within the space of a mere three weeks appeared to be a particularly daunting one. However as the RFU had agreed to the programme there was little option other than to buckle down and get on with the job. Matters were not helped by the fact that several first-choice players were going to be unavailable for one reason or another. Current skipper Peter Dixon had a university commitment, the two Keiths, Fielding and Fairbrother, were both injured and Duckham felt jaded, if not exhausted, after eighteen months of non-stop rugby and declined the trip in order to recharge his batteries.

Others such as Jorden, Rossborough and Brinn were unable to travel either. As a final straw, the highly promising Roger Uttley, who had been one of the few successes from the trip to Japan and Hong Kong, was added to the party but then had to withdraw due to injury within days of being selected. When the team was announced it included only three prop-forwards – Burton, Cotton and Stack himself. Stack would also have fellow Cornishman Tommy Palmer, the Gloucester and Cornwall fly-half, along with him. Palmer was destined to do very well on his own account in South Africa and was possibly unlucky not to win a full cap in Johannesburg.

Accordingly the group with which he met up at the Star & Garter Hotel in Richmond was something of a mishmash comprising around half of the current team; recalled old stagers like Larter, Watt, Barton and Spencer were teamed together with no fewer than eight others who had as yet to even pull on an England shirt. The tour manager was an ex-England flanker named Alec Lewis, who seemed undaunted by all this and put his trust in his most experienced player, John Pullin, to captain the team. It turned out to be an inspired choice. Pullin was never an overly demonstrative England leader of the 'God, King Harry and St George' variety but was universally respected as possibly the best technical hooker in world rugby. The England team would soon respond magnificently to his quiet but persuasive style of leadership and thrive on adversity. Pullin's appointment was music to Stack's ears.

The touring party also knew they could expect plenty of trouble on the political front. The players had all received a round-robin letter from a 'Stop the Tour Committee' urging them not to go in reasonably moderate terms. However, when they assembled at their hotel and later visited the South African embassy they were besieged by groups of protestors waving banners, screaming abuse and even lying down in front of the team bus. Two new boys to touring were Lionel Weston and the Coventry centre Peter Preece, neither of whom had ever been exposed to anything like that before and found it all quite unnerving. Having already played twice against the Springboks in England and seen at least some of it before, Stack was a little more phlegmatic.

Some of Edward Heath's government were not overly keen on the tour taking place either, but had more pressing issues such as the chaos in Ulster and the bitterly resisted Industrial Relations Act to contend with, and so declined to get themselves involved. Like most of the players, Stack wanted to test himself once again in opposition to the big Afrikaners and was more bemused than shocked at all the vitriol being spewed in the players' direction. When they eventually landed in South Africa they began to appreciate what all the fuss had been about.

South Africans are naturally hospitable people and were keen for the tourists to visit their homes, where a sumptuous barbecue or *braai* would invariably be served. However, they tried to steer their guests well away from areas where you would see 'whites only' notices and Stack and the other players were constantly being asked 'What do you think of South Africa?' in a way which betrayed their evident unease.

Stack's objections to segregation were strong but as much practical as political. England centre John Spencer recalled:

> I went with Stack into a post office to get some stamps and we were told by some 'jobsworth' that we had come in by the wrong entrance and that we had to go back out again and come in via the one set aside for the white population. He told the guy that this was just a stupid waste of time and basically to bugger off. He then just vaulted calmly over the railing and joined the queue of surprised-looking whites. Nobody uttered a word.

The first port of call was Durban, down on the coast at sea level, and on the first morning they came downstairs to be fed with a large cooked breakfast.

Unfortunately, they then had to go straight out onto a burning-hot pitch for their initial training session of interval running and, to make matters worse, a large crowd including plenty of local reporters had gathered to watch. They could hardly have been impressed by what they saw. Those old amateur ways were not quite dead yet. For all that the first match against Natal at the Kings Park Stadium in Durban proved to be something of a revelation.

The tour was to be crammed into just three weeks. The first ten days would comprise four matches, all to be played at sea level, followed by a further three at altitude up on the Transvaal. The tour would conclude with a full international at Johannesburg. Natal were led by the ex-Oxford Rhodes scholar Tommy Bedford, who had built up a huge reputation in the UK during the past few seasons and had a strong team around him, which was confidently expected to win.

The match was played against a provincial team and, as such, did not count as a full international, but it was nevertheless the best performance an England XV had shown for a very long time. Reporting in the *Daily Express*, veteran correspondent Pat Marshall led with the flattering headline 'Granite Stevens sets up England Triumph'. It was possibly his finest game in an England shirt to date as he, Pullin and Cotton bullied their larger Natal opponents out of their stride. A 19-0 victory constituted a very encouraging start, but they all knew there were far higher mountains yet to climb.

Just three days later they ran out again at the famous Newlands ground in Cape Town. They had read all about the size of the Western Province pack that the local press confidently believed would grind the English upstarts into the turf. For this match, Mike Burton had been selected and in his entertaining book *Never Stay Down* he recounted meeting them for the first time:

> John Pullin said a few words and we went out into the tunnel. The home side ran past and Stack Stevens and I, the props of the day, looked at each other. Morne du Plessis, the giant number eight, went lurching by followed by Immelman and de Villiers, the two huge locks. Stack and I were searching for the numbers one and three on the Western Province backs, so that we could size up our own opposition.
>
> Then the sun set, and darkness fell on the face of the earth – or that is what seemed to happen. Actually, blotting out the light were van Jaarsveldt and Walter Hugo, the Western Province props who were thirty-seven stone and four yards between them. They were monstrous. Stack was not big by some standards but compared with those two he reminded me compellingly of a starving maggot with me as his slightly larger, elder but also starving brother.
>
> As they lumbered past Stack's jaw dropped. 'I don't like the look of yours much mate,' he said revealing his considerable ability to crack jokes in terribly unfunny situations.'

At times like that, years of accumulated experience comes into its own. Stack knew that if he and Pullin went really low, much of the weight and power from those two monsters would be effectively neutralised. He had learned it all the hard way back in Cornwall years before and now it came to his aid much in the way that his pal Mighty Mouse had dealt with the enormous Jazz Muller on the Lions tour the previous summer. It was to be a tough afternoon but he and Burton came through without mishap and a second (albeit much narrower) win was chalked up.

That season, Burton had been the stand-up comic and most outrageous comedian of the party but he had a fair number of willing accomplices. Between the matches, the practice sessions and similar commitments, the team were invited to see something of the country despite the short period of time they were going to be there. At one point they were taken down a deep gold mine and the tour guide switched out all the lights to demonstrate what total darkness actually felt like. They also found out that the Bantu miners who toiled away for hours in that pitch-black underground dungeon were paid the princely sum of one rand per day – then the equivalent of around 50p. They flew over the Great Hole of Kimberley, which was then the largest man-made pit in the world, visited a safari park and an ostrich farm and, while in Cape Town, took the cable car up to the top of Table Mountain.

On the way up one very large forward – not Stack – decided to grab the team's little scrum-half, Jan Webster, and dangle him over the side. 'The drop was hundreds of feet and once I had been hauled back I spent the rest of the journey to the top hunched up on the floor having a panic attack,' was Webster's heartfelt recollection.

Having found his bearings, Peter Preece also became a bit of a joker on his own account and found a ready soulmate in Stack. Most front-row forwards had a tendency to stick together, but, having by then found his touring feet in California and New Zealand, Stack was an easy mixer and the two shared any number of pranks together, which continued for the rest of their England careers. Peter was the son of the ex-British Lion and England captain Ivor Preece and, as with all sons following in the footsteps of famous parents, he had to overcome constant comparisons with his father, but soon showed his own considerable talents as the tour progressed.

This was a whirlwind tour and certainly not all one of excursions and jokes which merely served to lighten the intensity of their main mission. This was a deadly serious expedition, not only with respect to straining every sinew in trying to overcome the Springboks but, as this was South Africa, the spectre of politics soon loomed large once more.

The tour organisers had scheduled two matches against non-white teams for almost the very first time and as such this could be construed as making a small degree of progress. The previous winter a touring team called the Proteas had visited the UK and the first match was to be something of a return fixture.

Unfortunately, that winter tour had not gone very well and there had been a number of misunderstandings both off and on the pitch. Their forwards were small and heavily outweighed, which caused problems right away, but also, partly due to being continually forced to play on rough bone-hard pitches back home, they had a habit of head-high tackling which was considered highly dangerous by their hosts and one match against Berkshire had descended into an unseemly brawl.

The non-white rugby administration was shared between two organisations and opinion was sharply divided between them as to whether fielding a team assembled on entirely racial grounds against the English merely served to further crystallise apartheid, or whether it would signify meaningful progress towards their declared goal of mixed-race teams selected purely on merit. Feelings ran extremely high, many selected players felt threatened and some indeed withdrew altogether.

The England tourists inevitably travelled in something of a sheltered cocoon but could hardly miss the fact that they were being either wildly applauded or coldly shunned wherever they travelled, that the non-whites were corralled into the most inhospitable parts of the stadiums and cheered in direct opposition to their own local teams or indeed the Springboks themselves. Furthermore, they had all become acutely conscious of the fact that every facility, transport, shop, hotel, school and even public toilets and ambulances were rigidly divided on racial grounds. After his post office episode, Stack and all the other players found this increasingly hard to stomach, but generally kept their counsel and concentrated upon the rugby.

Stack was not selected to play in either of those two matches against non-white teams which were held in rather primitive stadiums in Cape Town and at New Brighton, which is a township on the outskirts of Port Elizabeth. As the first-choice loosehead prop, he was being held back for the big match with Northern Transvaal. This was to be held at the towering Loftus Versfeld Stadium in Pretoria and as such constituted his first-ever game played at altitude.

If the mighty front row at Cape Town, so graphically described by Mike Burton, was a severe test, Northern Transvaal was the spiritual home of the Afrikaner rugby 'volk' who worshipped their much-loved Blue Bulls with an almost spiritual homage to the mythology and power of the set scrum. Stack's old adversaries Myburgh and Potgeiter had been weaned and hardened in that brutal environment but they had now retired to be replaced by the equally huge and forbidding Bezuidenhout and Le Roux. Packing down between them was the current Springbok hooker – the splendidly nick-named 'Piston' Van Wyk.

This game was dubbed by the locals as the 'Extra Test Match' and it indeed turned out to be the hardest struggle of the entire tour. It was a match in which the English were relieved to scrape a late draw, having trailed 3-13 well into the second half. The thin air allowed the ball to travel seemingly miles further than at sea level and, thanks to three huge penalties from the Moseley full-back Sam Doble, they stayed in the hunt. The decisive breakthrough came when Stack ripped the ball expertly away from a maul and sent out a perfect pass to fashion a rampaging late try from Ripley and a thrilling 13-13 draw was duly secured.

Although the England back row stole the honours, the front trio, which this time included Fran Cotton, had naturally been under massive pressure but had never buckled and at the end came up still smiling for more. As the Bulls had included at least five of the prospective Springbok pack for the match scheduled a week later, this draw was, in the overall context, a hugely encouraging result.

At the time, Stack had never captained Cornwall, or indeed the Pirates back in Penzance, so it was a great compliment to be given the honour of leading out the tourists in the penultimate match in Kimberley. The town had built itself almost entirely around the diamond-mining business and the little local stadium was called De Beers after the family who held almost all of the mining rights. The touring party had just been joined by the youthful but supremely self-confident Steve Smith, who had come out as a replacement for the injured Weston and the team Stack led out in truth had a distinctly 'midweek' look to it.

It is often said that a team can only play what is in front of them and there is always the possibility of getting sucked into a scrappy mess of a game, as indeed the tourists had themselves found out against the Proteas a week earlier. Stack's team, however, never let up and ran away with a huge 60-21 victory, scoring nine tries to two in the process. One of these he claimed himself by finishing off a fine bout of inter-passing with backs and forwards joining in the fun. So he had the satisfaction of leading his country and appearing on the score-sheet for the first time all on the same afternoon.

One of the more innocent, but nonetheless enjoyable, party games on any tour of this nature used to be the Players' Court and, perhaps reflecting his fast-developing status as one of the senior men on the tour, Stack was elected as a presiding judge. Once appointed, he dispensed merciless justice rather like a latter-day Judge Jeffreys upon his hapless colleagues. Big David Watt was sentenced to be summarily deported for having had an excessive number of medical appointments, centre J. P. A. G. Janion was arraigned for the heinous crime of having far too many names, the future vicar Peter Knight for twice being late for church and fellow-prop Fran Cotton for wilfully appearing on a smart golf course in a horrible yellow surfing vest and pair of red carpet slippers.

But now it was time for all thoughts to be turned to the big game at the historic Ellis Park, Johannesburg. The old stadium was totally rebuilt in the 1980s, but back in 1972 it still comprised of one large but old-fashioned stand running down one touchline with enormous open banks of spectators on the other three sides, onto which the 1955 Lions had reportedly attracted a crowd of 100,000 people. All the non-whites were predictably banished to one rather remote area high up in the Gods. Equally predictably, they all cheered loudly for England and by the end of the afternoon they would have much to cheer about.

Lewis and Elders, with a bit of help from Pullin, named four new caps and plumped for Burton in front of Cotton for the hotly contested tighthead prop berth. The backs had really struggled on a couple of occasions and the most experienced centre, John Spencer, appeared to have temporarily lost both form and confidence. Accordingly, the selectors gambled on a centre partnership combining the wiles of Coventry's talented youngster Peter Preece and the direct muscularity of Jeremy Janion, and switched Peter Knight from full-back to one wing and introduced Bristol's high-scoring Alan Morley onto the other.

These all rose magnificently to the occasion but the two new sensations of the day were the six-feet-four-inch full-back Sam Doble with power to burn and a kick like a siege gun, together with Gloucester's hard-grafting flanker John Watkins. Some 70,000 thronged the terraces and the match got off to a stormy start when little Jan Webster was callously kicked and stamped on, prompting an early fight. The plucky scrum-half bounced back and led the way to become the clear man of the match, not least for following up his high kick-through to pick up on the full-back's fumbling error and send Morley over for the only try of the match.

At one point Stack got a very nasty kick in the head and had to leave the field for several minutes to either be patched up or permanently replaced. Mike Burton still remembered it vividly:

> I was just going into a pile-up for the ball when I heard this sickening 'clunk' and Stack was prone on the deck with a horrible gash on his head with a white bit in the middle which I am sure was his skull. The blood started pumping and the referee insisted he went off to have it seen to. Stack didn't want to go but in the end trotted off to the touchline with some uniformed bloke in tow.

In those days there were no automatic temporary substitutions for head injury assessments and a doctor had to authorise any replacement to take place, which could usually take several minutes. With the concept of uncontested scrums still decades into the future, all fourteen stone of Watkins stepped manfully up into the front row to face the eighteen-and-some lump of Bezuidenhout while Burton moved over to cover for his wounded Cornish pal. After what must have felt to Watkins like an eternity, Stack bounded back onto the park and pitched right back into the battle. As Burton went on, 'We both had a pretty good idea who had done it so we gave him some back for his trouble.'

Unlike at Pretoria, once they had a full scrum, England held the Springboks up front without undue trouble. Indeed, Stack looked very comfortable against Transvaal's Tinus Sauermann and despite some harassment from Mr Moolman, the referee, over his hooking positions, Pullin came out on top in the hooking duel. Long before the end, thousands of bitterly disappointed Afrikaners were streaming glumly out of the gates while the English-speakers and non-whites cheered themselves hoarse. It was all slightly surreal as England had ripped up the form book to run out as surprisingly decisive 18-9 winners.

The Springboks and their legions of fans were desolate. They then let further criticism rain down upon them by failing to attend the traditional after-match function with their visitors, much to the fury and embarrassment of Dr Danie Craven, who was the paramount figure and spokesman in South African rugby circles for a generation. The press and pundits were a little more gracious and paid tribute to the tenacity of the English players.

However, for Stack and his colleagues it was a deeply satisfying moment. After that dreadful Five Nations whitewash they had somehow bounced back against all the odds, not only to beat the mighty Springboks decisively on their home patch of veldt, but to also go through an entire seven-match tour unbeaten. It is noteworthy that even to this day no team representing Scotland, Ireland or even Wales has ever managed that particular feat. Furthermore, prior to the match at Twickenham two years earlier, England themselves had never emerged victorious against the mighty men in the dark green jerseys, but had now done so twice in successive matches – and he had played a major role in both of them.

Late in the tour Stack had given another interview to his friendly journalist John Reason of the *Daily Telegraph* and had confessed that at thirty-two he was toying with the idea of calling it a day:

I have a lot to do on the farm in Cornwall and if I do go on next season I shan't be able to travel to London for club football. I may join Bristol.

The tug of war upon his time and responsibilities had not eased up one little bit. No doubt Pullin would have loved to have brought him to Bristol, but even that involved a trip of around four hours each way, even for a home match. Fortunately for all his friends and admirers, all thoughts of retirement were quickly forgotten and his England career was only halfway through while his club rugby would continue for another eight years. Furthermore, it would all be back with the Pirates.

13

All Blacks and Greens

The England party returned home to a champagne reception and then dispersed for the summer. For Stack it was back to the farm, the beach runs and thoughts of the new rugby season to come. It promised to be a special one, not least because the New Zealanders were due to return to make a full tour of the British Isles for the first time since carrying all before them nine years previously. At that time, Stack had missed out on the chance to confront them at Exeter, and despite touring New Zealand with the Lions he had still to take the field against the actual vaunted All Blacks.

He returned to rugby in a measured way by playing only one game in September for the Pirates against Esher and then two for Cornwall. The first of these was a fairly routine fixture against the Army in Penzance but a week later it was against the Romanian international team at Redruth. The long-running communist dictatorship of Nicolae Ceauşescu had already brought about a shattered economy and untold misery to his people but, in a perverse way, rugby had flourished – often under the auspices of the armed forces and his hated Securitate secret police. The state-backed Romanians had played numerous fixtures against Italy and France and accordingly it was a powerful and experienced team who ran out winners to the tune of 18-3 by the end of the afternoon.

The season also marked the centenary of the Scottish Rugby Union and several celebratory matches and Sevens tournaments were arranged to mark the occasion. The biggest of these occurred in mid-October at Murrayfield with a special match in which a combined Scottish and Irish team took on the pick of England and Wales. These sorts of matches were always an honour for those chosen to play and, although taken seriously, spectators could confidently anticipate plenty of open-running rugby with lots of spectacular tries – in other words, the sort of game Stack relished. His front-row partners would be his old mate Pullin and the hefty Welshman John Lloyd (he of Mr Greedy fame) and he would be in direct opposition to the man he had replaced in New Zealand – Sandy Carmichael.

It was a thrilling match which lived up to all expectations but the Scots and Irish won the day thanks largely to the exceptional form of the brilliant Mike Gibson. Stack enjoyed the running game and moreover proved to the watching England selectors that, despite not playing senior club rugby on a weekly basis, his form and fitness were as sharp as ever.

A couple of those selectors would have scrutinised him again a week later at Kingsholm in Gloucester when Cornwall went down to a powerful Gloucestershire team that went on to reach the final. Indeed it was an ideal opportunity as he was positioning himself directly against Burton, Pullin and the up-and-coming Robin Cowling who, like Stack himself in the recent past, was to be plying his trade around the circuit for several years before later emerging as a genuine rival for his Number 1 shirt. It is always difficult to shine in a team that keeps losing and Cornwall, with a relatively weak three-quarter line, lost all three of their Championship matches to finish bottom of the South West group. Nevertheless, he had shown enough form to retain his place in the national squad without undue alarm.

By this time, the All Blacks had arrived in Britain utterly determined to avenge those defeats by the Lions on their home soil a mere couple of years previously. Two of their great talismen, Colin Meads and Brian Lochore, had finally departed from the international scene but in skipper Ian Kirkpatrick, winger Bryan Williams, scrum-half Sid Going and hooker Tane Norton they still had several men in their ranks acknowledged as among the very best in the world. As the tour progressed, feisty little winger Grant Batty and the towering Peter Whiting would also become household names.

One other name in the party intrigued the press and doubtless Stack as well. He was an enormous bear of a prop forward named Keith Murdoch, who sported a luxuriant black Mexican moustache and allegedly a dangerously short fuse. That conditional term 'allegedly' had to be applied as nobody from Britain could ever have claimed to have actually clapped eyes upon him. He had been selected several times to play against the 1971 Lions but had mysteriously withdrawn each time and had never materialised. As with the Abominable Snowman, various reports of his whereabouts had filtered through – but of the elusive Mr Murdoch there was no sign.

That particular All Blacks team were a peculiarly grumpy lot at the best of times, and their mood was not improved when they were well beaten both at Llanelli and Workington early in the tour. Their manager Ernie Todd was understandably worried about what Murdoch might say in any interview and, fearing the worst, had wisely made it abundantly clear to him that he should avoid ever speaking to the press. What Todd hadn't bargained for was that when an august and elderly Rugby Union official first tried to make polite conversation with his surly guest with the innocent question, 'Now how are you enjoying your first visit to Britain, Mr Murdoch?' all he would get was the instant reply, 'I don't talk to reporters – so f**k off.' The hovering press gang loved it.

With that the myth grew and Stack must have sat and pondered over his likely direct opponent when the All Blacks were to face England at Twickenham. No doubt his mother cherished him dearly but, by then, the British media were making poor old Murdoch sound rather like a cross between Ronnie Kray and the Missing Link. For good or ill, that meeting between them was destined never to happen as Murdoch proceeded to beat up a security guard at the team's hotel in Cardiff and was promptly sent home in disgrace to vanish back into the mists once more.

When the England game did get around to being played early in the New Year, the English approached the match with rather more confidence than usual. The All Blacks had only just scraped through against Wales in Cardiff with a fair degree of luck and some weak refereeing and had then stolen a win at Murrayfield when the alert Sid Going had intercepted a wayward pass from lock forward McHarg to streak away and bag the winner. Added to this, England's shock win in Johannesburg during the summer gave hope that a corner had at last been turned.

Stack had waited a decade to get his chance to face the All Blacks but now, rather as with the approach of London buses, he was selected to face them twice in four days. The first was to be for the South West Counties at Redruth on the Wednesday and then for England on the Saturday. Clearly that was out of the question and so he had to withdraw from the fixture in Cornwall. Thus the Combined Counties team lost first their star forward and then the match itself by seven tries to one. That match did, however, showcase a fine young blond Cornish flanker named Peter Hendy who would soon be joining Stack in the England squad.

At the beginning of January, Britain at last joined what was then known as the European Economic Community (EEC), thereby realising a long-held ambition of the Prime Minister Edward Heath. New Zealand was of course a key member of the British Commonwealth and, relying heavily upon the UK for its meat and dairy exports, must have viewed the development with some mixed feelings. For all that, there was some serious rugby to be played.

Just before the international match, Fran Cotton withdrew and was replaced by Orrell's Frank Anderson, who had done particularly well in the North West team that had won at Workington. As so often happens, the keenly anticipated match turned out to be a bit of a damp squib. Sam Doble had a disappointing day with his goal-kicking and Preece had a try disallowed by the referee. Thereafter, the combined play of the big All Black back row in unison with Going tipped the balance and England, despite attempting all manner of back-row moves themselves, sagged to defeat.

In the absence of Murdoch, Stack's opposite number was a relative newcomer called Kent Lambert, who had only made his international debut as a replacement at Murrayfield three weeks earlier. Against Lambert, Stack had a sound enough match himself and was as ever prominent around the field without ever being able to seriously disrupt the stranglehold the tourists were able to exert in the rucks and mauls as England were inexorably ground down to a 9-0 defeat.

It was now time for the Five Nations Championship. One major stadium he had as yet to appear at was the National Stadium in Cardiff. It was in the process of its transformation from the old Cardiff Arms Park but was still over a quarter of a century away from becoming the spectacular indoor Millennium Stadium of recent times. Wales were going through a golden era and somehow seemed to get even stronger year by year. Barry John had sadly and prematurely called it a day but was immediately replaced by his brilliant heir-apparent Phil Bennett and the already powerful and settled pack had been further augmented by the hugely talented Derek Quinnell. All the other big guns – Edwards, J. P. R. Williams, Mervyn and Gerald Davies, etc – were still very much around and indeed reaching the pinnacle of their stellar careers. On paper at least England did not stand much of a chance.

The fact remained that the Welsh had only narrowly missed out against New Zealand and the England pack with little to lose and, with Stack very much to the fore, tore into them from the start. However, as the game progressed, the match slipped away and by the end they were well beaten, having conceded five tries and failing to claim a single one of their own. Late in the game he and his colleagues were left chasing shadows while 50,000 passionate Taffies belted out 'Bread of Heaven' in homage to their red-shirted heroes. It was another chastening experience.

Only a week later, he might have been back at the same stadium once again. The All Blacks had failed to win many friends in Britain and Ireland over the previous four months but had won three and drawn one of the Internationals. Now, in their final match before decamping to France, they faced a powerful Barbarians team and, to their great credit, entered into the spirit of what rapidly became regarded as one of the all-time classic rugby matches.

It is not widely known that Stack had received an invitation to play in that wonderful match and has kept the postcard informing him of his selection as a souvenir. However, due to a combination of workload and a misunderstanding over what travelling expenses might be allowed, he decided to decline. With the benefit of hindsight it was probably the very worst decision of his entire rugby career. The old Lions originals of McLoughlin, Pullin and Carmichael were reunited to play their full part in a glorious spectacle, which would have been ideally suited to Stack's mobility, and is still recalled, discussed and watched endlessly on YouTube to this day. Regrettably, he was never to play for the Barbarians again.

The following Saturday, it was back down to earth with a bump when he played at Truro for the Pirates, where they gained an easy victory in front of around ten men and a wet dog. His life was certainly one of extraordinary contrasts but nothing could have prepared him for the dramas that were now about to unfold.

The 'troubles' in Ulster had turned increasingly ugly and the Province had been teetering on the edge of all-out civil war. The British Army had reluctantly become a virtual occupying force as it struggled to keep some semblance of peace but, as so often happens, soon became cast in the unwanted role of being regarded as the oppressors and the enemy. This was by now especially felt by the Catholics who, although only a sizeable minority in Ulster, comprised the overwhelming majority of the populace in Dublin and the rest of the Republic.

The previous season Scotland and Wales had both shied away from visiting Dublin and even the New Zealanders – with absolutely no role in the tragic affair – had needed heavy armed protection for their match in Belfast and only slightly less for the Ireland game in Dublin. The English Rugby Union had come out and declared defiantly that they would fulfil the fixture without apparently consulting the players beforehand. The RFU then stated it would be left up to each individual and that anyone withdrawing would have their decision respected. As with the tour to South Africa, the team all wanted to play rugby but this time it was a personal safety issue rather than any moral dilemma which faced them.

The players held a conflab among themselves and winger David Duckham was asked to phone the great Willie John McBride to seek his views and advice. The two men had toured in New Zealand together and a great mutual respect had developed between them. Duckham recalled the conversation as though it happened only yesterday:

> When I got through McBride was understanding and sympathetic but in his soft Ulster brogue came directly to the point. 'Your boys have to come Duckers – don't let the terrorists win.'

That one brief sentence coming straight from the heart settled it. Perhaps it is no exaggeration to state that it probably saved the Irish Rugby Union from financial meltdown and arguably even rescued the immediate future of the Five Nations Championship as well. The vast majority of the England team which had been defeated in Cardiff agreed to go although not before some deep conversations and soul-searching had taken place with wives and families.

Stack courageously agreed to go but, as usual, the newspapers had pumped up and possibly exaggerated the drama. His father CB made a poignant entry in his farm diary the day before the match: 'Strict security preparations for the England Rugby team to Dublin. Silly to go – my opinion.' There were plenty of people up and down the country who would have shared CB's pessimistic views with him. Two players – Sam Doble and Peter Larter – decided reluctantly against making the trip and, despite those assurances from the RFU, soon

Right: Three-year-old Brian with his first rugby ball.

Below: With some mates parading a giant pasty at the Cornwall v. Warwickshire final at Coventry, 1958. Brian is fourth from the left in a new duffle coat.

Mounts Bay Colts, 1957. The already powerfully built seventeen-year-old Brian is the second player from the left in the back row.

The winning team after the match with the shirt of defeated Reds' skipper Harold Stevens (no relation). Stack is second from right in back row behind his friend Tony Stevenson – the man credited with inventing his nickname. Squatting with the cigarette is hooker Jimmy Hosking.

Lineout at Coventry. Alvin Williams jumps for the ball with Stack and Bonzo Johns behind him eager to help.

Above left: Celebrating his call-up for the British Lions with a pint of milk.

Above right: All smartly kitted out in a Lions blazer and tie, although props' necks rarely allowed them to do up their shirts properly!

Below left: Action with the Lions against Manawatu.

Below right: Back with the Pirates in a match against Falmouth. His fellow prop with the beard is the future star comedian Jethro.

Cornwall team group for the final with Lancashire. Back row: Ray George, Gerry McKeown, Roger Harris, Roger Hosken, Barrie Ninnes, Colin Kneebone, Vernon Parkin. Seated: Derek Prout, Gareth Jones, Stack Stevens, Graham Bate, Bonzo Johns, Ken Plummer. Front: David Chapman, Tommy Palmer.

Ready to face the Springboks. England front row of Keith Fairbrother, John Pullin and Stack in some rather tattered training shirts.

Meeting the Queen before England play a President's XV at Twickenham, 1971.

The team that could have died. England in Paris 1974. Back row: Stack Stevens, David Duckham, Andy Ripley, Roger Uttley, Chris Ralston, Peter Dixon and Mike Burton. Seated: Keith Smith, Peter Squires, Geoff Evans, John Pullin, Tony Neary and Tony Jorden. Front: Steve Smith and Alan Old.

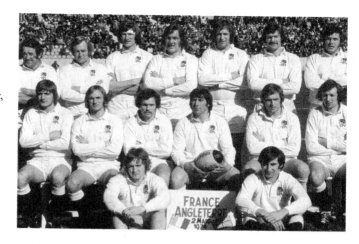

In action for England XV against Natal in Durban, May 1972.

On the attack against the All Blacks at Twickenham with opposite number Kent Lambert poised to pounce.

Going over for a historic try in Auckland with Ian Hurst (13) and Sid Going (9) unable to do a thing about it.

Ireland's Ray McLoughlin dives in to tackle Stack at Twickenham with scrum-half Johnny Moloney and hooker Ken Kennedy poised to help him out. Steve Smith wonders what is going to happen next.

Tidying up a line-out against France in 1975. England players Uttley, Ralston, Cotton and Watkins provide a white wall of cover.

Enjoying some time off with fellow Lions Gordon Brown and Delme Thomas and a couple of Maori friends.

All kitted out in evening dress as John Watkins wields a scary-looking tribal weapon, although Peter Knight, Tommy Palmer, John Pullin and Stack don't seem to be too bothered.

Off duty in Christchurch, New Zealand, with his best mate, John Pullin.

Above left: A young CB in naval uniform.

Above right: Mother Beatrice at Land's End.

Left: Back at home with wife Jane and young sons Sam and John.

A proud father with Sam and John plus Tinker the Jack Russell.

found their international careers were at an end. The RFU nevertheless realised that the players were coming under extreme pressure and were far more flexible than usual. The recently married David Duckham was even allowed to take his wife along, which was almost unheard of at the time.

Those strict security precautions entailed the team training on the Friday in London rather than Dublin and then flying over later in the day. They were met by a phalanx of Irish soldiers as well as the Garda at a separate terminal and were ushered swiftly onto a waiting bus which, with true Irish logic, had a large notice proclaiming ENGLAND RUGBY TEAM emblazoned boldly across the front. It was all getting very tense as Andy Ripley, who was sitting by a window, started twitching and rocking in his seat when the bus pulled up at some traffic lights. When asked what was the matter he replied he was just making it 'more difficult for the snipers'. It was meant just as a joke but it raised some very nervous laughs.

That celebrated rugby player and business tycoon Tony O'Reilly once remarked that Irish rugby was always desperate but never serious and that was eloquently borne out over that highly charged weekend in Dublin. When the bus pulled up at the luxurious Shelbourne Hotel on St Stephen's Green in the city centre, the players, all rigged out in their smart England blazers and ties, spilled out onto the pavement clutching their RFU-monogrammed kitbags and wondering quite what they were supposed to do next. Just then, a little man with a small dog shuffled past, stopped and, gazing up into the eyes of the six-foot-six towering Englishman Chris Ralston, enquired 'Would ye fellas be over here for the rugby then?'

When they got inside they found that, in the interests of security, the Irish team would be taking the unusual step of staying in the same hotel, presumably on the reasonable assumption that the IRA were unlikely to try to blow up their own team. Nevertheless, the hotel was crawling with armed police and secret agents and Stack and the others slept with them posted like the KGB outside their bedroom doors.

There was still an important game to be played and accordingly it had been agreed that the two parties should be kept apart until after the match. The two teams had their rooms on different floors, ate their meals in separate restaurants and were not permitted to leave the hotel. After dinner each group retired to their own room to a have a private team talk followed by a movie before going off to bed. David Duckham was sat at the back beginning to doze off when a lone figure slipped in through the dark and silently plonked himself down in the empty chair beside him. When he looked across Duckham realised to his alarm that it was Fergus Slattery, who had been his touring mate with the Lions and was to be a flanker in the Irish team the following afternoon. 'Christ Slats,' hissed Duckham, 'You can't be seen in here mate.' He was met with a loud voice asking 'Jasus Duckers is yer man's fillum any good? Ours is a load of fecking shite.'

The next day security at Lansdowne Road was everywhere and when Pullin came to lead Stack and the others out onto the pitch they really did not know what to expect. In Cardiff, their entry onto the field had been greeted by some half-hearted clapping mingled with a few boos and the usual bit of light-hearted abuse. This time, as they emerged, blinking into the winter sunlight, they were met with an ear-splitting roar that seemed to shake their studs in the turf. True rugby fans made their feelings known – these particular fifteen Englishmen were very, very welcome. In spite of all the precautions the teams were still expected to line up and stand still for presentations and Peter Preece recalled being reprimanded for not standing still during the anthems as he nervously scanned the roof of the grandstand looking fearfully for anyone who might be ready to take a potshot at him.

The match thankfully passed off without incident but England yet again came off second best and for once Kennedy out-hooked Pullin while Stack had his hands full with his old Lions 'victim', Sean Lynch. Lock-forward Roger Uttley had made his international debut that afternoon and recalled being much more concerned about marking Willie John McBride than he was about any imaginary snipers.

The team were disappointed with their display and once again had been undone largely by another peerless display from Mike Gibson. Of course, the important thing was that the match was actually played and nothing untoward had occurred. Skipper John Pullin's after-dinner comment that 'we are not much good but at least we turn up' is of course part of rugby folklore and has been recounted a million times ever since. Pullin swears that it was entirely spontaneous and that he never rehearsed his speeches in advance. Be that as it may, in those eleven short words the farmer from Gloucestershire had somehow succeeded in capturing the very soul of rugby football.

The players – with the sociable Mr Slattery very much in attendance – celebrated their renewed bond with their Irish hosts well into the night and then flew back to London as fast as possible. Back in Godolphin, CB was much relieved to see his son striding into the kitchen late on the Sunday evening none the worse for wear.

The selectors retained the pack that had somewhat underperformed in Dublin for the visit of the French, but made three changes in the backs, including recalling Geoff Evans to partner his Coventry colleague Preece in the centre and replacing Morley with the speedy but lightweight Yorkshire cricketer Peter Squires on the wing. The most significant change was to include a converted winger from Moseley named Martin Cooper into the crucial Number 10 shirt.

Perhaps the team took inspiration from all this because they then rose to the occasion in magnificent fashion to outplay a powerful French team that had arrived at Twickenham as hot favourites. Stack had one of his very best games for England and could be seen popping up all over the field as the pack outplayed the men in blue. He was even on hand to give Duckham a perfect scoring pass for the Coventry winger to sail over for one of his brace of spectacular tries. His direct opponent in the scrums was a man named Darrieussecq from Biarritz, who was making his debut and got a bit of a pasting in the process, and was thus never called upon to appear for France again.

England made it two in a row when the pack comprehensively overran their Scottish adversaries at Twickenham. Scotland was by now being captained by Ian McLauchlan, who had only recently been diagnosed with a cracked bone in his leg. By some medical miracle, he was out there on the pitch but was understandably a little below par, as indeed were many of those around him. The stranglehold gained by Stack, Cotton and indeed the back row of Dixon, Ripley and Neary was such that their backs should have claimed two or three more tries than the four they were actually awarded. New fly-half Martin Cooper was a natural runner with the ball but, perhaps as recent English results had been so paltry, he was also under strict orders to keep kicking it. Peter Dixon scored two tries and late in the game nearly claimed a third when he appeared to be stamped on by a frustrated Scots defender who was immediately poleaxed by Stack for his pains. He was never one to start any trouble (there were plenty of those around at the time) but he was clearly a man you did not take liberties with either.

England finished by beating the Scots for the first time in four years but, as the crowd poured out of Twickenham, the more perceptive among them would have appreciated that, had the overly cautious management allowed Steve Smith and Cooper to play their natural game, then Duckham, Preece and the rampaging Ripley might have done a lot more damage.

Stack finished the season back with the Pirates and played half a dozen matches for them before the season ended. These included matches against Gloucester and Wasps but, due to those ever-present farming commitments, missed out on a pleasant late-season trip to Guernsey in the Channel Islands. On the international stage, he had undoubtedly been one of England's most consistent performers in a season which had begun with high hopes, had dipped alarmingly but had then redeemed itself in the two final matches at Twickenham. At thirty-three his innate fitness was still self-evident, as was his technical ability. The question remained how long he could continue to tolerate the strain of constantly trying to live his life in two places at once.

14

Now Is the Hour

The RFU had accepted an invitation from Argentina to make a short tour at the commencement of the following season. Both Wales and Scotland had visited Buenos Aires over the past few seasons and had found the Pumas to be seriously tough opponents. For all that, with happy memories of the success in South Africa the previous summer, Stack and his colleagues looked forward to the experience and a series of matches they felt reasonably confident they could win.

In truth they did not know a huge amount about them. One of the men who had preceded Stack by playing for both the Pirates and England (and had also been his boyhood hero) was John Kendall-Carpenter, who was later to be instrumental in the establishment of the Rugby World Cup. Kendall-Carpenter had toured Argentina with a combined Oxford and Cambridge universities team back in the late forties and had enjoyed a glorious time. Apart from winning all their matches, he had left the tour for a few days to try to track down some family ancestors out in the country only to return several days later riding on a mule and dressed in a poncho and gaucho hat.

They had also been warmly received by President Peron and his glamorous wife Eva and, according to Kendall-Carpenter's son, the celebrated Evita took something of a liking to the handsome Cornishman and invited him to fly in her private aeroplane. He must have been tempted by the idea but, no doubt sensing that getting himself involved with the young wife of a notorious neo-fascist dictator was probably not a good long-term career option, politely declined.

An England tour was likely to be a lot less colourful than that but nonetheless intriguing for all those involved. Unfortunately they never got the chance to find out. Yet again politics and civil unrest seemed to be constant companions to Stack's rugby career. Argentina had been through two *coups d'état* and no fewer than five presidents in just a couple of years; the economy was in ruins and brutal riots, shootings and kidnappings had become the order of the day.

The Rugby Union hierarchy received due warning from the Foreign Office that urban guerrillas in Buenos Aires had kidnapped a number of overseas businessmen and other prominent figures and had since made specific threats against the England rugby players. This time the RFU decided discretion was the better part of valour and reluctantly cancelled the tour. Having prepared themselves for the tour, the team and management now found themselves with no fixtures.

The New Zealand Rugby Union had been going through some heavy political issues of its own. Their prime minister, Norman Kirk, had ordered the NZRU to withdraw its invitation to South Africa unless the Springboks would accept the principle of selecting its team entirely on merit and with no consideration of a colour bar. This agreement was never going to happen and so the tour was abruptly cancelled. So both they and England were all dressed up but with nowhere to go.

With the prospect of an empty calendar, the New Zealanders stepped up at short notice and invited England down for a full international match in Auckland preceded by a short series of provincial matches to become acclimatised. An added bonus would be an extra match against Fiji in the capital city of Suva as a first stop. Early September was not an ideal time for a high-pressure tour and it was all somewhat hurriedly put together but, with the management and team already chosen, all the necessary arrangements were soon sorted out. Stack now contemplated a return to the country where he had done well with the Lions but had still narrowly failed to win a place in the Test team two years before.

This time he was to have another young farmer from Cornwall to travel along with him. This was Peter Hendy, whose family had a farm way out on the Lizard peninsular and as such could probably lay claim to being the owners of the most southerly farm in the entire British Isles. Hendy was the lively flank-forward who had distinguished himself in a losing cause at Redruth six months previously and had since done enough to persuade coach John Elders that he was now worth his own place in the England squad as of right.

England took only twenty-five players, which included the three established props in Stack, Burton and Cotton but, apart from Hendy, almost the entire party had been capped already and fourteen of the team that had defeated Scotland in March were also on the plane. Neither Nigel Horton nor Peter Larter were available and so the extra locks were two ex-Cambridge Blues named Nick Martin and Bob Wilkinson. Bob had excelled for the Barbarians in Cardiff against the All Blacks and was seen very much like Hendy as one for the future.

The party landed in the burning heat of Suva after a punishing air journey via Los Angeles with all the inevitable effects of tiredness and jet lag. It did not seem to dampen Stack's spirits as he, showing unusual agility for a prop, shinned up a nearby coconut tree and began lobbing coconuts at his teammates. The players were also intrigued to discover that among the welcoming party were some of the largest women they had ever set eyes upon. There was a lavish sit-down meal with a local chief soon after they landed and enormous plates of what appeared to be some form of stew were laid out before them. Jet lag had so caught up with John Watkins that he crashed face down right into his plate of stew and promptly fell fast asleep.

Refreshed after a good long rest, the party began their first training session and it was not one they were likely to forget. The recent spell of very hot dry weather had been interrupted by a torrential downpour and suddenly the entire field was covered by hundreds – if not thousands – of large croaking frogs. They were everywhere and players kept treading on them with gory results, and it all became a bit of a farce. Stack exacted due revenge on scrum-half Steve Smith by shoving one down the back of his shirt when he wasn't looking. Smith had arrived late for the warm up, was thus unaware of the frogs and had already gained a reputation for having rather a lot to say for himself. Because of all this his screams of terror – he apparently imagined it was a snake – got precious little sympathy.

England, with both Stack and Hendy in the side, scraped through the match to just snatch a win by 13-12 thanks to a late try from winger Peter Squires, and it was then time to move on to Auckland. It was not the most auspicious welcome as, yet again, anti-apartheid demonstrators, who if anything were even more vociferous than those back in Britain, picketed them as they arrived at the airport. This had absolutely nothing to do with the current tour but was on the presumption that some of the England team would be expected to tour South Africa with the Lions the following summer. Stack would have certainly been on that shortlist.

The first match was played out at New Plymouth in torrents of rain and a sea of mud against the regional team representing Taranaki. John Pullin had been injured playing for Bristol at Twickenham in the John Player Cup Final at the end of the previous season and the Fiji match had been his first match back in business. He gave a superb hooking performance in the mire to take seven scrums against the Taranaki put-in ably assisted by Burton and Stack. Outside the scrum things did not work so well and, having squandered numerous chances, they lost by two penalties to one. Just to add to their woes, big Nick Martin was rushed off to hospital with what was initially thought to be concussion, went briefly into a coma but happily it then turned out that he was suffering nothing worse than dehydration and low blood pressure.

Martin quickly became one of the characters of the tour and he, together with Stack and Peter Preece, earned a dubious reputation as the tour's self-appointed 'Fire Brigade', which as usual specialised in rearranging other players' bedrooms when the occupants were otherwise engaged. By this time Stack was definitely one of the old hands and, with his beaming smile and warm Cornish accent, could seemingly get away with most things. This even extended to watching his teammates train from the back of a stand when he should have been out there sweating blood with the rest of them. Elders and manager Sandy Sanders knew he would still be one of the fittest on the park and with an 'ah well, that's just Stack' tended to let him do his own thing.

He also managed to secure a particularly noteworthy souvenir. One of New Zealand's most senior officials was a gentleman named Frank Kilby, who was rarely seen out and about without a rather fetching trilby hat. Stack somehow managed to acquire this particular item and wore it proudly for the rest of the tour.

The weather continued to be vile and, after missing a second defeat at Wellington, he returned to face Canterbury at Lancaster Park in Christchurch, where it will be recalled the Lions front row had been physically beaten up two years before. Some of the old protagonists like McCormick and Wyllie were still there although the notorious Alistair Hopkinson had by then moved on. The match was hard but there was thankfully no repeat of the nastiness of the Lions match.

Although England lost yet again, there were definite signs of improvement, especially in the second half when England scored three excellent tries having trailed 12-0 at the interval. Indeed, only poor goal-kicking prevented them from pulling off an unlikely victory. For one of those tries Stack played a vital role, steaming up beside his centre Geoff Evans, pulling in the covering defence and expertly offloading to Martin Cooper, who then sent Squires surging over for the score. Stack may have sat out a training run or two but it is highly debatable whether any other prop forward in Europe at the time could have had the anticipation, stamina and rugby skills to have resurrected a threequarter movement in quite that manner.

Defeated on the day but far from beaten in spirit, Pullin took his troops off to the pleasant seaside resort of Waitangi in the Bay of Islands area to rest and recuperate. Upon arrival and just to cheer everyone up the sun at last came out. Some pleasant days fishing and sailing interspersed with training and planning provided just the tonic the team required. Stack had been out fishing in the bay and had landed a large and ugly-looking snapper. This was kept fresh in John Pullin's en-suite toilet and then found its way into Steve Smith's bed just before he turned in for the night. The resulting scream was well worth all the effort.

A further cause for optimism had been the form shown by the bouncy scrum-half Jan Webster, who had done so much to bring about the victory in Johannesburg the previous year. At Twickenham, Sid Going had been allowed to boss matters and had given Webster a difficult afternoon, but plans were now put in place to neutralise the often brilliant little Maori and Webster's part in this was to prove vital.

The All Blacks had not had an easy time themselves. In their last international match they had lost to France in Paris and their recent trials had been a bit of a mess. Many of their star names including Kirkpatrick, Bryan Williams, Tane Norton and Grant Batty as well as Going were all ready and waiting but they also included two debutants called Bob Lendrum and Murray Jones in the key full-back and loosehead prop roles with the almost equally untested John Dougan at fly-half. All this gave further cause for hope. Stack would again be up against Kent Lambert – the same man who had opposed him in London but had not presented him with any undue cause for concern.

On Saturday 15 September the teams took to the field at Eden Park in Auckland. On their only previous visit ten years before, England had gone down bravely by 21-11 and so the 56,000 spectators settled confidently in the expectation of a similar outcome. Despite having a couple of relative newcomers in the All Blacks team, nobody expected anything other than a routine victory. Pullin and his men had other ideas and for Stack this was probably his finest hour.

Things seemed to be going according to the script when Wyllie picked up at the base of a scrum and fed Sid Going, who sent Batty zipping across the turf to score. Minutes later, Jan Webster (who again was everybody's man of the match) made a crisp break to open up a score for Peter Squires, which was capped off by a fine touchline conversion from Peter Rossborough. The All Blacks then grabbed a second try to lead 10-6 at the interval.

Eight minutes into the second half, the two new All Blacks got themselves into a horrible mess. Webster put a searching kick downfield which got fly-half Dougan into a tangle and he then threw a wild pass to debutant Lendrum, whose clearance kick was gobbled up by the England pack tearing up behind Stack as he hurtled upfield. He passed to the long-striding Chris Ralston and then received a perfectly timed return to round the defence and crash over for what turned out to be the critical score. It was his first international try but it has to go down as a historic one. The England pack with John Watkins, Andy Ripley and Tony Neary much to the fore then took a stranglehold on the game, despite repeated and desperate attempts by the home team to break through. A few minutes before time, the luckless Lendrum made a hash of another high ball for the magnificent Webster to set up a further try via Alan Old for the ever-available Neary to put the icing on the cake.

Just to rub it all in, the burly Fran Cotton careered upfield in the dying minutes selling two outrageous dummies (one sent the rather morose Sid Going spinning in the wrong direction) before threading a delicate fly-half's kick through the defensive cover, which nearly resulted in yet another. It was just that kind of afternoon.

Predictably, the New Zealand press castigated their own team and their selectors but some still found the good grace to praise a very spirited England display. Stack and the rest of the squad did not care a hoot – this was one hell of a victory.

The Maoris have a haunting melody named 'Po Atarau', which was adopted to send off ANZAC troops to Europe and to fight and die at Gallipoli in 1915. In recent times, it is often sung through misty eyes at the end of rugby tours to New Zealand. It is called 'Now is the Hour' and for Stack and his colleagues those words surely captured both their performance and that fleeting moment of triumph so far away from home and against all the odds.

15

But for the Grace of God

John Pullin's England team had returned home with renewed confidence. Wales were still very much on top of the tree in Europe but, with successive victories over France, Scotland and now the New Zealanders, there was every hope that a more settled side might at last challenge the Welsh for a Grand Slam.

Stack had now gained no fewer than fifteen caps and had taken part in victories over every senior rugby-playing country except for those infuriatingly consistent Welshmen and also Australia. In fact, the Wallabies were a team against whom he had as yet never even taken the field but this might now be rectified as they were scheduled to make a brief autumn tour to England and Wales.

He kept himself in trim with matches for the Pirates against local rivals Redruth and at Plymouth Albion before leading Cornwall for the first time in a Championship match against Somerset at Taunton – where he had made his county debut a whole fourteen years before. He had never been one for the convoluted theories of rugby and so neither coaching nor captaincy were ever really his forte but, if he was called upon to lead, it would be very much from the front and by example. It did not bring about any tangible success as Cornwall lost all three county matches – albeit narrowly – despite a virtually unchanged team being kept together throughout the brief series.

Life in Britain was getting increasingly difficult. The generation of power still relied heavily upon coal (and to a lesser extent oil) and the cost of fuel impacted hugely upon every single business, home and journey undertaken. In a coordinated political response to the American support given to Israel during the short Yom Kippur War, the Middle East oil-producing countries quadrupled the price of crude oil, which sent the Western economies into a panic. Although Britain had its North Sea oil reserves, these had yet to actually produce a single barrel and so for the entire country it was bad news all round.

The cost of farming and transportation of produce to markets was affected just as badly as everything else, and so CB and Stack now had this additional pressure to contend with.

Meanwhile, the Wallabies had arrived as something of an unknown quantity. The only man to have toured in the UK before in 1966 was their chunky scrum-half John Hipwell, and even then he had only done so as cover for the outstanding Ken Catchpole. Of the rest, the giant lock Garrick Fay was known to be more than useful, as was their goal-kicking winger Jeff McLean. Good reports had also been received about the promise of their blond full-back Russell Fairfax who had actually made his international debut while still at school. Apart from them, their resources at the time were felt to be fairly modest.

The Stevens-Pullin-Burton trio were reunited to play against them for a scratch team designated as the 'South and South-West Counties' at Bath's picturesque Recreation Ground. In truth, it was essentially a combined Bristol and Gloucester team with only Stack and centre Peter Johnson from the Clifton club deemed worthy of being interlopers. Historically, teams from the South West had a poor record against tourists from the southern hemisphere but this time they took the spoils by a single point courtesy of a try from flanker John Watkins.

The Bath ground is set in the very centre of the city next to all the best shops and restaurants. The after-match meal provided by the Bath club was apparently not up to much, so Stack led his partner-in-crime Mike Burton next door, waltzing into a smart restaurant that just happened to be owned by the ex-England manager Alec Lewis. They sat down, ordered a good bottle of wine and a T-bone steak and tucked in cheerfully. Immediately recognising the pair from the tour to South Africa, Lewis asked them what the hell they were doing in there. With a beaming smile Stack just said, 'Sorry Alec, we must have got confused and turned right instead of left when we came out of the changing room.' Of course, they got away with it.

Three weeks later hostilities were resumed at a barely three-quarters-full Twickenham when England notched up their fourth victory in a row with something to spare. The Wallabies' confidence must have been at a low ebb as they had been hammered 24-0 at Cardiff the previous weekend and they were unable to cope with England's forward dominance as Neary, Ripley and Alan Old all claimed tries in a 20-3 victory that could well have been far more. For Stack, it must have been one of his easiest afternoons in an England shirt. For some unfathomable reason the selectors had left the hero of Auckland Jan Webster on the bench and recalled Sale's Steve Smith only to immediately reverse the change once again a few weeks later at Edinburgh.

Fellow Cornishman Peter Hendy was by now part of the England squad and they began to travel together to those regular 'get-togethers' which were now part and parcel of the international scene. Sitting in his kitchen down by the Lizard, he recalled:

> Travelling with Stack was always something of an experience in itself. He sometimes made an excuse not to come at all and on one occasion got off the train at Bodmin and went back home again. If we decided to go by car it was always me who ended up doing the driving as Stack's cars were always claimed to be off the road for one reason or another.
>
> His fame went before him and sometimes it came to our aid. On one occasion we were belting back from Twickenham along a stretch of the then only partially completed M5 in Somerset. Soon I saw the tell-tale blue lights flashing and was waved onto the hard shoulder by a police car. The cop got out and peered into the window and began to ask me for my licence. As luck would have it he happened to be a keen rugby fan and when he looked across to the passenger seat he immediately recognised those familiar craggy features and cheery smile. Within a few minutes all thoughts of a speeding ticket were forgotten and Stack was autographing the policeman's notebook. He then looked at me and said 'Perhaps I should have yours as well son – you might be famous too one day.' We did the rest of the journey quite a bit slower.

Britain's miners had seized upon the opportunity of the pressure on fuel costs to flex their muscles and had 'worked-to-rule' for several months so that by Christmas stocks of coal were already running dangerously low. The customary salutations of a 'Happy New Year' rang strangely hollow as the government, in a desperate effort to conserve power supplies, was forced to adopt what became known as the Three-Day Week. Of course, farming had to continue around the clock for seven days a week but, with the inevitable squeeze on employment and spending power coming on everywhere, it was anything but a happy time. Floodlit sport was banned in the drive to save power but as all international rugby was still played in daylight, the effects on the men in white were minimised.

For some reason, England had held an extra trial at Burton-on-Trent before the Five Nations got under way. Usually this began with the Wales match in January with the Calcutta Cup game being played in March but this time the fixtures were swapped around. Despite having Uttley withdraw with an injury, they travelled up to Edinburgh hoping to make it five in a row. They nearly made it as, once again, the England front five took a firm grip. The lead see-sawed until, with just minutes to go, England nosed in front thanks to a towering drop-goal from Peter Rossborough before losing it with the very last kick of the match.

That defeat was a personal nightmare for England's David Duckham. Not only was he a brilliant player but, already boasting nearly thirty caps to his name, was one of the most experienced men in the squad. In his book, *Dai for England*, he does not spare himself.

> A penalty was awarded to Scotland during the first half. We were forced to retreat behind our own line as if a conversion was being taken. For some unaccountable reason I was a bundle of nervous energy, and in the heat of the moment I actually mistook the penalty and charged the kick. Even as Wilson Lauder prepared for the attempt, Stack Stevens warned me to keep still, yet I was already resolved to run and ignored Stack's advice. Only when the referee ruled that the kick should be retaken did I realize what I had done.

In the dying moments of the match England were closing out with a 14-13 lead when the French referee once again pulled Duckham up – this time for carelessly wandering offside out by the touchline but deep in England's half. Andy Irvine struck the winning kick straight and true to snatch a last-gasp winner. As England trooped wearily back to their dressing room, the Scots celebrated wildly as though William Wallace and Bonnie Prince Charlie had both turned up together at Murrayfield for the party. Poor David, so often the hero of the hour, was inconsolable.

The British Lions were due to tour South Africa in the summer and of course there were all the inevitable humanitarian and political objections being raised. The nominated coach for the trip was to be Syd Millar, who was himself a vastly experienced Ireland and Lions loosehead prop not long retired from playing. Furthermore, he had personally played no fewer than six Tests in South Africa and so if anyone knew precisely what was required from the front row to win a series out there then that man was Syd. He knew that Stack had already proven himself in that hugely testing environment and had both the scrummaging and ball skills to succeed. Accordingly he was sounded out at an early stage as to whether he could make the trip.

There were four potential candidates to captain the tourists. One was certainly Stack's comrade-in-arms John Pullin. Another might have been Gareth Edwards of Wales, who was certain of his place in any Test team, as might also be said of Ian McLauchlan, especially if Stack was unable to go. Finally there was Willie John McBride who, although by then thirty-four years old, was probably equally sure of his position as the front jumper and enforcer in the pack. All this gave some extra interest to the match at Twickenham when Ireland came to visit as the winning skipper would undoubtedly have gained some extra kudos when the team finally came to being chosen.

Once again, England were undone by their 'nemesis' Gibson, who twice sliced his way through the bemused England defence before half-time. Although England stormed back with a late rally it was another great day for the Irish. Up front, Stack and his colleagues had more than matched their opponents but the difference in class behind the scrum tipped the balance. This made it one up to McBride in the captaincy stakes.

Furthermore, Pullin was now potentially under pressure for the Test-hooking berth from a tough newcomer onto the scene named Bobby Windsor. He was the first member of the celebrated and widely feared Pontypool front row to be selected for Wales and clearly had that hard edge which would be so necessary when facing the Springboks. Another point in McBride's favour was that he and Millar had played together for well over a decade, not only with Ireland and the Lions but also back at their home club of Ballymena as well. They knew and trusted one another completely.

For a while Stack hesitated on his decision but then, with extreme reluctance, felt he just had to turn down the golden chance. The pressures of maintaining the farm, especially in the recent economic downturn, were now almost overwhelming. He explained this to his ever-supportive scribe John Reason in yet another interview for the *Daily Telegraph*:

> I would have loved to go on the Lions tour. It would be nice to finish the job we started in 1971. The trouble is I've hardly been able to do any work on the farm for the past three years with tours of one sort or another and we just can't get the labour to work on the land. Fifteen years ago there were twenty men working on the land in our village. Now there are none. They've all gone to the towns. My father is seventy-eight and still working. I can't leave him to do it all on his own.

A number of people tried hard to get him to change his mind but none could offer a practical solution to his dilemma. Over the past four summers he had indeed been to California, New Zealand (twice) and South Africa, but it was nevertheless a gut-wrenching decision. He knew perfectly well that with so many of their strong 1971 contingent still at their peak, and with younger additions like Ripley, J. J. Williams, Cotton, Irvine and the dazzling Phil Bennett all coming to the fore, the Lions squad would present the Boks with some major problems. He ached to be a part of it. If only his brother Roy had still been around, perhaps a way through might just have been found to avoid him being left behind chewing his nails. However, all of this might well have paled into insignificance with what so very nearly happened next.

France had moved their home fixtures from the crumbling old Stade Colombes out in the suburbs to a freshly rebuilt Parc des Princes near the centre of Paris. It was now a swanky all-seater affair offering superb views from every seat in the near-50,000-capacity stadium. It certainly made poor old Twickenham really look like a sad old pre-war relic, which of course by then it clearly had become.

Mike Burton was recalled for England's visit to the new stadium to pack down alongside Stack and Pullin. Stack had already come up against some colourful characters in his time but Armand Vacquerin from Beziers would be one he would be unlikely to forget. He was listed in the programme notes as a bar owner but was mainly used as the bouncer and had got himself into a series of brawls during a recent tour of Australia. Indeed, he had become something of a legend in the south of France as a bona fide hard case at a time when French club rugby was populated with some of the most violent characters in the entire world of sport. He had nevertheless won a string of honours with Beziers, proved to be a very mobile rugby player around the field but was to give Stack no problems in the set scrums where England enjoyed a clear advantage. Sadly Vacquerin was later to die as violently as he had lived by blowing his brains out during a drunken game of Russian roulette.

The night before the match, several of the England players spent the evening with John Cooper, who was still supplying them with Adidas kit. When it came to the game itself England snatched a 12-12 draw which, in the light of the thrashings they had been given on their two previous visits to Paris, was looked upon as a cause for celebration. In fact they all went out on the town to savour the delights of 'Gay Paree', and in Stack's particular case it was a night out which possibly saved his life.

Britain was still beset by strikes and one within BEA meant that all their flights were suspended, thereby leaving the England party, which numbered around seventy people (once all the committee men, their wives and assorted hangers-on were accounted for), potentially stranded at Orly airport. To these could be added hundreds, if not thousands, of supporters who needed to be back for work on the Monday morning.

With everybody scrambling around for seats, one of the earlier Sunday morning flights was with Turkish Airlines and the RFU made urgent enquiries to try to get onto it. It so happened that it could only take around half of the sizeable England party and so, by some happy miracle, an RFU official made the crucial decision to keep the group all together and opt for a slightly later flight. Stack, however, was always under pressure to get back home to the farm as soon as he possibly could and had therefore arranged to be woken up to try for an early flight. By a happy stroke of fate the effects of the previous evening's revelry made him sleep through his alarm call and so he had no option other than to come back along with everyone else.

Later that morning they all flew uneventfully back to Heathrow on a Pakistani Airlines jet to be met at the barrier by an ashen-faced RFU official who just croaked to them all, 'Please everybody phone home immediately.' Everyone was still oblivious to the fact that the earlier Turkish Airlines flight 981 from Orly to London had crashed just a few minutes after take-off, killing every single one of the 346 people on board. Among the dead was the players' friend John Cooper.

As so often happens, instant newsflashes can be cruelly misleading and, to make matters worse, one report had mentioned a rugby team as having been on board. It was of course no consolation to the cruelly shattered people of Bury St Edmunds in Suffolk when it turned out to be their sons, brothers, husbands and boyfriends who had perished on their way home from supporting their countrymen, rather than the England team itself. For all that, English rugby had somehow narrowly avoided its own version of the Munich Air Disaster.

Back in Godolphin Stack's father and sister had passed an agonising couple of hours waiting for news until the phone rang with his cheerful voice on the line. He was safe. The following day (3 March), CB made a poignant entry into his diary:

I am feeling shocked at the air disaster. It has given me the creeps. I can't help thinking how lucky we were over this great air disaster with over 350 all dead. The rugby team were to have been on that plane.

He then, almost as an afterthought, added one short word in capital letters: 'GOD'.

16

The Senior Pro

If the England team had been shaken by the spectre of what so easily might have taken place on that trip back from Paris, they were clearly stirred as well. Two weeks later they strode out at Twickenham and gave a thoroughly assured forward performance to overturn Wales for the first time in eleven years. That victory gave Stack the then unique honour in that he – along with Pullin and Duckham – had figured in England victories over every single International Board country in the world of rugby.

Wales had endured an up-and-down season but, with the notable exception of their superb but injured full-back J. P. R. Williams, were able to field all their major stars. Directed by the ever-brilliant Edwards, Phil Bennett was now throwing off the shadow of Barry John to blossom into the most exciting fly-half in Europe. Their young wing J. J. Williams (so named to differentiate him from J. P. R.) was reckoned to be the fastest thing on two feet playing rugby and they still had the mesmeric Gerald Davies who was now, by his late twenties, at the zenith of his powers. He had always had an electric burst of pace and a dazzling sidestep in either direction. Spectators and opponents would often rub their eyes and swear they saw blue sparks coming from his dancing boots. He really was that good.

Good old England were more prosaic but were now much better organised and gave a fine exhibition of controlled yet passionate rugby with the rampaging Andy Ripley carrying all before him. Stack faced a new Welsh front row of not only Bobby Windsor but Glyn Shaw of Neath and his direct opponent was Phil Llewellyn from Swansea. Wales actually shaded the scrums but, with a better quality of possession, England came out on top. They had a scare when J. J. Williams had a possible try controversially disallowed by the Irish referee but somehow held on for a rare 16-12 victory. The season had thus opened and closed with victories over the All Blacks and Wales. If only what had come in between had been half as good.

The Lions management had made a final plea for Stack to go to South Africa but he still felt unable to leave his farm and father behind for three long months and the touring party was thus named without him. McBride was nominated as captain with Pullin left at home with David Duckham, who needed an operation on a nagging injury. The other two England props, Cotton and Burton, were selected along with the two Scots from 1971 in 'Mighty Mouse' McLauchlan and the ubiquitous Sandy Carmichael.

The RFU and the French authorities agreed upon a special benefit match at the end of the season as an extra England v. France international to raise money for an Air Disaster Fund set up to help the families of the crash victims. Several of the England players seemed to have their minds fixed on their forthcoming trip with the Lions and, in a somewhat desultory performance, the home team sank to a 7-26 defeat.

In fact the most entertaining feature of the entire match was the sudden appearance of a long-haired male streaker cavorting merrily along the touchline as though welcoming the coming of spring. The following morning the newspapers had a glorious time with photographs of him being apprehended by a posse of earnest young policemen, one of whom had the presence of mind to whip off his helmet and plonk it strategically over the streaker's prize possessions. Meanwhile a portly RFU official could be seen puffing to their aid clutching an old gabardine raincoat. One could just imagine the scene back at Twickenham police station the following Monday morning with the branch inspector addressing his men: 'Well done on showing good initiative PC Jones – but I think you should put in for a new hat.'

That summer, Stack had to work in Cornwall as television footage and newspaper reports came flowing back glorifying in the success of the Lions as they carried all before them in South Africa. The Test series was won 3-0 with the final match being officially drawn although the tourists will swear that the irrepressible Fergus Slattery scored in the last breathless moments of the Final Test only to have it ruled out by the South African referee. By all accounts it was a wonderful tour, and Stack yearned to have been out there with them.

The following autumn he was playing more regularly for the Pirates, appearing in a number of local matches against teams like St Ives, Hayle, Redruth and Newquay and he also captained Cornwall against the South Wales Police at the Mennaye Field in Penzance. Cornwall had by then begun to hold squad sessions at Redruth to prepare for the County Championship matches and his propping colleague Terry Pryor recalled:

Our rucking had been highlighted as a weakness and the Coach asked Stack to lead a session to work on it. His response was simple – we were just not fit enough to get a sufficient number of us there in the first place. He then led us in a brutal series of runs around the field. People kept dropping back but he just plugged on regardless. He never seemed to do any organised training – he must have been doing it in secret. Coaching and rugby theory never really interested him. He always turned up at the very last minute and sometimes had left half his kit behind and on more than one occasion he trained with us in a battered old pair of suede shoes. He seemed very laid back – almost casual – much of the time. But when he really had to turn it on – look out!

Cornwall beat local rivals Devon and then travelled to Bristol where Stack was lined up once more against Mike Burton who was now playing his way back into rugby after his Lions tour. The big Gloucester prop rather enjoyed putting one over on opponents and soon tried it on with Cornwall's new young hooker Trevor Tonkin, who immediately waded back into Burton to Stack's evident approval. He knew his England colleague would never have had a go at him in the same way but was well aware that Gloucestershire packs were often out to isolate him by trying to intimidate some of his less experienced colleagues. Little did he realise that he would soon profit personally from one of Burton's little brushes with the powers that be.

For the past couple of seasons the England selectors had begun their trials process by selecting four regional teams to play one another and accordingly Stack took his place in a South West team which went down to a London team at Rosslyn Park's ground in early December. He missed the final trial at Twickenham just before Christmas and it was evident that change was in the air. Significantly, Pullin had been replaced in the prospective England XV by Leicester's Peter Wheeler and the two chosen loosehead props were Wheeler's clubmate Robin Cowling and Colin White of Gosforth. Most importantly of all, the new captain to replace Pullin was prop Fran Cotton who, like Stack, could play happily on either side of the scrum.

England had recalled John Burgess to once again coach the England team in place of John Elders. For several years he had known and nurtured Cotton, who had recently enjoyed a magnificent series against the Springboks playing at tighthead in all four Tests. They had both shared in the triumph over the All Blacks at Workington two years before and certainly it was a leadership combination that made a fair degree of sense.

England were due to return to a Dublin that had reduced but still significant security procedures in place and a nominated front row of Cotton, as captain, Pullin and Burton. In those days international teams were announced nearly two weeks before a match was due to take place. In the meantime, Gloucestershire played a county quarter-final at Bristol, during which Burton got himself – perhaps harshly – sent off. He then compounded his problems by bowing mockingly to the assembled committeemen in the stand, which went down like the proverbial lead balloon. Whatever the rights and wrongs of the case, the England hierarchy felt he should be withdrawn from the team for Dublin. They then called for neither White nor Cowling but Stack.

After so many disappointments, the Gods had smiled upon him for a change and he eagerly grasped the renewed opportunity. By this time he (along with Pullin, Duckham and, to a certain extent Cotton, Ralston and Neary) was definitely one of the wise old pros in the England squad. That core of experience was clearly going to be much needed when facing McBride, Slattery and company on their home soil, especially now they had been joined by two very large hellraising new boys in Willie Duggan and Moss Keane.

Apart from Burton, Roger Uttley also had to pull out with an injury, thus affording the future England skipper Bill Beaumont his very first taste of the 'big time'. England should have potentially won the game as they were leading 9-6 with just ten minutes to go courtesy of a fine try from Stack, who once again showed uncanny anticipation, mobility and ball skills to take a pass from winger Peter Squires to sail over near the posts and quieten the noisy Lansdowne Road crowd. Unfortunately, with just minutes to go, England heeled the ball for the umpteenth time but Webster's pass, for once, went awry. Rossborough then slipped on the turf for the Irish fly-half Bill McCombe to pick up and score the winner to send thousands of green hats and scarves flying into the air and for all the partying to begin.

Stack retained his place for the French visit to Twickenham with Cotton continuing to lead the side from the tighthead position, but now with Peter Wheeler making his long-delayed debut at hooker. He was a very different type of player from Pullin – taller, lighter and faster with the unusual ability to be a decent goal-kicker as well as a solid line-out thrower. Despite a mop of blonde hair and a deceptively babyish face (which had earned him the nickname of 'White Angel') he was also hugely competitive and, in the Leicester tradition, tough as old boots.

France once again included the ill-starred Monsieur Vacquerin but this time he was joined in the front row by an equally fearsome individual called Gerard Cholley, who made a habit of graphically reminding everyone how he had been a heavyweight boxing champion. Their most intriguing newcomer, however, was the exotic Jean-Pierre Rives who soon became the unchallenged pin-up boy of French rugby. He was here, there and everywhere and, after a brief opening flurry, England were well beaten and a try count of only 4-2 barely reflected French dominance. Stack had a sound enough game himself but, with a back row having to give second best, and a back line frequently in a degree of panic, there was little he could do. During the match he suffered a badly gouged eye, which he recalled later as being one of the most painful injuries from foul play he had ever suffered in his life.

With the next match due in Cardiff, the England selectors reacted by mysteriously dropping Andy Ripley, moving Uttley into the back row and recalling the uncompromising Nigel Horton once again at lock. However, by then Wales had recruited the Pontypool front row en bloc with Bobby Windsor being propped by judo black belt Charlie Faulkner and the young but extravagantly gifted tighthead, Graham Price. Price had marked his debut in Paris a few weeks before with an extraordinary seventy-yard kick-and-chase try and was soon to establish himself as a truly world-class prop-forward over the next decade. When he met Stack for their one and only time he was still learning his trade but already posed a formidable technical challenge.

The Welsh were understandably keen to put right their recent reverse at Twickenham and stormed into a 16-0 lead with classic tries from, yet again, J. J. Williams and Gerald Davies. Despite having to take off Wheeler and Webster with nasty-looking injuries, England dug in and made more of a contest of it in the second half, but never looked remotely like getting back into contention. This all added up to three matches and three straight losses. For the Lancashire-based coach and captain combination of Burgess and Cotton, this was a thoroughly depressing return.

Their last opportunity to turn things around was against Scotland at Twickenham and, no doubt in a bit of a panic following the run of losses, the selectors made sweeping changes – some deliberate and some enforced. Cotton and Duckham were injured and Ripley was immediately recalled, as were winger Alan Morley and the Bedford scrum-half Jacko Page. Rather more bizarrely, they also turned back to Bristol's silver-haired back-row man David Rollitt, who had put a few venerable noses severely out of joint with some outspoken comments after that debacle in Cardiff six years before and had not been selected since. Indeed, his last international had been way back before Stack had even made his debut. Stack retained his place with Mike Burton (now deemed to have 'served his time') back in the fold beside him and once again with the restored John Pullin. The captaincy was however passed to that other Burgess protégé Tony Neary.

Scotland, perhaps surprisingly, had just overcome Wales at a highly charged Murrayfield in front of an enormous and raucous crowd of over 80,000 packed onto the steep banking. With another win over the Irish, they came down to London with a rare chance of taking the Triple Crown. It turned out to be poor fare and, although England snatched a 7-6 victory, thanks to a booted-through try by Morley, it was clear that the England squad was in desperate need of an overhaul.

Although he did not know it at the time, this turned out to be Stack's swansong in an England shirt. He was still superbly fit, his form was as sound as ever and his experience was invaluable. Furthermore it was patently clear that, beyond Cotton and the potential powder keg that was Mike Burton, the selectors had no clear vision of who should be taking his place. Robin Cowling had sat and squirmed like many before him on the substitutes' bench but had to date been given no opportunity to actually play any more than had Colin White, Les Barlow or any of the other possible contenders for Stack's loosehead berth.

Down in Cornwall, the Pirates had reached the final of the still relatively new Cornwall Cup for the first time and Stack joined them to face Penryn in their match at Camborne. The Pirates' coach got held up in traffic and they arrived in something of a rush and were thus rather poorly prepared when they took the field and went down to the tune of 11-0 after a disappointing display.

News soon came through of the England party picked to tour Australia and to say that it raised a few eyebrows would be the understatement of the year. In a seemingly desperate attempt to find some new young blood, they had somehow contrived to throw out all the bathwater and filled it up with all the babies. Perhaps lulled into a sense of false security by the Wallabies' poor showing in the UK eighteen months before, they had seen fit to travel without Duckham, Ralston, Dixon, Old, Webster, Smith, Watkins, Horton, Rossborough, Cooper and Stack himself. Nobody ever took the trouble to explain why a man was omitted from an England team – you just never received your next invitation.

At thirty-five Stack's England career was in all probability now at an end, but at least he was in very good company.

17

Rugby for Fun

The short tour to Australia was an unmitigated disaster from just about every point of view. Key players such as Cotton and Neary were early casualties, both Tests were lost, the refereeing was appalling and several matches were played in a vile atmosphere of virtual warfare. Also, with the notable exception of Bill Beaumont and to a slightly lesser extent, Phil Blakeway, Bob Wilkinson and Alistair Hignell, none of the new boys revealed they could ever truly perform at international level. Indeed, several immediately disappeared seemingly without trace.

Stack had not given up hope of getting his place back and those selfsame Wallabies were due back for an extended tour in the autumn. Several administrators and press correspondents had questioned the wisdom of having them back so soon after all the unbridled thuggery which had so disfigured the second international in Brisbane. Calmer counsels prevailed and fortunately the tour went ahead as planned.

Sure enough he was fit and ready to play five games for the Pirates in September as well as captaining a 'Stack Stevens's XV' against Redruth to help celebrate the Reds' centenary. One of those who came down for that match was his friend Fran Cotton, although he was still not ready to resume playing after his Australian injury. Fran remembered it well:

I went to visit Stack and we popped next door to the pub for a couple of pints. In the corner was the landlord's dog fast asleep in his basket. I did a double-take and realised that its sleeping blanket was one of his England rugby shirts. He really didn't give a hoot about all that souvenir stuff.

Stack then went on to lead from the front in a re-energised Cornwall team. The Cornish went down narrowly 6-9 to Gloucestershire at Redruth, having been undone by three well-struck penalty goals from the new England full-back

Peter Butler. They then bounced back to defeat both Somerset and Devon at Bridgwater and Torquay respectively. The win over their cross-Tamar rivals was the biggest since the season Cornwall had reached the final seven years before.

None of this appeared to interest the England selectors, who reverted to Cotton and Burton but, having exacted due revenge for the naked brutality in Brisbane, the team then slumped to lose every single Five Nations match to finish up with the dreaded Wooden Spoon. Would Stack have made any appreciable difference? We shall never know.

The day after Boxing Day, he took his place in a final South West Counties game against the Australians at Exeter in what turned out to be his very last senior representative match. He and Redruth's Terry Pryor packed down against Stuart McDougall and Steve Finnane, who had been two of the worst culprits in Australia back in the summer. Fortunately, there were no serious incidents this time but the Counties sagged to a comprehensive defeat by four tries to none.

The Pirates had enjoyed something of a revival during the season and had only just lost out at Beacon Park against Plymouth Albion and had subsequently won at Taunton. More significantly, they disposed of Falmouth and Penryn in the County Cup and had come out on top from a keenly fought semi-final with Hayle in a tie which had gone to a replay. As a result, for a second year running they had reached the Cornwall Cup Final – this time to face Redruth at neutral Camborne.

Stack had played in each of these cup ties and, although never particularly taken with coaching, he made an extra special effort to help in getting the Pirates pack better organised and in the right frame of mind to try to banish the disappointment of the previous season. This time their preparation was much better; they arrived in plenty of time and were backed by the biggest crowd which had come to a Cornish club match for several years. This was a game in which the ex-England prop pulled out all the stops as he rampaged around the field and, just as importantly, his colleagues were inspired to follow him. Redruth were undoubtedly the pre-match favourites but the crowd of well over 5,000 witnessed a titanic struggle. For all Stack and the others' efforts, Redruth were leading by a single penalty until, late in the game, the Pirates pack thundered upfield and transferred the ball out to a speedy young wing named Nobby Roberts, who scorched away to score the winning try, ending the match a 4-3 victory for the Pirates. It must be recalled that this was still a time before any formal League structure was in place and as such it was the only time in his long, distinguished career that Stack ever had a hand in winning an actual trophy.

That County Cup victory guaranteed an automatic place in the preliminary round of the RFU's John Player Cup, which had been launched only four years before and organised broadly along the same lines as the FA Cup in football. The previous season their 1975 conquerors Penryn had gone on to the third round before losing to the ultimate finalists, Rosslyn Park. Hopes were therefore high that the Pirates could build some real momentum in the same way, especially as they were given a home draw. Their opponents were a relatively junior club named Gordon League from Gloucester and as such were one of the successful feeder clubs for the city's beloved Cherry and Whites.

The game took place at the beginning of May and Penzance's Mennaye Field was well filled for the occasion but sadly it was not to be and the Pirates went down by a single point to fall at the very first hurdle. Once again, Stack raced about the field but, despite three booming penalties from their talented full-back Malcolm Nicholls and the shrewd promptings of their diminutive fly-half Roger Pascoe, it was never quite enough.

The year of 1976 was a historic one for the people of North America. The USA was celebrating the bicentenary of gaining independence and Canada hosted the Olympic Games in Montreal, virtually bankrupting the city in the process. On the rugby front, the Barbarians sent a powerful team to its own tea party in Boston and then traversed the whole of Canada from British Columbia to Nova Scotia, stopping off to defeat Canada in Toronto along the way.

Hooking for Canada had been ex-Pirate Mike Luke, who had not only played beside Stack in Cornwall but had also had a spell with the Harlequins. Later that summer, the Quins made their own short tour to Canada, taking in Ottawa, Hamilton, Toronto and Montreal and Luke was going to be there to guest again for the visitors. It will be recalled Stack had stayed back at home during the summers of 1974 and 1975 and felt he was due the chance to play overseas for one more time. It was four years since he had pulled on the famous multicoloured old shirt but this was too good a chance to miss.

Compared with the high-pressure tours with England and the British Lions, this was a reasonably relaxed trip led by his old Quins partners of Earle Kirton as team manager and the prop Rhys Williams as captain. They also included the two Claxton brothers as further props so he was not required for every game and it was an enjoyable way to finish his six-year stint of globetrotting.

Season 1976/77 marked Stack's last appearances in a black-and-gold Cornwall shirt and he responded by playing in all six games. For several years he had missed many of the pre-Championship friendly matches but now, spared from all the commuting to England squad sessions, he was able to give the old competition one last shot. One of those warm-up games was a victory over an England Under 23 team, which was yet another recently introduced experiment to develop future international players. Stack led Cornwall that evening to a 12-7 victory and then to a further one over the Navy a fortnight later.

However, the Championship itself was a bitter disappointment. Cornwall were trounced by Gloucestershire at Bristol and then sagged to home defeats against both Somerset and Devon. The latter match was appropriately at Cornwall's spiritual rugby home at Redruth and this proved to be his eighty-third and very last county match. He ended with the second-highest appearance record for his county, a mere five behind his old propping companion Bonzo Johns. Had he not been obliged to refuse so many invitations to play for one reason or another, his final total for Cornwall would have almost certainly passed the century mark – a feat only achieved many years later by the Redruth lock Tony Cook.

That season he made no fewer than thirty-two appearances in the Pirates team, which was by far the highest number he had made for over a decade and followed this up with a further twenty-nine the following year. His captain at the time was winger Jimmy Walton, who recalled:

> We were often on tenterhooks as to whether he would arrive on time but sure enough at ten minutes to three he would burst through the door calling out 'Bosun where's my shirt?' and our faithful first-aid and kit man would drop whatever or whoever he was attending to in order to sort him out. He always seemed to cut it to the very last minute but he never once let us down.

The season of 1978/79 was his last in the first XV at the Pirates and he actually led the side on a few occasions in the absence of the elected captain Dave Drew. By unhappy chance, one of these was an away fixture against London New Zealand, played on the morning before an England v. France match in the afternoon. Unfortunately, the Pirates lads thought it would just be a gentle runabout and went on the beer the night before only to discover that the Kiwis had some seriously good players in their ranks. Just to make matters worse, Stack's boyhood idol Kendall-Carpenter had turned out to watch and he must have been less than impressed to see the Pirates annihilated to the tune of 70-0. This is still the worst ever result in their seventy-year history. At Easter he played what looked to be his last senior match for the club against the Wasps on the Mennaye Field some twenty years after meeting them for the first time.

That sense of almost poetic symmetry continued the following season when he played regularly for the third team, led by Roger Roberts – the same man who had been his classmate at school and had found a bladder for an old rugby ball to give to Max Biddick back in Leedstown.

Roger takes up the story:

> Those games were never too serious but were hugely enjoyable and many ex-first team players insisted that this was the only team they now wanted to play for. Another lad who had been with us back at Leedstown School all those years ago named Tony Pollard also came back and joined us although he hadn't played any rugby for years.

Games were played against the second and third teams of the other Cornish clubs and against local junior clubs such as Helston – which was actually the nearest rugby team to his home at Godolphin – Stithians, Perranporth and St Just. Although by now in his late thirties, he was still miles ahead of those around him. 'It was a bit like taking a Ferrari down to Tesco's – he never needed to get out of third gear,' was how one old colleague described it. Those games also gave him the chance to enjoy his afternoons and indulge in a few party tricks which would never be tolerated in a more serious match.

One favourite was to crouch down in a loose maul and then hide the ball up the front of his shirt while all the players and referee were all milling around looking for it. Another was to stand directly behind the referee grinning while the poor man was peering anxiously into a ruck trying work out what was going on. He once picked up a much-loved local referee named Tommy May (who was a real character in his own right) and dropped him gently into the middle of a ruck from which he emerged all muddy and dishevelled. In the manner of Captain Mainwaring from *Dad's Army*, he spluttered, 'I know it was you Stevens and if I had actually seen you I would have sent you off!'

One player had just taken delivery of a shiny new company car and had wanted to show it off to his teammates. Thus it was proudly driven to a small club, which had some particularly basic changing facilities, and Stack decided to strip off after the game and chuck all his muddy kit into the poor lad's car, only to be followed by all the rest of the team.

On another occasion he did absolutely nothing in the first half except kick the ball through the scrum to the opposition. Somebody asked him what the matter was and he replied that he had just eaten a very large pasty after working on the farm all morning and was 'just waiting for it to settle'. Sure enough, after the change of ends, he tore about the pitch like a whirling dervish and won the game virtually on his own.

He also used to love running with the ball in one large mitt, throwing one-handed dummies before offloading it. One story about this sounds a bit far-fetched, but ex-colleague Paul Greaves swears that it is true:

We were playing a junior team – I think it might have been a works team called Ormdales – when somebody got a bang and had to be revived with the old magic sponge. Stack grabbed the sponge as the trainer ran off and stuck it in his pocket. A minute or so later he ran up field with the ball in one hand and the sponge in the other selling dummies. As he approached their full-back, he tossed the sponge to a supporting player who instinctively caught it and was promptly flattened by that full-back. Meanwhile Stack strolled off with the ball chuckling to himself and scored under the posts. When the referee had somehow managed to stop laughing enough to blow his whistle he apparently disallowed the try saying that he hadn't a bloody clue what Law he had just broken but in any case it was a penalty to Ormdales.

Life back at Godolphin continued much as before. During the summer the farm always needed additional temporary help to deal with the potato harvest and other sundry crops and in 1977 two young sisters duly arrived looking for a holiday job. They just happened to be the daughters of Stack's old second team captain – the same man who had recommended that the Pirates give him a shot in the first team over twenty years before. To date little has been said about Stack's love life and it is certainly true that the farm and rugby dominated most of his waking thoughts at a time when many of his contemporaries had settled down and were raising families.

Jane Vingoe, however, struck a very different chord when she and her elder sister began working on that potato crop. She was extremely pretty, blonde, enthusiastic and a person who loved sport (she was a very good runner and netball player), horses and the outdoor life in general. Having grown up in a rugby-loving household, as her father had gone on after his playing days to be a Cornwall committee man, she had some idea about what life with a rugby player in his late thirties might possibly entail.

Jane recalled fondly:

I remember Brian's sunny disposition, the twinkle in his eye and his enormous capacity for fun and that made the hard work very easy and enjoyable. He always had a beaming smile on his face and plenty of funny comments and asides.

Jane quickly showed that she was perfectly happy to get stuck in and work really hard at the farm, which soon won CB's approval. She continued:

At this time he had another Austin A40 pickup and always had Tinker his Jack Russell with him. Looking back, even after his international days were over all his work was aligned to maintain his fitness. I think he invented power walking as I had to jog just to keep up with him. If he was loading trailers it was all done as if it was a training circuit.

In August 1980 they got married quietly in Helston with John Pullin and his wife Brenda, who were staying down on holiday at the time, acting as witnesses.

Because of all this, he played no more rugby until the following January, when he once again returned to play for the Pirates' lower teams. He had also turned out in several celebration games or special matches to raise money for some charitable cause. In November 1979 he had gone with a number of the 1971 British Lions team over to St Helier to celebrate the centenary of Jersey Rugby Club, where he renewed his partnership with John Pullin in the front row. He and Pullin also ventured up to Melrose in Scotland to play in a special match for a family member of one of their ex-Lions colleagues, Frank Laidlaw.

There was also a special match to help the families of two policemen who had been washed into the sea in their panda car and drowned during a storm at the local fishing village of Porthleven, and yet another game was at Lionel Weston's Stowe school near Buckingham for a seriously injured pupil. Then, just after Christmas 1981, a Cornwall team played a President's Fifteen in Penzance for the widows of the local Penlee Lifeboat that had gone down with all hands a mere eleven days before. That gallant crew actually included one ex-Pirate player and made national and international headlines and is still commemorated every December in Cornwall. Stack was always ready to lace up his boots and 'do his bit' for worthy causes such as these.

He actually made a fleeting reappearance in the first team at the Pirates during an injury crisis in early 1982 when he returned to face Redruth but, after a handful more, finally played his last senior match in a game over Easter against Maidstone. The Pirates only won eighteen of their forty matches that season but, whether by mere coincidence or not, they secured a victory in every one of the six matches in which he took part. He was now forty-two and while by then his pace around the field had dropped a little, and he had lost most of his hair, he could still get around the park for eighty minutes as well as men half his age. Furthermore, that infectious grin through enjoying the game for its own sake still shone through undiminished.

Since moving into adult rugby he had played no fewer than 579 matches for the Pirates, 83 for Cornwall, 25 for England, 14 for the Harlequins, 6 for the British Lions, 3 for the Barbarians plus dozens of trials, non-cap internationals, regional fixtures and benefit matches probably amounting to well over 850 in all.

His very last rugby match of all was not until 9 March 1986, when he took part in a special celebration fixture to mark the fact that his old teammate and fly-half Roger Pascoe was playing a mind-boggling 1,000th match for the Pirates. In the interim he had been serving as an England selector and had played virtually no sport but now, at the grand old age of forty-six, it was time to finally call it a day.

It was exactly thirty years since he had first run around a rugby field with his old friend Terry Luke for the Young Farmers Club back in 1956 – a time when most of the players around him in that final match had not even been born.

18

Family and Farming

Following their marriage, Stack and Jane moved in together to live in one of the two farms, which was called Treweeth. They both loved the outdoors and sports life and now Jane would often accompany him on his beach runs, followed by a dip in the sea if the weather was reasonable. Jane had a job at an estate agents in Penzance but now joined him and CB on the farm.

No sooner had Stack finished with all his fun and frolics in the Pirates' third team than he was approached via his old friend Don Rutherford to join the England selection panel. The England team had continued to struggle for the three or four years immediately following his final cap in 1975 but, under Coach Mike Davis and led by Bill Beaumont, they had won a Grand Slam in 1980 with an experienced team that had included several of Stack's old colleagues.

However, by 1982 Cotton, Uttley, Neary and Beaumont had all gone and, apart from the dynamic Peter Winterbottom, their replacements were hardly of a similar calibre. Accordingly, the new head coach looked to scour the country for some fresh talent. He was Dick Greenwood – the father of World Cup-winning centre Will – and he asked Stack and Roger Harris to help find a few gems in the West Country.

It was at this juncture that Bath began to make huge waves on the English rugby scene. Under their demanding and somewhat dictatorial coach, Jack Rowell, they began to construct a squad which was not only tremendously talented but savagely competitive as well. For as long as anybody could remember, Bath had hovered on the edge of the senior rugby scene without ever seriously challenging the Coventrys, Wasps and Leicesters of this world, nor indeed their local rivals Bristol and Gloucester. Now all this was about to change.

Unlike players, selectors could claim all reasonable expenses, stay and eat in good hotels and even bring along their wives to numerous functions. He and Jane enjoyed getting around the country and also visiting places like

Cardiff, Edinburgh and Dublin. With his eyes on Bath he quickly spotted the burgeoning talents of Nigel Redman, Gareth Chilcott, Paul Simpson and John Hall and urged Rowell to take a good long look at Launceston's young hooker Graham Dawe. Rowell did so and Dawe was destined to play well over 300 times for Bath as well as later being capped for England.

In some ways, being a selector was a surprising role for him to assume given his lack of enthusiasm for committees and paperwork. Indeed, the world of 'blazers' and their wives all seemed rather remote from all the old easy banter among the players. Nevertheless, he was determined to make the most of it and quite enjoyed the experience. This continued for two years and several new faces from Bath and Gloucester obtained international recognition but, apart from a surprise victory over the All Blacks in 1983, the England team's results continued to be mediocre.

Life on the farm followed a routine governed by the seasons. Now with Jane by his side, he kept large numbers of pigs, which had to be fed and looked after, as well as a sizeable herd of beef cattle. Then there was the growing of barley for cattle feed plus several winter crops including potatoes, cabbages and cauliflowers. In the winter, Stack would spend hours in his workshop repairing machinery and other vehicles, including a succession of old cars, tractors and trucks. He was very good with his hands and had a talent for making things work, although in recent years he has never gone anywhere near a computer. In fact, he rarely sat around watching television – although in the past he had enjoyed *Sergeant Bilko* and *M*A*S*H* – but his restless energy always meant that he was much happier up and about and actually doing something.

In the 1980s, they also ventured into keeping sheep for the first time. One of his successors in the England team as loosehead prop was Robin Cowling, who retired from rugby in 1981 and before long had also moved down to farm in Cornwall. During Stack's last season with England, Robin had been a frustrated bench reserve at a time when replacements were only made following an injury that a doctor had confirmed as being too serious for the injured man to return to the field.

After a couple of matches Robin's impatience began to boil over and before one game he went up to Stack and asked him, 'Why don't you get bloody injured, Stevens, and let me get on so I can at least get a cap?' 'Tell you what Robin, perhaps I will – but it'll cost you a pound a minute, mate,' he grinned back. Sure enough, early in the second half Stack took a bang and, temporarily winded, went down on his haunches while the trainer ran on to look at him. He then glanced over to the bench where Cowling was desperately trying to pull off his tracksuit and winked at him. He then just got up and trotted back into the next scrum and went on to finish the match and indeed the next couple of games with no problem whatsoever.

Now, about ten years later, Cowling rang up the Stevens household and enquired whether they could do with some contract help with shearing their new flock. Jane answered the phone and, having quickly consulted her husband, said he wanted to know what he would charge. 'Tell the old bugger it'll cost him a pound a minute' he shot back. Like elderly elephants, old props never forget.

He had always been quite adept at building and had once constructed a bungalow on some nearby land owned by CB at Germoe. This was eventually sold to none other than Don Rutherford and his wife Sue, and they have remained friends and neighbours ever since. Another sideline was a camping site which, being close to several beautiful beaches, proved very popular. Several of his old international colleagues used to bring their growing families down for a week or so in the summer. John and Brenda Pullin and their children were regular visitors to the farm, as indeed was Lionel Weston's family who used to park their caravan in one of the fields.

Lionel recalled:

The first year we went he had built a handy little ablutions block with toilets and showers. The second year it had a roof and in the third the toilets even had seats and by year four it even had doors as well. We all really enjoyed it and the children loved the animals but, being rather a 'townie', I had a bit of a shock when I was asked to help deliver a calf which had got itself stuck while being born. I am a bit squeamish and nearly passed out.

In addition to being the sole witnesses at the wedding, the Pullin family had many happy holidays on the beach and going out on various boats on the Helford River, although John was never quite sure which were actually owned by the Stevens family.

By this time Jane had produced two young sons in Samuel, who was born in 1992, and John, born two years later. On the day of Sam's arrival, Stack announced at Helston market that he had just acquired a bull calf, and when John made his first appearance, he told everyone he 'had another flanker'. He had thus become a father for the first time in his early fifties and all the bathing and nappy changing did not come easily. As they grew he loved playing with them and their dog especially at football, throwing a ball about and even used to take them swimming.

Jane mentioned:

He was a great dad to them but not always terribly practical. On one occasion when they were bit older and had started school I had been for a short holiday with some friends in Italy. Brian brought the boys to meet me at Newquay but I had warned him they wouldn't want to be seen at the airport

still in their school uniforms so to bring along a change of clothes for them.
He only went and brought their pyjamas.

For Brian, rugby, and all that being 'Stack' entailed, had largely departed the
scene apart from the odd England or Lions reunion. The Pirates were going
through a lean time, although conversely Cornwall had won an enthralling
County Championship Final over Yorkshire at Twickenham in 1991. If the
crowds following Cornwall in the 1960s had been impressive, these were
truly enormous, and it is estimated that over 50,000 Cornish fans descended
on the capital to watch a thrilling victory only snatched deep into extra time.
Furthermore, they all came back again a year later to see them nearly repeat the
success – this time over those 1969 opponents Lancashire – but all in vain. How
Stack would have loved to have been around to have taken part in all that!

In 1990, CB had passed away at the grand old age of ninety-four and Stack
and Jane finally inherited the two farms. He had become a partner in the business
in 1978 and had worked flat out for thirty-five years – much of it for not much
more than agricultural wages – so he had certainly earned his inheritance in full
measure. In due course, he took great care to ensure that Sam and John enjoyed
the benefits of the education which he felt so strongly had been unfairly denied
him. Both were to go on to college and higher education.

Both boys also became very good rugby players in their own right, playing
with both the Pirates and Redruth. Sam is a scrum-half and John, as his
father had predicted, a flanker and, at the time of writing, both are playing
at National League level. John initially made his sporting name as a young
horseman, winning the Pony Club national show-jumping competition at his
age group. He has since gone on to study surveying at Plymouth University
while Sam spent an extended period working and playing in Australia before
returning to work on the farm.

Running a busy farm does not lend itself to family holidays but they all made
ample use of the sea on their doorstep for boating, fishing and swimming, and
would regularly visit the Royal Cornwall Show every June.

In the mid-1990s Rugby Union finally embraced professionalism and the
Pirates were themselves at last staging a spirited comeback. Having teetered on
the brink of bankruptcy, they had the good fortune that a wealthy ex-player
(and sometime teammate of Stack) called Richard Evans stepped in as a
sponsor and benefactor. In due course, Evans took over the club and later
funded its reincarnation as the Cornish Pirates professional club that we know
today, playing in the English Championship.

In 1995, the club had celebrated its Golden Jubilee with a dinner in the
town, which Stack attended along with many of his old playing colleagues.
Evans had become president just as Rugby Union had finally (but ultimately
in a somewhat unseemly rush) declared itself as an 'open' sport. Players could
then be paid, Rugby League players could come back to Union whenever they

wished and there would now be the whole paraphernalia of contracts, agents, owners, sponsors and lawyers involved. Nobody really knew quite what was going to happen next. All that old song and dance about white stripes on rugby boots and hitching rides on lorries to Twickenham suddenly seemed like something from another age – even from a past century. Five short years later along came the millennium and by then it really was.

In 2003 Stack began to experience balance problems and difficulty in keeping his eyes open and, despite seeing a succession of specialists, it took a while to get it properly diagnosed. Eventually, in 2008, he was told he had a rare degenerative neurological condition called Progressive Supranuclear Palsy, which is a cruel disease that affects speech, the eyes, balance, swallowing and movement. He has dealt with this condition with heroic stoicism and courage but it has clearly shaped both his own and the family's life for the past decade. He continues to follow rugby closely, sometimes is taken along to matches and loves to be visited by his old colleagues and friends.

It was all down to those old colleagues and friends that it has been possible to tell his story.

19

The Final Word

Stack's pursuit of an England rugby career coming from a Cornish farming base was hard enough, but in today's professional environment it would be totally impossible. Since his time, two other front-row men from Cornish farming stock went the whole way to play for their country. The first, Graham Dawe, actually continued to farm on the Cornwall and Devon border but commuted to Bath to train and play. His was also a heroic effort but Godolphin was another hour and a half further to travel each way. Phil Vickery also hailed from the far eastern end of Cornwall but, although he played initially for Redruth, he immediately decamped to Gloucester just as rugby was turning professional and deservedly earned himself a very good career in the process.

At the time of writing there are in fact two more young men from the Penzance area who have recently been involved with England – Jack Nowell and Luke Cowan-Dickie. Both men played for the Pirates at junior age group levels but, having made their mark, then moved straight into the academy system at Exeter Chiefs and progressed from there. There is now a much more clearly defined pathway to the top but it is equally clear that it is well-nigh impossible for a man playing outside of the Premiership to even be considered.

Even back in the early 1970s, Stack was one of the last to be capped from outside the circle of elite clubs. Peter Squires of Harrogate and Chris Wardlow from Carlisle were other examples at the time with the massive Wade Dooley of Preston Grasshoppers probably being the very last of all. For all that, none of them faced remotely the same competing work pressures as were endured by Stack.

It is probably because of all this that he is so revered throughout Cornwall even today. Several other men from the area have made it all the way to the England team but Stack was always seen by his fellow Cornishmen as being very much 'one of us'. Cornwall was, and indeed remains, rather parochial in its affections and for some reason there has always been a certain coolness towards players and officials from Penzance. However, Stack always seemed able to transcend all of that and would be welcomed as warmly in Redruth or Falmouth as he would back at the Pirates.

It has been mentioned on several occasions that his relationship with the Pirates was not always easy. In fact it was only in very recent times that he was elected to Life Membership of the club some thirty years after he had ceased playing. For all that, he was as loyal as he could afford to be, given the constant counter-demands upon his time and energy. He never considered moving to any other Cornish club, had no interest in Rugby League and opened and indeed closed his career as a very regular team member. He was always very popular with his teammates, who probably understood him better than some officials and indeed supporters who could sometimes be rather ambivalent about him.

In fact, honours like that Life Membership have been few and far between. Few players from his generation ever got MBEs or 'Hall of Fame' awards and the like and he was no exception. He has however had one unusual compliment paid in that his name was adopted by the Muppets. In 1996 a movie called *The Muppet Treasure Island* was released which featured some strong Robert Louis Stevenson-inspired Cornish overtones with Squire Trelawney and the Admiral Benbow part of the plot. One of the scurvy Pirates is called 'Short Stack Stevens' and creates a fair amount of mayhem until he is finally despatched with a passionate kiss and a flying headbutt by Miss Piggy. Such is fame!

Much has been made of his quiet and easy-going demeanour, his ready smile and his ability to get along with people from all walks of life remarkably easily. He actually cared very little for 'pomp and circumstance', although it is noticeable that he has kept all the menus and seating plans of the dozens of formal dinners he was expected to attend.

Touring around the world probably allowed him enough freedom from all the pressures of farm and father to bring out the best of his naturally sunny disposition. When officialdom got too pompous, some young players might try to lash out and rebel – Stack would just have a quiet little chuckle to himself and let them get on with it.

Some old players retain all their old international shirts wrapped up lovingly in tissue paper or present them in glass cases to adorn the walls of their old rugby clubs. Then they have all their old programmes and press cuttings stuck religiously into scrapbooks and albums and keep wearing all their old ties and blazers well into their dotage. Stack appeared to value these things – but only up to a point. The walls of his house are decorated with numerous rugby photographs but he has long since given away many of his shirts and ties and just kept his old programmes and cuttings in a couple of boxes.

Friendships, however, were much more precious. Without a single exception every ex-player contacted for this book immediately said how much they really liked him – and moreover clearly meant it. Indeed, this usually got mentioned well before any objective analysis of his relative merits as a rugby player. When a group of young men have to travel and room together for weeks on end, it is not unnatural that some of them get on one another's nerves especially when they are also in fierce competition for places in the international matches. Stack, however, seemed to rub along easily with everyone regardless of their age, position or country of origin. Until his recent illness he loved to attend the regular reunions that continue to bond players of his era together, even though they are now mainly well into their seventies.

His two sons have returned to Cornwall and are helping Jane to run the farm and Stack is evidently immensely proud of them all. When he reflects on his life he has so many achievements to look back upon – and knows deep down how much his mother and brother Roy would have been proud of him.

The last word has to be again about rugby. One evening several years ago Terry Luke – his lifelong friend from the Young Farmers who took him along to play his first-ever game of rugby – and with some other old Pirates players was attending a reception for the visiting New Zealanders. There, holding court in a corner of the room, was Colin Meads – arguably the greatest lock-forward to have ever pulled on a pair of rugby boots. The conversation turned to the England players of his time and Meads is reported by two or three of them as saying:

There was only one England forward in my day that could ever have been a regular fixture in an All Black pack ... and that was Stack Stevens.

We can all drink to that.

APPENDIX 1

The Things They Said

'In many ways he was a player before his time. He could get around the field so well he would have thrived in the modern game. He was quiet but when he spoke everybody listened.'

Gareth Edwards

'He was a great bloke who was so easy to get along with. He just gelled with everyone.'

Bob Hiller

'Stack was always being talked about by the older guys when I was a kid growing up.'

Jason Leonard

'He was one of God's honest forwards with a great attitude. The Saturday team was pretty well settled by the time he joined the 1971 Lions but if we had needed him for a Test we wouldn't have hesitated for a second.'

Willie John McBride

'The best tight head prop I ever played with was Tony Horton. The best-loose head was Stack Stevens.'

John Pullin

'All the Welsh boys on the 1971 tour took to him immediately – he knew his job too.'

John Dawes

'Never saw him having to struggle in the scrums. I didn't know him as well as some of the forwards did but we backs really appreciated his work up front.'

Mike Gibson

'I only ever played with Stack the one time when I got my England first cap. Cornwall never seemed to beat Gloucestershire so Lancashire always ended against them.'

Bill Beaumont

'He was the strong silent type who you could always rely on to do his job.'

Chris Ralston

'He was an excellent technical prop who knew all the tricks. The crafty blighter used to try to overcharge me for his spuds though.'

Keith Fairbrother

'We both came from farming backgrounds and I really enjoyed his friendship. We were room-mates on many occasions but our first meeting was him joining some pre-tour training at Eastbourne when he arrived at my room door two days late and at two o'clock in the morning.'

Delme Thomas

'He was strong, brave and technically very competent. It is never easy to join a tour halfway through but he was always fun and had a bit of mischief about him which immediately made him very popular.'

Ian 'Mighty Mouse' McLauchlan

'He was already one of the old pros when I first played for England. Lovely guy – always with a smile on his face although he had a rather bony backside to scrum behind.'

Roger Uttley

'Great guy and bit of a scallywag but I don't ever want to help him deliver a calf again!'

Lionel Weston

'He still owes me for that taxi fare when we landed in New Zealand.'

Geoff Evans

'He was a quiet bloke for much of the time but he used to come out with some priceless one-liners! You immediately recognised his upper body strength but the more you played with him the more you appreciated his contribution around the pitch as well.'

Tony Neary

"He was one of the very best technical props around who was always fun to be with. We had a lot of laughs together and became great mates – we played with and against each other loads of times and I never wanted to hit him!'

Mike Burton

'The England team had been having quite a few problems in the scrum and we had taken quite a pasting down in Wales. When Stack came along it all seemed to get solved immediately.'

John Spencer

'He was a rock-hard prop on the field but one of the very nicest guys off it – always a pleasure to be with.'

Peter Rossborough

'When I was a seventeen-year-old kid starting to play for Cornwall Stack took me under his wing and let me know he would look after me. I will never forget that.'

Kenny Plummer

'Often seemed so laid back and casual but when the time came to turn it on – watch out.'

Terry Pryor

'I have vivid memories of playing against Stack for the East Midlands in a semi-final at Redruth.'

David Powell

'He was both very strong and technically excellent. Most loosehead props in the UK I had found relatively easy to unsettle but Stack was different. Whether you went in at him high, low or at an angle he was still just as strong.'

Tony Horton

'Some props used to like to show off but Stack was never a braggart. He always let his rugby do the talking.'

Ray McLoughlin

'Even when he was a teenager he could be a crafty sod.'

Alvin Williams

APPENDIX 2

Statistical Summary

England International Matches 1969–75

20 DECEMBER 1969 – SOUTH AFRICA – TWICKENHAM, LONDON – WON 11-8

England: R. B. Hiller, K. J. Fielding, J. S. Spencer, D. J. Duckham, P. M. Hale, I. R. Shackleton, N. C. Starmer-Smith, C. B. Stevens, J. V. Pullin, K. E. Fairbrother, A. M. Davis, P. J. Larter, A. L. Bucknall, R. B. Taylor, B. R. West. *Rep*: C. S. Wardlow.

Scorers: T: Larter, Pullin; C: Hiller; P: Hiller.

South Africa: H. O. de Villiers, S. H. Nomis, O. A. Roux, E. Olivier, A. E. van der Watt, P. J. Visagie, D. J. de Villiers, J. L. Myburgh, D. C. Walton, J. F. K. Marais, A. E. de Wet, I. J. de Klerk, P. J. F. Greyling, T. P. Bedford, A. J. Bates. *Rep*: M. J. Lawless.

Scorers: T: Greyling; C: Visagie; P: Visagie.

14 FEBRUARY 1970 – IRELAND – TWICKENHAM, LONDON – WON 9-3

England: R. B. Hiller, K. J. Fielding, J. S. Spencer, D. J. Duckham, P. M. Hale, I. R. Shackleton, N. C. Starmer-Smith, C. B. Stevens, J. V. Pullin, K. E. Fairbrother, A. M. Davis, P. J. Larter, A. L. Bucknall, R. B. Taylor, B. R. West.

Scorers: T: Shackleton; DG: Hiller 2.

Ireland: T. J .Kiernan, A T. A. Duggan, F. P. K. Bresnihan, C. M. H. Gibson, A. J. F. O'Reilly, B. J. McGann, R. M. Young, S. Millar, K. W. Kennedy P. O'Callaghan, M. G. Molloy, W. J. McBride, R. A. Lamont, K. G. Goodall, J. F. Slattery.

Scorers: P: Kiernan.

28 FEBRUARY 1970 – WALES – TWICKENHAM, LONDON – LOST 13-17
England: R. B. Hiller, M. J. Novak, J. S. Spencer, D. J. Duckham, P. M. Hale, I. R. Shackleton, N. C. Starmer-Smith, C. B. Stevens, J. V. Pullin, K. E. Fairbrother, A. M. Davis, P. J. Larter, A. L. Bucknall, R. B. Taylor, B. R. West.
Scorers: T: Duckham, Novak; C: Hiller 2; P: Hiller.
Wales: J. P. R. Williams, S. J. Watkins, S. J. Dawes, W. H. Raybould, I. R. Hall, B. John, G. O. Edwards, D. B. Llewellyn, J. J. Young, D. Williams, W. D. Thomas T. G. Evans, W. D. Morris, T. M. Davies, W. D. Hughes. *Rep*: R. Hopkins.
Scorers: Davies, Hopkins, John, J. P. R. Williams; C: J. P. R. Williams; DG: John.

21 MARCH 1970 – SCOTLAND – MURRAYFIELD, EDINBURGH – LOST 5-14
Scotland: I. S. G. Smith, M. A. Smith, J. N. M. Frame, J. W. C. Turner, A. G. Biggar, I. R. Robertson, D. S. Paterson, N. Suddon, F. A. L. Laidlaw, A. B. Carmichael, P. K. Stagg, G. L. Brown, T. G. Elliot, P. C. Brown, R. J. Arneil.
Scorers: T: Biggar, Turner; C: P. C. Brown; P: P. C. Brown 2.
England: R. B. Hiller, M. J. Novak J. S. Spencer, D. J. Duckham, M. P. Bulpitt, I. R. Shackleton, N. C. Starmer-Smith, C. B. Stevens, J. V. Pullin, K. E. Fairbrother, A. M. Davis, P. J. Larter, A. L. Bucknall, R. B. Taylor, B. R. West. *Rep*: B. S. Jackson.
Scorers: T: Spencer; C: Hiller.

18 APRIL 1971 – RFU PRESIDENTS XV – TWICKENHAM, LONDON – LOST 11-28
England: R. B. Hiller, J. P. A. G. Janion, J. S. Spencer, D. J. Duckham, P. B. Glover, A. R. Cowman, N. C. Starmer-Smith, C. B. Stevens, J. V. Pullin, F. E. Cotton, P. J. Larter, C. W. Ralston, R. N. Creed, P. J. Dixon, A. Neary.
Scorers: T: Hiller; C Hiller; P: Hiller 2.
Presidents XV: P. Villepreux, S. O. Knight, J. J. Maso, J. S. Jansen, B. G. Williams, W. D. Cottrell, D. J. de Villiers, R. B. Prosser, P. G. Johnson, J. F. K. Marais, C. E. Meads, F. C. du Preez, G. V. Davis, B. J. Lochore, I. R. Kirkpatrick.
Scorers: T: Williams 3, Kirkpatrick 2, Marais; C: Villepreux 5.

15 JANUARY 1972 – WALES – TWICKENHAM, LONDON – LOST 3-12
England: R. B. Hiller, J. P. A. G. Janion, M. C. Beese, D. J. Duckham, K. J. Fielding, A. G. B. Old, J. G. Webster, C. B. Stevens, J. V. Pullin, M. A. Burton, A. J. Brinn, C. W. Ralston, P. J. Dixon, A. G. Ripley, A. Neary.
Scorers: P: Hiller.

Wales: J. P. R. Williams, T. G. R. Davies, R. T. E. Bergiers, A. J. L. Lewis, J. C. Bevan, B. John, G. O. Edwards, D. J. Lloyd, J. J. Young, D. B. Llewellyn, W. D. Thomas, T. G. Evans, W. D. Morris, T. M. Davies, J. Taylor.
Scorers: T: Williams; C: John; P: John 2.

12 FEBRUARY 1972 – IRELAND – TWICKENHAM, LONDON – LOST 12-16
England: R. B. Hiller, K. J. Fielding, M. C. Beese, D. J. Duckham, R. E. Webb, A. G. B. Old, J. G. Webster, C. B. Stevens, J. V. Pullin, M. A. Burton, A. J. Brinn, C. W. Ralston, P. J. Dixon, A. G. Ripley, A. Neary.
Scorers: T: Ralston; C: Hiller; P: Hiller 2.
Ireland: T. J. Kiernan, T. O. Grace, M. K. Flynn, C. M. H. Gibson, A. W. McMaster, B. J. McGann, J. J. Moloney, R. J. McLoughlin, K. W. Kennedy, J. F. Lynch, C. F. P. Feighery, W. J. McBride, S. A. McKinney, D. J. Hickie, J. F. Slattery.
Scorers: T: Grace, Flynn; C: Kiernan; P: Kiernan; DG: McGann.

26 FEBRUARY 1972 – FRANCE – STADE COLOMBES, PARIS – LOST 12-37
France: P. Villepreux, B. Duprat, J. J. Maso, J.-P. Lux, J. Sillieres, J.-L. Berot, M. Barrau, J. Iracabal, R. Benesis, J.-L. Azarete, A. Esteve, C. Spanghero, J.-P. Biermouret, W. Spanghero, J.-C. Skrela.
Scorers: T: Duprat 2, Biermouret, Lux, Sillieres, W. Spanghero; C: Villepreux 5; P: Villepreux.
England: P. M. Knight, K. J. Fielding, M. C. Beese, D. J. Duckham, R. E. Webb, A. G. B. Old, L. E. Weston, C. B. Stevens, J. V. Pullin, M. A. Burton, J. J. Barton, C. W. Ralston, P. J. Dixon, A. G. Ripley, A. Neary. *Rep:* N. O. Martin.
Scorers: T: Beese, C, Old; P: Old 2.

18 MARCH 1972 – SCOTLAND – MURRAYFIELD, EDINBURGH – LOST 9-23
Scotland: A. R. Brown, W. C. C. Steele, J. N. M. Frame, J. M. Renwick, L. G. Dick, C. M. Telfer, A. J. M. Lawson, J. McLauchlan, R. L. Clark, A. B. Carmichael, A. F. McHarg, G. L. Brown, N. A. McEwan, P. C. Brown, R. J. Arneil.
Scorers: T: P. C. Brown, McEwan; P: P. C. Brown 3, A. R. Brown; DG: Telfer.
England: P. M. Knight, K. J. Fielding, G. W. Evans, J. P. A. G. Janion, D. J. Duckham, A. G. B. Old, L. E. Weston, C. B. Stevens, J. V. Pullin, M. A. Burton, A. J. Brinn, C. W. Ralston, P. J. Dixon, A. G. Ripley, A. Neary.
Scorers: P: Old 3.

3 JUNE 1972 – SOUTH AFRICA – ELLIS PARK, JOHANNESBURG – WON 18-9
South Africa: R. A. Carlson, S. H. Nomis, O. A. Roux, J. S. Jansen, G. H. Muller, D. S. L. Snyman, J. F. Viljoen, N. S. E. Bezuidenhout, J. F. B. van Wyk,

J. T. Sauermann, J. G. Williams, P.G. du Plessis, P. J. F. Greyling, A. J. Bates, J. H. Ellis.
Scorers: P: Snyman 3.
England: S. A. Doble, A. J. Morley, P. S. Preece, J. P. A. G. Janion, P. M. Knight, A. G. B. Old, J. G. Webster, C. B. Stevens, J. V. Pullin, M. A. Burton, P. J. Larter, C. W. Ralston, J. A. Watkins, A. G. Ripley, A. Neary.
Scorers: T: Morley; C: Doble; P: Doble 4.

6 JANUARY 1973 – NEW ZEALAND – TWICKENHAM, LONDON – LOST 0-9
England: S. A. Doble, A. J. Morley, P. S. Preece, P. J. Warfield, D. J. Duckham, J. F. Finlan, J. G. Webster, C. B. Stevens, J. V. Pullin, W. F. Anderson, P. J. Larter, C. W. Ralston, J. A. Watkins, A. G. Ripley, A. Neary.
Scorers: None.
New Zealand: J. F. Karam, B. G. Williams, B. J. Robertson, R. M. Parkinson G. B. Batty, I. N. Stevens, S. M. Going, G. J. Whiting, R. W. Norton, K. K. Lambert, H. H. McDonald, P. J. Whiting, A. J. Wyllie, A. R. Sutherland, I. A. Kirkpatrick.
Scorers: T: Kirkpatrick; C: Karam; DG: Williams.

20 JANUARY 1973 – WALES – NATIONAL STADIUM, CARDIFF – LOST 9-25
Wales: J. P. R. Williams, T. G. R. Davies, R. T. E. Bergiers, A. J. L. Lewis, J. C. Bevan, P. Bennett, G. O. Edwards, D. J. Lloyd, J. J. Young G. Shaw, W. D. Thomas, D. L. Quinnell, W. D. Morris, T. M. Davies, J. Taylor.
Scorers: T: Bevan 2, T. G. R. Davies, Edwards, Lewis; C: Bennett; P: Taylor.
England: S. A. Doble, A. J. Morley, P. S. Preece, P. J. Warfield, D. J. Duckham, A. R. Cowman, J. G. Webster, C. B. Stevens, J. V. Pullin, F. E. Cotton, P. J. Larter, C. W. Ralston, J. A. Watkins, A. G. Ripley, A. Neary. *Rep*: G. W. Evans.
Scorers: P: Doble 2; DG: Cowman.

10 FEBRUARY 1973 – IRELAND – LANSDOWNE ROAD, DUBLIN – LOST 9-18
Ireland: T. J. Kiernan, T. O. Grace, R. A. Milliken, C. M. H. Gibson, A. W. McMaster, B. J. McGann, J. J. Moloney, R. J. McLoughlin, K. W. Kennedy, J. F. Lynch, K. M. A. Mays, W. J. McBride, J. H. Buckley, T. A. P. Moore, J. F. Slattery.
Scorers: T: Grace, Milliken; C: McGann 2; P: McGann; DG: McGann.
England: A. M. Jorden, A. J. Morley, P. S. Preece, P. J. Warfield, D. J. Duckham, A. R. Cowman, S. R. Smith, C. B. Stevens, J. V. Pullin, F. E. Cotton, R. M. Uttley, C. W. Ralston, P. J. Dixon, A. G. Ripley, A. Neary.
Scorers: T: Neary; C: Jorden; P: Jorden.

24 FEBRUARY 1973 – FRANCE – TWICKENHAM, LONDON – WON 14-6
England: A. M. Jorden, P. J. Squires, P. S. Preece, G. W. Evans, D. J. Duckham, M. J. Cooper, S. R. Smith, C. B. Stevens, J. V. Pullin, F. E. Cotton, R. M. Uttley, C. W. Ralston, P. J. Dixon, A. G. Ripley, A. Neary.
Scorers: T: Duckham 2; P: Jorden 2.
France: M. Droitecourt, R. Bertranne, C. Dourthe, J. Trillo, J.-P. Lux, J.-P. Romeu, M. Barrau, J. Iracabal, R. Benesis, A. Darrieussecq, A. Esteve, J.-P. Bastiat, J.-P. Biermouret, W. Spanghero, O. Saisset. *Rep*: R. Astre.
Scorers: T: Bertranne; C: Romeu.

17 MARCH 1973 – SCOTLAND – TWICKENHAM, LONDON – WON 20-13
England: A. M. Jorden, P. J. Squires, P. S. Preece, G. W. Evans, D. J. Duckham, M. J. Cooper, S. R. Smith, C. B. Stevens, J. V. Pullin, F. E. Cotton, R. M. Uttley, C. W. Ralston, P. J. Dixon, A. G. Ripley, A. Neary.
Scorers: T: Dixon 2, Evans, Squires; C: Jorden 2.
Scotland: A. R. Irvine, W. C. C. Steele, I. R. McGeechan, I. W. Forsyth, D. W. Shedden, C. M. Telfer, D. W. Morgan, J. McLauchlan, R. L. Clark, A. B. Carmichael, A. F. McHarg, P. C. Brown, N. A. McEwan, G. M. Strachan, J. G. Millican. *Rep*: G. L. Brown.
Scorers: T: Steele 2; C: Irvine; P: Morgan.

15 SEPTEMBER 1973 – NEW ZEALAND – EDEN PARK, AUCKLAND – WON 16-10
New Zealand: R. N. Lendrum, B. G. Williams, I. A. Hurst, R. M. Parkinson, G. B. Batty, J. P. Dougan, S. M. Going, M. G. Jones, R. W. Norton, K. K. Lambert, H. H. McDonald, S. C. Strahan, I. A. Kirkpatrick, A. J. Wyllie, K. W. Stewart. *Rep*: T. G. Morrison.
Scorers: T: Batty, Hurst; C: Lendrum.
England: P. A. Rossborough, P. J. Squires, P. S. Preece, G. W. Evans, D. J. Duckham, A. G. B. Old, J. G. Webster, C. B. Stevens, J. V. Pullin, F. E. Cotton, R. M. Uttley, C. W. Ralston, J. A. Watkins, A. G. Ripley, A. Neary. *Rep*: M. J. Cooper.
Scorers: T: Neary, Squires, Stevens; C: Rossborough 2.

17 NOVEMBER 1973 – AUSTRALIA – TWICKENHAM, LONDON – WON 20-3
England: P. A. Rossborough, P. J. Squires, D. F. K. Roughley, J. P. A. G. Janion, D. J. Duckham, A. G. B. Old, S. J. Smith, C. B. Stevens, J. V. Pullin, F. E. Cotton, R. M. Uttley, C. W. Ralston, J. A. Watkins, A. G. Ripley, A. Neary.
Scorers: T: Neary, Old, Ripley; C: Rossborough; P: Rossborough 2.
Australia: R. L. Fairfax, L. E. Monaghan, R. D. L'Estrange, G. A. Shaw, J. J. McLean, P. G. Rowles, J. N. B. Hipwell, R. Graham, C. M. Carberry,

S. G. McDougall, S. C. Gregory, G. Fay, M. R. Cocks, A. A. Shaw, B. R. Battishall. *Rep*: M. E. Freney.
Scorers: P: Fairfax.

2 FEBRUARY 1974 – SCOTLAND – MURRAYFIELD, EDINBURGH – LOST 14-16
Scotland: A. R. Irvine, A. D. Gill, I. R. McGeechan, J. M. Renwick, L. G. Dick, C. M. Telfer, A. J. M. Lawson, J. McLauchlan, D. F. Madsen, A. B. Carmichael, A. F. McHarg, G. L. Brown, N. A. McEwan, W. S. Watson, W. Lauder.
Scorers: T: Irvine, Lauder; C: Irvine; P: Irvine 2.
England: P. A. Rossborough, P. J. Squires, D. F. K. Roughley, G. W. Evans, D. J. Duckham, A. G. B. Old, J. G. Webster, C. B. Stevens, J. V. Pullin, F. E. Cotton, N. E. Horton, C. W. Ralston, P. J. Dixon, A. G. Ripley, A. Neary.
Scorers: T: Cotton, Neary; P: Old; DG: Rossborough.

16 FEBRUARY 1974, IRELAND – TWICKENHAM, LONDON – LOST 21-26
England: P. A. Rossborough, P. J. Squires, D. F. K. Roughley, G. W. Evans, D. J. Duckham, A. G. B. Old, S. J. Smith, C. B. Stevens, J. V. Pullin, F. E. Cotton, R. M. Uttley, C. W. Ralston, P. J. Dixon, A. G. Ripley, A. Neary.
Scorers: T: Squires; C: Old; P: Old 5.
Ireland: A. H. Ensor, T. O. Grace, R. A. Milliken, C. M. H. Gibson, A. W. McMaster, M. A. Quinn, J. J. Moloney, R. J. McLoughlin, K. W. Kennedy, J. F. Lynch, M. I. Keane, W. J. McBride, S. A. McKinney, T. A. P. Moore, J. F. Slattery.
Scorers: T: Gibson 2, Moloney, Moore; C: Gibson 2; P: Ensor; DG: Quinn.

2 MARCH 1974 – FRANCE – PARC DES PRINCES, PARIS – DRAWN 12-12
France: M. Droitecourt, R. Bertranne, J. Pecune, J.-P. Lux, A. Dubertrand, J. P. Romeu, J. Fouroux, J. Iracabal, R. Benesis, A. Vaquerin, A. Esteve, E. A. Cester, V. Bofelli, C. Spanghero, J.-C.Skrela.
Scorers: T: Romeu; C: Romeu; P: Romeu; DG: Romeu.
England: A. M. Jorden, P. J. Squires, K. Smith, G. W. Evans, D. J. Duckham, A. G. B. Old, S. J. Smith, C. B. Stevens, J. V. Pullin, M. A. Burton, R. M. Uttley, C. W. Ralston, P. J. Dixon, A. G. Ripley, A. Neary.
Scorers: T: Duckham; C: Old; P: Old; DG: Evans.

16 MARCH 1974 – WALES – TWICKENHAM, LONDON – WON 16-12
England: W. H. Hare, P. J. Squires, K. Smith, G. W. Evans, D. J. Duckham, A. G. B. Old, J. G. Webster, C. B. Stevens, J. V. Pullin, M. A. Burton, R. M. Uttley, C. W. Ralston, P. J. Dixon, A. G. Ripley, A. Neary.
Scorers: T: Duckham, Ripley; C: Old; P: Old 2.

Wales: W. R. Blyth, T. G. R. Davies, R. T. E. Bergiers, A. A. J. Finlayson, J. J. Williams, P. Bennett, G. O. Edwards, G. Shaw, R. W. Windsor, P. D. Llewellyn, W. D. Thomas, I. R. Robinson, W. D. Morris, T. M. Davies, T. J. Cobner. *Rep*: G. A. D. Wheel.
Scorers: T: T. M. Davies; C: Bennett; P: Bennett 2.

18 JANUARY 1975 – IRELAND – LANSDOWNE ROAD, DUBLIN – LOST 9-12
England: A. H. Ensor, T. O. Grace, R. A. Milliken, C. M. H. Gibson, J. P. Dennison, W. M. McCombe, J. J. Moloney, R. J. McLoughlin, P. C. Whelan, R. J. Clegg, M. I. Keane, W. J. McBride, S. A. McKinney, W. P. Duggan, J. F. Slattery.
Scorers: T: Gibson, McCombe, C: McCombe 2.
England: P. A. Rossborough, P. J. Squires, P. S. Preece, P. J. Warfield, D. J. Duckham, A. G. B. Old, J. G. Webster, C. B. Stevens, J. V. Pullin, F. E. Cotton, C. W. Ralston, W. B. Beaumont, P. J. Dixon, A. G. Ripley, A. Neary.
Scorers: T: Stevens; C: Old; DG: Old.

1 FEBRUARY 1975 – FRANCE – TWICKENHAM, LONDON – LOST 20-27
England: P. A. Rossborough, P. J. Squires, P. S. Preece, P. J. Warfield, D. J. Duckham, M. J. Cooper, J. G. Webster, C. B. Stevens, P. J. Wheeler, F. E. Cotton, C. W. Ralston, R. M. Uttley, J. A. Watkins, A. G. Ripley, A. Neary.
Scorers: T: Duckham, Rossborough; P: Rossborough 4.
France: M. Taffary, J.-F. Gourdon, C. Dourthe, J. M. Etchenique, R. Bertranne, L. Paries, R. Astre, G. Cholley, A. Paco, A. Vaquerin, A. Esteve, A. Guilbert, J.-P. Rives, C. Spanghero, J.-C. Skrela.
Scorers: T: Etchenique, Gourdon, Guilbert, Spanghero; C: Paries 4; P: Paries.

15 FEBRUARY 1975 – WALES – NATIONAL STADIUM, CARDIFF – LOST 4-20
Wales: J. P. R. Williams, T. G. R. Davies, S. P. Fenwick, R. W. R. Gravell, J. J. Williams, J. D. Bevan, G. O. Edwards, A. G. Faulkner, R. W. Windsor, G. J. Price, A. J. Martin, G. A. D. Wheel, T. P. Evans, T. M. Davies, T. J. Cobner. *Rep*: D. L. Quinnell.
Scorers: T: T. G. R. Davies, Fenwick, J. J. Williams; C: Martin; P: Martin 2.
England: A. M. Jorden, P. J. Squires, P. S. Preece, K. Smith, D. J. Duckham, M. J. Cooper, J. G. Webster, C. B. Stevens, P. J. Wheeler, F. E. Cotton, C. W. Ralston, N. E. Horton, J. A. Watkins, R. M. Uttley, A. Neary. *Rep*: S. J. Smith, J. V. Pullin.
Scorers: T: Horton.

15 MARCH 1975 – SCOTLAND – TWICKENHAM – WON 7-6
England: A. M. Jorden, P. J. Squires, P. J. Warfield, K. Smith, A. J. Morley, W. N. Bennett, J. J. Page, C. B. Stevens, J. V. Pullin, M. A. Burton, R. M. Uttley, C. W. Ralston, D. M. Rollitt, A. G. Ripley, A. Neary.
Scorers: T: Morley; P: Bennett.

Scotland: A. R. Irvine, W. C. C. Steele, J. M. Renwick, D. L. Bell, L. G. Dick, I. R. McGeechan, D. W. Morgan, J. McLauchlan, D. F. Madsen, A. B. Carmichael, A. F. McHarg, G. L. Brown, N. A. McEwan, D. G. Leslie, M. A. Biggar. *Rep*: I. A. Barnes.
Scorers: P: Morgan 2.

British Lions Matches in New Zealand 1971

30 JUNE 1971 – SOUTHLAND – RUGBY PARK, INVERCARGILL – WON 25-3
Southland: D. Nicol, L. Booth, M. Mitchell, J. Polson, R. Hardie, B. Small, D. Langford, I. Gutsell, K. McRae, J. McKenzie, G. Dermody, G. McAllister, H. Miller, R. Kingdon, K. Stewart.
Scorers: P: Nicol.
Lions: J. P. R. Williams, T. G. R. Davies, S. J. Dawes, J. S. Spencer, A. G. Biggar, B. John, R. Hopkins, C. B. Stevens, J. V. Pullin, J. F. Lynch, W. D. Thomas, G. L. Brown, J. Taylor, T. M. Davies, J. F. Slattery. *Rep*: W. J. McBride.
Scorers: T: Biggar 2, Taylor, Dawes, Davies; C: John 5.

6 JULY 1971 – NEW ZEALAND UNIVERSITIES – ATHLETIC GROUND, WELLINGTON – WON 27-6
NZ Universities: E. Taylor, D. L. Palmer, T. Joseph, G. F. Kember, M. P. Collins, R. E. Burgess, R. M. Barlow, P. A. Lindesay, P. Barrett, A. McLellan, J. Sherlock, R. Lockwood, A. Mathieson, G. McGee, R. T. de Cleene.
Rep: P. Anderson.
Scorers: T: Collins 2.
Lions: J. P. R. Williams, D. J. Duckham, S. J. Dawes, C. M. H. Gibson, J. C. Bevan, B. John, R. Hopkins, J. McLauchlan, F. A. L. Laidlaw, C. B. Stevens, W. D. Thomas, G. L. Brown, J. Taylor, T. M. Davies, J. F. Slattery.
Scorers: T: John, Duckham, Bevan; C: John 3; P: John 3; DG: John.

14 JULY 1971 – WAIRARAPA-BUSH – MEMORIAL PARK, MASTERTON – WON 27-6
Wairarapa: V. D. Marfell, K. E. O'Shea, B. G. Martin, N. A. Purvis, M. Barnes, R. T. Couch, L. H. Karatu, W. N. Rowlands, G. E. Falconer, W. J. Crawley, B. J. Lochore, D. P. Oliver, P. J. Ryan, R. R. Brock, C. N. Gray.
Rep: M. R. Sanson.
Scorers: T: Couch; P: Marfell.
Lions: R. B. Hiller, J. S. Spencer, A. J. Lewis, C. W. W. Rea, A. G. Biggar, B. John, G. O. Edwards, C. B. Stevens, J. V. Pullin, M. G. Roberts, T. G. Evans, G. L. Brown, R. J. Arneil, D. L. Quinnell, J. F. Slattery.
Scorers: T: John 2, Biggar 2, Rea, Spencer, Edwards; C: John 2, Hiller.

21 JULY 1971 – POVERTY BAY, EAST COAST – RUGBY PARK, GISBORNE – WON 18-12
Poverty Bay: W. K. Mabey, P. S. Ransley, R. M. Parkinson, G. R. Newlands, A. J. Cross, P. A. Martin, P. J. Duncan, R. J. Ussher, G. Allen, D. Walker, K. Allen, K. G. McGrannachan, D. A. Kirkpatrick, D. I. Wirepa, I. A. Kirkpatrick.
Scorers: T: Ussher; P: Mabey 3.
Lions: R. B. Hiller, D. J. Duckham, S. J. Dawes, A. J. Lewis, A. G. Biggar, C. W. W. Rea, G. O. Edwards, C. B. Stevens, F. A. L. Laidlaw, J. F. Lynch, W. D. Thomas, T. G. Evans, D. L. Quinnell, P. J. Dixon, J. Taylor.
Scorers: T: Duckham 2, Edwards; P: Hiller; DG: Hiller, Dawes.

4 AUGUST 1971 – MANAWATU – SHOWGROUNDS, PALMERSTON NORTH – WON 39-6
Manawatu: J. Francis, J. F. Karam, J. Brennan, A. McLaren, R. Twentyman, G. Tuarau, B. J. Cuff, G. Rohloff, G. McKenzie, P. Harris, J. Callesen, M. Oram, J. Betty, K. Eveleigh, R. G. Myers.
Scorers: P: Karam; DG: Karam.
Lions: R. B. Hiller, J. S. Spencer, S. J. Dawes, A. J. Lewis, J. C. Bevan, C. M. H. Gibson, R. Hopkins, C. B. Stevens, F. A. L. Laidlaw, J. F. Lynch, W. D. Thomas, W. J. McBride, R. J. Arneil, P. J. Dixon J.Taylor.
Scorers: T: Bevan 4, Lewis, Spencer, Hiller, Gibson; C: Hiller 3; P: Hiller 3.

25 AUGUST 1971 – BAY OF PLENTY – THE DOMAIN, TAURANGA – WON 20-14
Bay of Plenty: B. Trask, M. Patterson, E. Stokes, L. Kaipara, G. Moore, G. Rowlands, C. Jacob, J. Helmbright, R. Walker, D. Mohi, G. Hicks, J. Maniapoto, A. M. McNaughton, M. Connor, M. Spence.
Scorers: T: Moore, Trask, Walker; C: Trask; P: Trask.
Lions: R. B. Hiller, A. G. Biggar, C. W. W. Rea, C. M. H. Gibson, J. C. Bevan, B. John, R. Hopkins, J. McLauchlan, F. A. L. Laidlaw, C. B. Stevens, W. D. Thomas, T. G. Evans, R. J. Arneil, P. J. Dixon, J. F. Slattery. *Rep*: M. G. Roberts.
Scorers: T: Biggar, Gibson; C: Hiller; P: Hiller 3; DG: John.

Other England XV Matches

17 MAY 1972 – NATAL – KINGS PARK, DURBAN – WON 19-0
Natal: M. R. Swanby, M. B. Warner, R. Greyling, P. I. Waterson, J. T. Viljoen, A. J. Smith, C. Holm, D. Hopper, B. E. Boyes, D. S. van den Berg, J. Kritzinger, J. A. A. Kapp, H. G. Norton, T. P. Bedford, J. van Oudtshoorn.
Scorers: None.
England XV: S. A. Doble, A. A. Richards, J. S. Spencer, P. S. Preece, P. M. Knight, A. G. B. Old, J. G. Webster, C. B. Stevens, J. V. Pullin, F. E. Cotton, P. J. Larter, D. E. J. Watt, J. A. Watkins, A. G. Ripley, A. Neary.
Scorers: T: Cotton, Knight, Ripley; C: Doble 2; P: Doble.

**20 MAY 1972 – WESTERN PROVINCE – NEWLANDS, CAPE TOWN –
WON 9-6**
W. Province: I. R. McCallum, F. Oeschger, R. Carlson, P. Whipp, E. Joyce,
D. S. L. Snyman, D. J. de Vos, C. van Jaarsveld, R. Cockerell, W. Hugo,
J. Immelman, A. de Villiers, J. Coetzee, M. du Plessis, S. Hillock.
Scorers: P: McCallum 2.
England XV: S. A. Doble, A. J. Morley, P. S. Preece, J. P. A. G. Janion,
P. M. Knight, A. G. B. Old, J. G. Webster, C. B. Stevens, J. V. Pullin,
M. A. Burton, P. J. Larter, C. W. Ralston, T. A. Cowell, A. G. Ripley, A. Neary.
Scorers: T: Knight; C: Doble; P: Doble

**27 MAY 1972 – NORTHERN TRANSVAAL – LOFTUS VERSFELD,
PRETORIA – DRAWN 13-13**
Northern Transvaal: T. Roux, C. F. Luther, A. van Staden, G. S. Thorne,
W. Stapelberg, D. Gradwell, J. Conradie, J. le Roux, P. van Wyk,
N. S. Bezuidenhout, J. G. Williams, J. J. Spies, T. C. Lourens, A. J. Bates,
L. Muller.
Scorers: T: Muller, Stapelberg; C: Luther; P: Luther.
England XV: S. A. Doble, A. J. Morley, P. S. Preece, A. G. B. Old, P. M. Knight,
T. C. Palmer, J. G. Webster C. B. Stevens, J. V. Pullin, F. E. Cotton, P. J. Larter,
D. E. J. Watt, J. A. Watkins, A. G. Ripley, A. Neary.
Scorers: T: Ripley; P: Doble 3.

**30 MAY 1972 – GRIQUALAND WEST – DE BEERS STADIUM,
KIMBERLEY – WON 60-21**
Griqualand West: T. Smith, B. Swartz, D. Wiese, J. Lategan, O. Fourie,
G. Serfontein, T. Johnson, B. Fourie, D. Slabbert, L. Swanepoel, J. van
Answegen, P. I. van Deventer, J. Theron, J. Markram, P. Smith.
Scorers: T: O. Fourie, van Deventer; C: P. Smith 2; P: P. Smith 3.
England XV: D. F. Whibley, A. J. Morley, J. S. Spencer, J. P. A. G. Janion,
A. A. Richards, A. G. B. Old, S. J. Smith, C. B. Stevens, A. V. Boddy, M. A. Burton,
C. W. Ralston, D. E. J. Watt, J. A. Watkins, J. J. Barton, T. A. Cowell.
Scorers: T: Spencer 2, Richards 2, Morley, Stevens, Watkins, Janion, Cowell;
C: Old 9; P: Old; DG: Old.

28 AUGUST 1973 – FIJI – NATIONAL STADIUM, SUVA – WON 13-12
Fiji: J. Visei, P. B. Tikoisuva, R. Latilevu, L. Namandila, T. Rabuli, W. Gavidi,
I. Batibasanga, P. Hughes, N. Ratudina, A. Racika, J. Naucabalavu,
N. Ravouvou, M. Kurisaru, I. Tuisese, R. Samuels.
Scorers: T: Kurisaru, Latilevu; C: Ratudina, Batibasanga.
England XV: A. M. Jorden, P. J. Squires, P. S. Preece, G. W. Evans,
D. J. Duckham, A. G. B. Old, S. J. Smith, C. B. Stevens, J. V. Pullin, F. E. Cotton,
R. M. Uttley, C. W. Ralston, P. J. Hendy, A. G. Ripley, A. Neary.
Scorers: T: Evans, Squires; C: Jorden; P: Jorden.

1 SEPTEMBER 1973 – TARANAKI – RUGBY PARK, NEW PLYMOUTH – LOST 3-6
Taranaki: N. Johnston, D. A. Vesty, R. Clough, T. R. Smith, P. J. Strange, P. G. Martin, D. J. Wards, A. J. Gardiner, F. O'Carroll, J. T. McEldowney, J. M. Thwaites, I. M. Eliason, R. Fraser, B. C. Grant, A. I. Scown. *Rep*: V. Baker.
Scorers: P: Johnston 2.
England XV: P. Rossborough, P. M. Knight, P. S. Preece, J. P. A. G. Janion, D. J. Duckham, M. J. Cooper, J. G. Webster, C. B. Stevens, J. V. Pullin, M. A. Burton, N. O. Martin, C. W. Ralston, J. A. Watkins, A. G. Ripley, A. Neary. *Rep*: G. W. Evans.
Scorers: P: Rossborough.

8 SEPTEMBER 1973 – CANTERBURY – LANCASTER PARK, CHRISTCHURCH – LOST 12-19
Canterbury: W. F. McCormick, T. W. Mitchell, I. A. Hurst, D. A. Hales, B. A. McPhail, O. D. Bruce, L. J. Davis, W. K. Bush, R. W. Norton, K. J. Tanner, H. H. McDonald, V. E. Stewart, S. E. G. Cron, A. J. Wyllie, J. K. Phillips.
Scorers: T: Hurst, McPhail; C: McCormick; P: McCormick 3.
England XV: P. Rossborough, P. J. Squires, M. J. Cooper, G. W. Evans, D. J. Duckham, A. G. B. Old, J. G. Webster, C. B. Stevens, J. V. Pullin, F. E. Cotton, R. M. Uttley, C. W. Ralston, J. A. Watkins, A. G. Ripley, A. Neary.
Scorers: T: Squires 2, Rossborough.

22 APRIL 1974 – FRANCE XV – TWICKENHAM, LONDON – LOST 7-26
England XV: W. H. Hare, P. J. Squires, K. Smith, G. W. Evans, D. J. Duckham, A. G. B. Old, J. G. Webster, C. B. Stevens, J. V. Pullin, F. E. Cotton, R. M. Uttley, C. W. Ralston, P. J. Dixon, A. G. Ripley, A. Neary. *Rep*: M. A. Burton.
Scorers: T: Duckham; P: Hare.
France XV: M. Droitecourt, J.-F. Gourdon, R. Bertranne, J.-P. Lux, J.-L. Averous, J.-P. Romeu, M. Barrau, P. Dospital, R. Benesis, J. Iracabal, A. Esteve, E. A. Cester, O. Saisset, C. Spanghero, J.-C. Skrela.
Scorers: Not known.

Other International Matches

14 OCTOBER 1972 – SCOTLAND/IRELAND XV – MURRAYFIELD, EDINBURGH – LOST 21-30
Scot/Ire XV: A. R. Brown, T. O. Grace, J. N. M. Frame, J. M. Renwick, W. C. C. Steele, C. M. H. Gibson, J. J. Moloney, N. Suddon, K. W. Kennedy, A. B. Carmichael, W. J. McBride, G. L. Brown, N. A. McEwan, P. C. Brown, J. F. Slattery.
Scorers: T: Gibson 3, Grace 2; C: A. R. Brown 2; P: A. R. Brown 2.

Eng/Wal XV: J. P. R. Williams, T. G. R. Davies, R. T. E. Bergiers, A. J. Lewis, P. M. Knight, P. Bennett, R. Hopkins, C. B. Stevens, J. V. Pullin, D. J. Lloyd, P. J. Larter, M. G. Roberts, J. Taylor, T. M. Davies, A. Neary. *Rep*: A. G. B. Old.
Scorers: T: T. G. R. Davies, Lloyd, Williams, Neary; C: Bennett; P: Taylor.

Barbarians Matches

27 MARCH 1970 – PENARTH – LAVERNOCK ROAD, PENARTH – WON 42-6
Barbarians: B. J. O'Driscoll, K. J. Fielding, J. N. M. Frame, C. S. Wardlow, K. Hughes, C. M. Telfer, N. C. Starmer-Smith, C. B. Stevens, R. F. S. Harris, P. L. Butler, M. M. Leadbetter, T. A. P. Moore, P. J. Hayward, P. J. Dixon, W. Lauder.
Scorers: T: Fielding 3, Starmer-Smith 2, Frame 2, Dixon; C: O'Driscoll 6; P: O'Driscoll; DG: Telfer.

30 MARCH 1970 – SWANSEA – ST HELENS, SWANSEA – WON 24-8
Barbarians: B. J. O'Driscoll, A. D. Williams, J. S. Spencer, C. S. Wardlow, M. P. Bulpitt, P. Bennett, R. M. Young, C. B. Stevens, R. F. S. Harris, P. O'Callaghan, M. G. Molloy, T. A. P. Moore, W. Lauder, P. J. Dixon, J. F. Slattery.
Scorers: T: Slattery 2, Dixon; C: O'Driscoll 3; P: O'Driscoll; DG: Bennett 2.

4 MARCH 1971 – EAST MIDLANDS – FRANKLINS GARDENS, NORTHAMPTON – WON 18-14
Barbarians: R. B. Hiller, J. P. A. G. Janion, S. J. Dawes, C. S. Wardlow, M. P. Bulpitt, R. H. Phillips, N. C. Starmer-Smith, C. B. Stevens, P. F. Madigan, J. F. Lynch, D. L. Quinnell, G. L. Brown, W. D. Morris, P. J. Dixon, A. L. Bucknall.
Scorers: T: Dixon, Bulpitt, Bucknall; P: Hiller 2.

South West Counties Matches Against International Teams

27 DEC 1969 – SOUTH AFRICA – COUNTY GROUND, EXETER – LOST 6-9
South West XV: G. Bate, K. C. Plummer, J. Bevan, B. Davies, D. H. Prout, R. P. Whitcombe, A. F. A. Pearn, C. B. Stevens, R. F. S. Harris, P. Baxter, J. Baxter, B. F. Ninnes, W. R. George, A. J. Hollins, A. Cole.
Scorers: P: Bate 2.
South Africa: H. O. de Villiers, S. H. Nomis, O. A. Roux, J. P. van der Merwe, A. E. van der Watt, M. J. Lawless, D. J. de Villiers, R. Potgeiter, C. H. Cockrell, J. B. Neethling, F. C. du Preez, M. C. J. van Rensburg, P. J. F. Greyling, M. W. Jennings, P. I. van Deventer. *Rep*: J. L. Myburgh.
Scorers: T: Lawless, Jennings; P: H. O. de Villiers.

18 APRIL 1970 – FRANCE B – RECREATION GROUND, REDRUTH – LOST 13-14

Cornwall: G. Bate, K. C. Plummer, V. C. Parkin, F. Johns, D. H. Prout, D. Thomas, D. R. Chapman, C. B. Stevens, C. Brown, J. P. O'Shea, B. F. Ninnes, J. Blackburn, W. R. George, S. E. Anderson, K. W. Trerise.
Scorers: T: Prout; C: George; P: Bate 2, George.
France B: R. Berges-Cau, S. Moly, J. Plantey, R. Charlems, R. Bertranne, H. Hassary, R. Crebier, F. Bergamasco, A. Torossian, A. Ross, J.-P. Bastiat, M. Satzaki, A. Quillis, M. Billiere, J.-C. Skrela.
Scorers: T: Bertranne 2, Quillis; C: Berges-Cau; DG: Hassary.

7 OCTOBER 1972 – ROMANIA – RECREATION GROUND, REDRUTH – LOST 3-18

Cornwall: P. J. Winnan, K. C. Plummer, J. P. Agnew, F. Johns, S. J. Tiddy, B. J. Jenkin, P. Sweeney, C. B. Stevens, J. Trevorrow, T. A. Pryor, M. T. H. Doney, J. Blackburn, N. S. Worrall, R. Hosken, T. K. Barnes.
Scorers: P: Winnan.
Romania: R. Durbac, C. Rascanu, A. Pavlovici, G. Dragomircu, G. Nica, R. Marica, S. Bargaunas, N. Baciu, M. Cretelcan, C. Dinu, A. Atanasiu, N. Postolache, C. Fugigi, F. Constantin, A. Pop.
Scorers: T: Rascanu, Basiu; C: Nica 2; P: Durbac, Nica.

27 OCTOBER 1973 – AUSTRALIA – RECREATION GROUND, BATH – WON 15-14

South West XV: D. G. Tyler, K. C. Plummer, P. Johnson, A. R. Swaffield, A. J. Morley, A. H. Nicholls, A. F. A. Pearn, C. B. Stevens, J. V. Pullin, M. A. Burton, A. J. Brinn, J. H. Fidler, D. M. Rollitt, R. C. Hannaford, J. A. Watkins. *Rep*: C. Williams, R. J. Hazzard.
Scorers: T: Watkins; C: Pearn; P: Pearn 3.
Australia: R. L. Fairfax, L. E. Monaghan, R. D. L'Estrange, D. R. Burnet, O. Stephens, P. G. Rowles, R. G. Hauser, S. G. McDougall, C. M. Carberry, R. Graham, G. Fay, R. A. Smith, A. A. Shaw, K. G. McCurrach, M. R. Cocks.
Scorers: T: L'Estrange, Monaghan; P: Fairfax 2.

27 DECEMBER 1975 – AUSTRALIA – COUNTY GROUND, EXETER – LOST 9-23

South West XV: P. J. Winnan, K. C. Plummer, J. S. Cocking, M. R. Shillabeer, M. J. Mills, B. G. Stevens, N. R. Vosper, C. B. Stevens, J. W. Lockyer, T. A. Pryor, J. P. Scott, C. J. Durant, P. J. Hendy, R. C. Corin, D. M. Jewell.
Scorers: P: Winnan 3.
Australia: P. E. McLean, J. R. Ryan, W. A. McKid, L. J. Weatherstone, P. G. Batch, L. J. Wright, R. G. Hauser, S. G. McDougall, C. M. Carberry, S. C. Finnane, R. A. Smith, G. S. Eisenhauer, G. C. Cornelson, M. E. Loane, R. A. Price.
Scorers: T: Batch 2, Loane, Cornelson; C: McLean 2; P: McLean.

Cornwall Semi-Finals and Final

3 FEBRUARY 1962 – WARWICKSHIRE (SF) – COUNDON ROAD, COVENTRY – LOST 0-8
Warwickshire: D. R. Cook, P. B. Jackson, R. J. Frame, A. Davies, M. Neale, T. J. Dalton, G. C. Cole, P. E. Judd, H. O. Godwin, M. R. McLean, C. M. Payne, T. A. Pargetter, P. G. D. Robbins, J. F. Gardiner, S. J. Purdy.
Scorers: T: Payne; C: Cole; P: Cole.
Cornwall: R. W. Hosen, D. H. Prout, G. G. Luke, J. G. Glover, R. J. Moyle, R. A. W. Sharp, P. J. B. Michell, C. B. Stevens, W. K. Abrahams, C. R. Johns, A. Williams, D. J. S. Mann, A. C. Thomas, W. N. Burley, P. E. McGovan.
Scorers: None.

3 FEBRUARY 3 1967 – SURREY (SF) – RECREATION GROUND, REDRUTH – DRAWN 6-6
Cornwall: G. Bate, K. C. Plummer, T. C. Mungles, J. G. Glover, D. H. Prout, T. A. Palmer, I. R. Davey, C. B. Stevens, R. F. S. Harris, W. J. Carling, J. Allen, A. E. Greep, W. R. George, R. S. Glazsher, G. R. McKeown.
Scorers: Stevens, Plummer.
Surrey: R. B. Hiller, J. B. H. Coker, T. J. Brooke, R. H. Lloyd, C. T. Gibbons, B. A. Richards, R. P. Lewis, G. C. Murray, P. L. Ostling, A. L. Horton, C. S. Dutson, G. Patterson, D. Richards, R. C. B. Michaelson, A. Hendrickse.
Scorers: P: Hiller 2.

17 FEBRUARY 1967 – SURREY (SF R) – ATHLETIC GROUND, RICHMOND – DRAWN 14-14
Surrey: R. B. Hiller, J. B. H. Coker, T. J. Brooke, R. H. Lloyd, C. T. Gibbons, B. A. Richards, N. J. Cosh, G. C. Murray, P. L. Ostling, A. L. Horton, C. S. Dutson, G. Patterson, D. Richards, R. C. B. Michaelson, A. J. Hendrickse.
Scorers: T: Coker; C; Hiller; P: Hiller 2; DG: B. A. Richards.
Cornwall: R. W. Hosen, K. C. Plummer, T. A. Palmer, J. G. Glover, D. H. Prout, R. A. W. Sharp, I. R. Davey, C. B. Stevens, R. F. S. Harris, R. Buckingham, J. Allen, A. E. Greep, W. R. George, R. S. Glazsher, G. R. McKeown.
Scorers: T: Prout, Plummer; C: Hosen; P: Hosen 2.

3 FEBRUARY 1967 – SURREY (SF R) – RECREATION GROUND, REDRUTH – LOST 3-14
Cornwall: R. W. Hosen, K. C. Plummer, T. A. Palmer, J. G. Glover, D. H. Prout, R. A. W. Sharp, I. R. Davey, C. B. Stevens, R. F. S. Harris, R. Buckingham, J. Allen, A. E. Greep, W. R. George, R. S. Glazsher, G. R. McKeown.
Scorers: P: Hosen.

Surrey: R. B. Hiller, J. B. H. Coker, T. J. Brooke, R. H. Lloyd, C. T. Gibbons, B. A. Richards, R. P. Lewis, G. C. Murray, P. L. Ostling, A. L. Horton, C. S. Dutson, G. Patterson, D. Richards, R. C. B. Michaelson, A. J. Hendrickse.
Scorers: T: Brooke, Lloyd; C: Hiller; P: Hiller 2.

1 FEBRUARY 1969 – EAST MIDLANDS (SF) – RECREATION GROUND, REDRUTH – WON 19-5
Cornwall: G. Bate, K. C. Plummer, V. C. Parkin, G. L. Jones, D. H. Prout, T. A. Palmer, D. Chapman, C. B. Stevens, R. F. S. Harris, C. R. Johns, C. Kneebone, B. F. Ninnes, W. R. George, R. Hosken, G. R. McKeown.
Scorers: T: McKeown 2, Bate, Chapman; C: Bate, George; P: Bate.
East Midlands: K. J. Taylor, N. R. Boult, J. R. Cooley, K. V. Allen, G. T. Robertson, P. D. Briggs, R. J. Kottler, D. L. Powell, K. N. Baughan, P. F. Duffy, N. E. Barker, P. S. Wolfenden, R. B. Taylor, M. J. Mason, D. P. Rogers.
Scorers: T: Robertson; C: K. J. Taylor.

8 MARCH 1969 – LANCASHIRE (F) – RECREATION GROUND, REDRUTH – LOST 9-11
Cornwall: G. Bate, K. C. Plummer, V. C. Parkin, G. L. Jones, D. H. Prout, T. A. Palmer, D. Chapman, C. B. Stevens, R. F. S. Harris, C. R. Johns, C. Kneebone, B. F. Ninnes, W. R. George, R. Hosken, G. R. McKeown.
Scorers: P: Harris, George; DG: Chapman.
Lancashire: A. Edge, A. A. Richards, C. R. Jennins, D. F. K. Roughley, C. P. Hanley, P. S. Mahon, E. W. Williams, M. J. Hindle, P. W. Barratt, B. S. Jackson, M. M. Leadbetter, A. R. Trickey, A. Neary, J. R. H. Greenwood, E. T. Lyon.
Scorers: T: Lyon, Richards; C: Jennins; P: Jennins.

Other Matches for Cornwall

1959
8 Sep, United Hospitals, Camborne, Drawn 11-11
1 Oct, Surrey, Penzance, Won 19-8
14 Nov, Somerset, Taunton, Won 12-11

1961
30 Sep, Lancashire, Redruth, Drawn 3-3
11 Oct, Sussex, Camborne, Won 29-6
28 Oct, Somerset, Weston-Super-Mare, Won 27-3
11 Nov, Devon, Exeter, Won 5-0
25 Nov, Gloucestershire, Camborne, Won 16-8

1962
10 Oct, British Police, Redruth, Won 11-3
27 Oct, Devon, Camborne, Lost 6-9

1963
26 Oct, Gloucestershire, Redruth, Won 6-3
9 Nov, Somerset, Bridgwater, Lost 6-8
23 Nov, Devon, Devonport, Won 9-6

1964
11 Jan, Gloucestershire, Bristol, Lost 3-9
26 Sep, Lancashire, Penzance, Lost 11-19

24 Oct, Somerset, Camborne, Won 16-9

14 Nov, Devon, Redruth, Won 6-3

28 Nov, Gloucestershire, Gloucester,
Lost 6-21

1965

15 Sep, Crawshays XV, Camborne,
Won 17-10

25 Sep, Dorset-Wiltshire, Falmouth,
Won 14-6

2 Oct, Berkshire, Penzance, Won 24-3

27 Nov, Somerset, Bath, Lost 6-8

1966

6 Sep, R. Hole's XV, Torquay, Won 24-8

15 Sep, Crawshays XV, Camborne,
Won 21-5

24 Sep, Lancashire, Penzance, Drawn 6-6

1 Oct, Oxfordshire, Falmouth, Won 22-5

22 Oct, Gloucestershire, Bristol, Won 9-3

12 Nov, Somerset, Redruth, Won 14-3

26 Nov, Devon, Camborne, Won 9-0

1967

14 Jan, Oxfordshire, Redruth, Won 16-6

30 Sep, Newbridge, Penzance, Lost 12-18

28 Oct, Somerset, Taunton, Lost 3-9

11 Nov, Devon, Devonport, Won 9-3

1968

27 Jan, Gloucestershire, Redruth,
Lost 3-9

28 Sep, Sussex, Penzance, Won 22-11

5 Oct, Newbridge, Falmouth,
Drawn 11-11

26 Oct, Devon, Redruth, Won 20-6

9 Nov, Gloucestershire, Gloucester,
Won 15-9

23 Nov, Somerset, Camborne, Drawn 6-6

1969

11 Jan, Hertfordshire, Redruth, Won 11-0

6 Sep, Tankards, Redruth, Drawn 11-11

17 Sep, Crawshays XV, Redruth,
Lost 9-16

27 Sep, The Army, Falmouth, Won 14-11

4 Oct, Dorset-Wiltshire, Penzance,
Won 44-0

25 Oct, Gloucestershire, Redruth,
Lost 9-12

8 Nov, Somerset, Bath, Won 9-8

22 Nov, Devon, Devonport, Lost 12-13

1970

28 Nov, Gloucestershire, Bristol, Lost 3-9

1971

13 Mar, Comite-du-Lyonnais, Vienne,
Lost 14-22

13 Nov, Gloucestershire, Redruth,
Won 13-10

27 Nov, Somerset, Weston-super-Mare,
Lost 0-6

11 Dec, Somerset, Redruth, Lost 3-9

1972

15 Apr, Comite-du-Lyonnais, Camborne,
Lost 13-14

30 Sep, The Army, Penzance, Won 25-9

7 Oct 7, Romania, Redruth, Lost 3-18

21 Oct 21, Gloucestershire, Gloucester,
Lost 6-24

11 Nov, Somerset, Camborne, Lost 4-10

25 Nov, Devon, Redruth, Lost 15-19

1973

10 Jan, Royal Navy, Devonport, Lost 10-20

20 Oct, Somerset, Taunton, Lost 3-11

10 Nov, Devon, Exeter, Lost 12-13

24 Nov, Gloucestershire, Camborne,
Lost 7-9

1974

5 Oct, South Wales Police, Penzance,
Drawn 9-9

26 Oct, Devon, Camborne, Won 18-12

9 Nov, Gloucestershire, Bristol, Lost 6-9

23 Nov, Somerset, Redruth, Lost 3-8

1975

4 Oct, South Wales Police, Penryn,
  Drawn 7-7

15 Oct, British Police, Penzance,
  Lost 12-13

25 Oct, Gloucestershire, Redruth,
  Lost 6-9

8 Nov, Somerset, Bridgwater,
  Won 22-14

22 Nov, Devon, Torquay, Won 20-9

1976

21 Jan, Royal Navy, Devonport,
  Won 17-9

8 Sep, Crawshays XV, Camborne,
  Won 7-4

15 Sep, England U-23, Redruth,
  Won 12-7

29 Sep, Royal Navy, Camborne,
  Won 22-3

9 Oct, Gloucestershire, Bristol,
  Lost 0-30

23 Oct, Somerset Camborne, Lost 0-6

13 Nov, Devon, Redruth, Lost 3-7

Penzance & Newlyn First XV Matches

1958

Nov 8, RAF Coastal Command,
  Penzance, Won 17-0

1959

31 Jan, RNAS Culdrose, Penzance,
  Won 14-3

7 Feb, St Ives, St Ives, Won 3-0

28 Feb, Redruth, Penzance, Won 6-0

7 Mar, Newton Abbot, Penzance,
  Won 22-5

14 Mar, Torquay Athletic, Torquay,
  Drawn 3-3

21 Mar, Truro, Penzance, Won 29-0

23 Mar, Imperial College, Penzance,
  Won 9-0

28 Mar, Wasps, Penzance, Won 14-5

30 Mar, St Thomas Hospital, Penzance,
  Lost 3-11

31 Mar, St Mary's Hospital, Penzance,
  Won 16-0

4 Apr, Cardiff, Penzance, Lost 6-13

6 Apr, Aberavon, Port Talbot, Lost 8-11

7 Apr, Cross Keys, Cross Keys, Lost 6-11

9 Apr, Treorchy, Treorchy, Drawn 6-6

10 Apr, Bridgwater & Albion,
  Bridgwater, Won 8-0

14 Apr, Devonport Services Penzance,
  Won 24-0

18 Apr, RAF Coastal Command,
  Penzance, Won 29-16

24 Apr, Bridgwater & Albion, Penzance,
  Lost 0-3

25 Apr, Cheltenham, Penzance, Won 9-5

1 Sep, AS Milano, Penzance, Won 18-6

4 Sep, Welsh Academicals, Penzance,
  Won 13-3

12 Sep, Dublin Wanderers, Penzance,
  Lost 8-31

19 Sep, Pontypridd, Penzance, Lost 6-9

21 Sep, Rosslyn Park, Penzance,
  Drawn 3-3

28 Sep, Penryn, Penryn, Won 11-8

7 Oct, RNAS Culdrose, Penzance,
  Won 13-8

10 Oct, Truro, Truro, Lost 3-11

13 Oct, Fleet Air Arm, Penzance,
  Won 16-0

17 Oct, Hayle, Hayle, Won 6-0

31 Oct, Bart's Hospital, Penzance,
  Won 14-3

7 Nov, St Ives, Penzance, Won 33-8

11 Nov, Cornwall Junior Group,
  Penzance, Won 9-0

21 Nov, Hayle, Penzance, Won 11-6

14 Dec, Oxford Greyhounds, Penzance, Lost 3-6

19 Dec, Taunton, Taunton, Drawn 0-0

26 Dec, Truro, Penzance, Won 11-0

28 Dec, St Ives, Penzance, Won 29-8

1960

2 Jan, Falmouth, Falmouth, Drawn 0-0

6 Jan, RNAS Culdrose, Penzance, Won 43-6

9 Jan, Barnstaple, Barnstaple, Lost 0-5

16 Jan, Camborne, Penzance, Won 20-0

23 Jan, Newton Abbot, Newton Abbot, Won 12-3

30 Jan, Camborne School Of Mines, Camborne, Won 8-0

6 Feb, Penryn, Penzance, Won 19-6

13 Feb, Imperial College, London, Won 11-0

20 Feb, Torquay Athletic, Penzance, Won 17-5

27 Feb, Redruth, Redruth, Lost 3-14

5 Mar, Hayle, Penzance, Won 22-8

19 Mar, Falmouth, Penzance, Won 11-0

21 Mar, Hayle, Penzance, Won 9-0

26 Mar, RAF Coastal Command, Penzance, Lost 6-8

6 Apr, Redruth, Redruth, Lost 6-11

9 Apr Penarth Penzance, Lost 5-14

16 Apr, Saracens, Penzance, Won 19-3

18 Apr, St Thomas Hospital, Penzance, Won 6-3

19 Apr, St Mary's Hospital, Penzance, Won 6-3

23 Apr, Cardiff, Penzance, Won 11-3

25 Apr, Ebbw Vale, Penzance, Drawn 6-6

28 Apr, Stroud, Penzance, Won 17-8

3 Sep, J. M. Williams XV, Penzance, Lost 3-27

1961

4 Feb, Exeter, Exeter, Lost 0-8

11 Feb, REME Corps, Penzance, Won 14-3

13 Feb, London University, Penzance, Won 6-0

25 Feb, RAF Coastal Command, Penzance, Won 33-0

4 Mar, Redruth, Redruth, Won 11-9

8 Mar, Exeter University, Penzance, Won 31-16

11 Mar, Hayle, Penzance, Won 42-3

18 Mar, Truro, Truro, Won 6-3

22 Mar, St Ives, St Ives, Won 24-0

25 Mar, Pontypool, Penzance, Won 9-6

29 Mar, Imperial College, Penzance, Won 36-5

1 Apr, Wasps, Penzance, Lost 6-10

3 Apr, St Thomas Hospital, Penzance, Lost 15-18

8 Apr, Cardiff, Penzance, Lost 3-15

10 Apr, Ebbw Vale, Penzance, Lost 6-29

18 Apr, Durham University, Penzance, Won 13-11

22 Apr, Bridwater & Albion, Penzance, Won 12-3

25 Apr, Falmouth, Penzance, Won 21-3

28 Apr, CRFU Sevens, Camborne, Winners

1 Sep, Welsh Academicals, Penzance, Won 6-3

2 Sep, Birmingham Old Boys, Penzance, Won 6-5

4 Sep, J. M. Williams XV, Penzance, Lost 0-20

9 Sep, Etceteras, Penzance, Won 11-3

11 Sep, London Scottish, Penzance, Lost 3-11

12 Sep, Esher, Penzance, Won 16-3

18 Sep, Rosslyn Park, Penzance, Won 9-8

21 Sep, Redruth, Redruth, Lost 6-25

23 Sep, Pontypridd, Penzance, Won 13-3

7 Oct, Oxford University, Penzance, Lost 3-9

18 Nov, St Ives, Penzance, Won 31-0

4 Dec, Camborne School of Mines,
Penzance, Won 24-0

9 Dec, Redruth, Penzance, Won 20-3

1962

20 Jan, Hayle, Penzance, Won 28-0

27 Jan, Camborne School of Mines,
Camborne, Won 14-3

7 Feb, Exeter University, Penzance,
Won 24-5

10 Feb, Liskeard-Looe, Liskeard,
Won 38-12

17 Feb, Falmouth, Penzance, Won 44-0

24 Feb, Penryn, Penzance, Won 11-5,

3 Mar, Camborne, Penzance, Won 19-0

10 Mar, Redruth, Redruth, Won 3-0

17 Mar, Torquay Athletic, Penzance,
Won 6-5

31 Mar, Cardiff, Penzance, Lost 3-17

2 Apr, Penryn, Penzance, Lost 0-11

4 Apr, Camborne, Camborne, Won 3-0

7 Apr, Newton Abbot, Penzance,
Won 32-0

11 Apr, Redruth, Penzance, Lost 0-6

14 Apr, Exeter, Penzance, Lost 0-8

4 Sep, Welsh Academicals, Penzance,
Won 16-5

8 Sep, London Scottish, Penzance,
Won 6-3

14 Sep, Metropolitan Police, Penzance,
Lost 3-8

15 Sep, Rosslyn Park, Penzance, Lost 0-19

18 Sep, Queens University Belfast,
Penzance, Lost 9-11

26 Sep, Odin Hannover, Penzance,
Won 11-6

27 Sep, Redruth, Redruth, Drawn 3-3,

24 Oct, RNE College, Penzance, Won 9-5

3 Nov, Bart's Hospital, Penzance,
Lost 9-10

17 Nov, Redruth, Redruth, Won 18-3

1 Dec, Camborne School of Mines,
Penzance, Won 45-0

15 Dec, Torquay Athletic, Torquay,
Won 6-0

17 Dec, Oxford University Greyhounds,
Penzance, Lost 6-13

22 Dec, Redruth, Penzance, Won 11-0

26 Dec, Truro, Penzance, Won 21-6

29 Dec, St Ives, St Ives, Won 11-3

1963

5 Jan, Camborne, Penzance, Won 25-0

16 Jan, CA San Isidro, Penzance,
Lost 6-12

26 Jan, Truro, Penzance, Won 16-0

9 Feb, Penryn, Penryn, Won 6-0

16 Feb, St Ives, Penzance, Won 6-3

20 Feb, Camborne School of Mines,
Penzance, Won 33-0

23 Feb, Penryn, Penzance, Won 3-0

2 Mar, Camborne, Camborne, Won 11-3

9 Mar, Plymouth Albion, Penzance,
Won 11-0

16 Mar, St Ives, St Ives, Won 13-3

20 Mar, Hayle, Penzance, Drawn 3-3

23 Mar, Newton Abbot, Newton Abbot,
Won 6-3

27 Mar, Hayle, Hayle, Won 3-0

30 Mar, Falmouth, Penzance, Won 8-6

4 Apr, Redruth, Penzance, Won 5-0

6 Apr, Torquay Athletic, Penzance,
Won 23-11

10 Apr, Falmouth, Falmouth, Won 6-0

13 Apr, Wasps, Penzance, Lost 6-16

16 Apr, St Mary's Hospital, Penzance,
Drawn 3-3

20 Apr, Cardiff, Penzance, Lost 5-13

22 Apr, Ebbw Vale, Penzance, Lost 3-25

27 Apr, Exeter, Exeter, Won 17-15

29 Apr, Bridgwater & Albion, Penzance,
Won 18-3

30 Apr, CRFU Sevens, Camborne,
Winners

3 Sep, Public School Wanderers,
Penzance, Won 14-11

7 Sep, J. M. Williams XV, Penzance,
  Lost 0-8
9 Sep, London Scottish, Penzance,
  Drawn 6-6
14 Sep, Metropolitan Police, Penzance,
  Won 6-5
21 Sep, Parachute Regiment, Penzance,
  Won 13-3
28 Sep, Exeter, Penzance, Drawn 8-8
5 Oct, Plymouth Albion, Plymouth,
  Lost 0-14
2 Nov, Bart's Hospital, Penzance,
  Won 19-8
14 Dec, Redruth, Penzance, Drawn 3-3
26 Dec, Truro, Truro, Lost 0-6
28 Dec, St Ives, Penzance, Won 27-8

1964
18 Jan, Truro, Penzance, Won 12-6
1 Feb, Camborne, Camborne, Won 3-0
8 Feb, Torquay Athletic, Penzance,
  Won 34-10
15 Feb, Hayle, Hayle, Drawn 3-3
22 Feb, Devonport Services, Penzance,
  Won 12-0
29 Feb, Falmouth, Penzance, Won 8-0
7 Mar, Redruth, Redruth, Won 17-9
11 Mar, RNE College, Penzance, Won 6-3
14 Mar, Falmouth, Falmouth, Won 6-3
21 Mar, St Ives, St Ives, Drawn 0-0
1 Sep, Falmouth, Falmouth, Lost 3-11
5 Sep, London Scottish, Penzance,
  Lost 3-5
7 Sep, Tankards, Penzance, Lost 6-11
11 Sep, Taunton, Penzance, Won 19-5
19 Sep, Rosslyn Park, Penzance,
  Lost 0-21
21 Sep, Old Belvedere, Penzance,
  Lost 6-8
29 Sep, Penryn, Penryn, Won 11-8
10 Oct, Hayle, Hayle, Lost 5-17
17 Oct, Teignmouth, Teignmouth,
  Won 21-3

31 Oct, Camborne, Camborne,
  Won 15-11
7 Nov, Launceston, Penzance, Won 41-6
9 Nov, Bart's Hospital, Penzance,
  Lost 0-11
21 Nov, Exeter, Exeter, Won 8-5
12 Dec, Redruth, Penzance, Drawn 6-6
19 Dec, Penryn, Penryn, Lost 0-16
26 Dec, Truro, Penzance, Lost 3-5

1965
2 Jan, St Ives, St Ives, Won 15-0
9 Jan, Teignmouth, Penzance, Won 9-0
23 Jan, Camborne School of Mines,
  Camborne, Won 37-9
30 Jan, St Ives, Penzance, Won 12-0
13 Feb, Camborne, Penzance, Won 6-0
20 Feb, Devonport Services, Devonport,
  Lost 6-11
24 Feb, RNE College, Penzance,
  Won 19-3
27 Feb, Hayle, Penzance, Won 9-5
6 Mar, St Ives, St Ives, Won 19-0
13 Mar, The Army, Penzance, Lost 0-8
1 Apr, Penryn, Penzance, Drawn 3-3
3 Apr, Barnstaple, Penzance, Won 11-6
14 Apr, Falmouth, Penzance, Drawn 0-0
17 Apr, Wasps, Penzance, Lost 3-8
19 Apr, St Thomas Hospital, Penzance,
  Lost 3-11
24 Apr, Gloucester, Penzance, Lost 3-12
26 Apr, Bridgwater & Albion, Penzance,
  Won 16-0
1 May, CRFU Sevens, Penzance,
  Lost Rd 1
6 Sep, Bath, Penzance, Lost 3-5
11 Sep, Metropolitan Police, Penzance,
  Lost 3-10
13 Sep, London Scottish, Penzance,
  Lost 3-14
20 Sep, Rosslyn Park, Penzance, Lost 3-8
9 Oct, Exeter, Penzance, Won 3-0
16 Oct, Hayle, Hayle, Won 17-6

30 Oct, Falmouth, Penzance, Lost 12-14

6 Nov, Bart's Hospital, Penzance, Won 11-9

20 Nov, Camborne, Penzance, Won 9-6

4 Dec, St Ives, Penzance, Won 11-8

11 Dec, Redruth, Redruth, Lost 3-6

13 Dec, Oxford University Greyhounds, Penzance, Won 8-0

27 Dec, Truro, Truro, Won 9-0

1966

1 Jan, St Ives, Penzance, Drawn 6-6

8 Jan, Penryn, Penryn, Lost 6-11

29 Jan, Devonport Services, Penzance, Won 13-3

5 Feb, Falmouth, Falmouth, Drawn 0-0

12 Feb, Penryn, Penzance, Drawn 3-3

19 Feb, Camborne, Camborne, Won 13-0

12 Mar, Torquay Athletic, Penzance, Won 12-3

19 Mar, St Ives, St Ives, Lost 3-6

26 Mar, Redruth, Penzance, Won 17-11

29 Mar, Newquay Hornets, Newquay, Won 13-8

5 Apr 5, Truro, Penzance, Won 25-0

9 Apr 9, Saracens, Penzance, Lost 0-1

11 Apr, St Thomas Hospital, Penzance, Lost 6-9

12 Apr, St Mary's Hospital, Penzance, Lost 9-15

21 Apr, Redruth, Redruth, Drawn 3-3

23 Apr, Bridgwater & Albion, Penzance, Won 11-9

25 Apr, Gloucester, Penzance, Won 11-6

3 Sep, Old Crescent, Penzance, Won 9-5

8 Sep, Metropolitan Police, Penzance, Lost 0-6

10 Sep, Taunton, Penzance, Won 11-8

17 Sep, Rosslyn Park, Penzance, Lost 6-19

19 Sep, Esher, Penzance, Lost 3-6

8 Oct, Falmouth, Falmouth, Lost 5-12

15 Oct, Torquay Athletic, Penzance, Drawn 5-5

29 Oct, Bridgwater & Albion, Bridgwater, Won 17-11

5 Nov, Bart's Hospital, Penzance, Won 24-10

3 Dec, St Ives, Penzance, Won 11-3

10 Dec, Redruth, Redruth, Drawn 6-6

12 Dec, Oxford University Greyhounds, Penzance, Drawn 3-3

17 Dec, Hayle, Penzance, Lost 15-21

24 Dec, Redruth, Penzance, Won 22-12

26 Dec, Truro, Penzance, Won 18-6

31 Dec, St Ives, St Ives, Won 3-0

1967

7 Jan, Penryn, Penryn Lost 0-6

21 Jan, Truro, Truro, Won 19-3

28 Jan, Penryn, Penzance, Lost 0-11

11 Mar, Torquay Athletic, Torquay, Lost 6-12

15 Mar, Fleet Air Arm Penzance, Won 8-3

18 Mar, Camborne, Camborne, Lost 9-11

21 Mar, Carnegie College, Penzance, Lost 0-14

1 Apr, Falmouth, Penzance, Won 12-0

3 Apr, Cross Keys, Penzance, Won 6-5

8 Apr, Devonport Services, Devonport, Won 3-0

12 Apr, Redruth, Penzance, Won 25-5

15 Apr, Barnstaple, Penzance, Won 11-3

19 Apr, St Ives, St Ives, Drawn 12-12

22 Apr, Gloucester, Penzance, Drawn 3-3

24 Apr, Bridgwater & Albion, Penzance, Drawn 3-3

29 Apr, Hayle, Penzance, Lost 6-20

7 Sep, Metropolitan Police, Penzance, Lost 6-21

9 Sep, London Scottish, Penzance, Lost 3-23

23 Sep, Exeter, Penzance, Lost 0-34

5 Oct, Redruth, Redruth, Won 16-8

14 Oct, Torquay Athletic, Penzance, Won 11-3

18 Nov, Camborne, Penzance, Drawn 6-6

2 Dec, St Ives, Penzance, Won 8-3

16 Dec, Oxford University Greyhounds, Penzance, Won 3-0

23 Dec, Falmouth, Penzance, Won 9-3

26 Dec, Truro, Truro, Lost 3-10

30 Dec, Redruth, Redruth, Won 22-3

1968

6 Jan, Penryn, Penryn, Lost 6-19

13 Jan, Devonport Services, Penzance, Won 6-0

20 Jan, Truro, Penzance, Won 9-6

17 Feb, Hayle, Penzance, Won 14-6

24 Feb, Plymouth Albion, Penzance, Lost 0-6

2 Mar, Camborne, Camborne, Won 8-3

9 Mar, Torquay Athletic, Torquay, Won 26-5

16 Mar, St Ives, Penzance, Won 8-3

19 Mar, Launceston (Cup), Penzance

23 Mar, Penryn, Penryn, Lost 6-11

30 Mar, Redruth, Penzance, Won 17-3

6 Apr, Griffins, Penzance, Won 16-6

13 Apr, Saracens, Penzance, Lost 6-17

15 Apr, St Thomas Hospital, Penzance, Won 6-5

23 Apr, Tredegar, Penzance, Lost 11-20

27 Apr, Gloucester, Penzance, Drawn 6-6

29 Apr, Bridgwater & Albion, Penzance, Won 14-8

7 Sep, Trojans, Penzance, Won 6-3

12 Sep, Metropolitan Police, Penzance, Lost 12-17

16 Sep, London Scottish, Penzance, Lost 9-22

19 Sep, Rosslyn Park, Penzance, Lost 6-38

23 Sep, Esher Penzance, Drawn 8-8

16 Nov, Camborne, Penzance, Won 6-3

30 Nov, Plymouth Albion, Penzance, Drawn 3-3

7 Dec, St Ives, St Ives, Lost 6-9

14 Dec, Penryn, Penzance, Drawn 0-0

26 Dec, Truro, Penzance, Lost 9-11

1969

8 Feb, Falmouth, Falmouth, Drawn 3-3

29 Mar, Redruth, Penzance, Lost 3-6

1 Apr, St Paul's College, Penzance, Won 12-9

2 Apr, Carnegie College, Penzance, Lost 3-14

5 Apr, Wasps, Penzance, Lost 9-11

7 Apr, St Thomas Hospital Penzance, Won 11-9

8 Apr, St Mary's Hospital, Penzance, Lost 6-18

12 Apr, Exeter, Penzance, Won 11-9

15 Apr, Tredegar, Penzance, Lost 3-16

17 Apr, Redruth, Redruth Lost 6-14

25 Apr, Bridgwater & Albion, Penzance, Won 17-8

26 Apr, Gloucester, Penzance, Lost 3-38

1 Sep, Penryn, Penzance, Lost 6-8

13 Sep, London Scottish, Penzance, Lost 9-38

11 Oct, Torquay Athletic, Torquay Lost 5-9

1970

3 Jan, Penryn, Penzance, Lost 6-14

10 Jan, Hayle, Hayle, Lost 3-9

7 Feb, Penryn, Penryn, Lost 3-9

7 Mar, Camborne, Camborne, Lost 12-20

14 Mar, Redruth, Penzance, Won 11-0

4 Apr, King Alfred's College, Penzance, Won 15-12

11 Apr, Exeter, Exeter, Lost 5-27

13 Apr, Penryn (Cup), Penryn, Lost 6-13

16 Apr, St Ives, Penzance, Lost 14-16

18 Apr, Redruth, Penzance, Lost 9-16

12 Sep, Taunton, Penzance, Won 17-6

12 Nov, Cornwall Junior Group, Penzance, Won 36-6

21 Nov, Camborne, Penzance, Drawn 6-6

5 Dec, St Ives, St Ives, Lost 0-17

12 Dec, Falmouth, Penzance, Lost 6-8

14 Dec, Oxford University Greyhounds, Penzance, Won 19-14

26 Dec, Truro, Penzance, Drawn 6-6

1971

9 Jan, Trojans, Penzance, Won 16-3

16 Jan, Exeter, Exeter, Lost 3-45

30 Jan, Barnstaple, Penzance, Lost 6-8

1 Mar, Redruth (Cup), Redruth, Lost 0-12

19 Apr, King Alfred's College, Penzance, Won 21-5

24 Apr, Gloucester, Penzance, Lost 3-14

25 Sep, Newton Abbot, Penzance, Won 42-0

1972

5 Feb, Truro, Penzance, Won 19-7

19 Feb, Devonport Services, Devonport, Lost 10-14

11 Mar, Redruth, Penzance, Won 10-6

25 Mar, Penryn, Penryn, Lost 3-15

30 Mar 30, Penryn (Cup), Penzance, Lost 3-34

1 Apr, Saracens, Penzance, Lost 3-36

8 Apr, Torquay Athletic, Penzance, Won 18-9

16 Sep, Esher, Penzance, Won 16-10

4 Nov, Falmouth, Penzance, Won 7-6

8 Nov, Cornwall Junior Group, Penzance, Won 35-6

18 Nov, Camborne, Penzance, Won 11-3

2 Dec, St Ives, Penzance, Won 11-8

9 Dec, Falmouth, Falmouth, Lost 3-4

23 Dec, Redruth Albany, Penzance, Won 43-4

26 Dec, Truro, Penzance, Won 9-0

1973

3 Feb, Truro, Truro, Won 18-6

17 Feb, Devonport Services, Penzance, Won 16-4

7 Mar, Exeter University, Penzance, Won 37-3

3 Apr, Penryn, Penzance, Lost 12-18

7 Apr, Barnstaple, Penzance, Lost 9-18

21 Apr, Wasps, Penzance, Lost 9-12

24 Apr, St Mary's Hospital, Penzance, Won 23-13

28 Apr, Gloucester, Penzance, Lost 19-48

29 Sep, Redruth, Penzance, Won 4-0

13 Oct, Plymouth Albion, Penzance, Lost 6-7

1 Dec, St Ives, St Ives, Won 6-3

8 Dec, Hayle, Hayle, Won 25-12

22 Dec, Falmouth, Penzance, Lost 4-6

29 Dec, St Ives, Penzance, Won 10-0

1974

23 Feb, Penryn, Penryn, Lost 7-15

30 Mar, Exeter, Penzance, Lost 12-21

13 Apr, Saracens, Penzance, Lost 4-15

15 Apr, Chester, Penzance, Won 9-4

7 Sep, Redruth, Penzance, Won 9-6

14 Sep, St Ives, Penzance, Lost 3-25

23 Sep, Esher, Penzance, Drawn 6-6

25 Sep, Hayle (Cup), Penzance, Drawn 13-13

19 Oct, Hayle (Cup), Hayle, Won 10-7

2 Nov, St Ives, St Ives, Drawn 4-4

16 Nov, Camborne (Cup), Penzance, Won 16-15

30 Nov, Redruth, Redruth, Lost 4-17

3 Dec, Newquay Hornets, Penzance, Lost 0-10

14 Dec, Penryn, Penzance, Won 10-3

1975

1 Jan, Falmouth GSOB, Penzance, Won 19-7

11 Jan, Hayle, Hayle, Lost 9-14

8 Feb, Falmouth (Cup), Falmouth, Won 18-9

1 Mar, Camborne, Camborne, Won 11-3

19 Mar, Penryn (Cup F), Camborne,
  Lost 0-11

26 Apr, Hayle, Penzance, Won 15-6

28 Apr, Tredegar, Penzance, Lost 0-9

13 Sep, Oxford, Penzance, Lost 3-9

17 Sep, St Ives, St Ives, Lost 3-8

20 Sep, Esher, Penzance, Won 9-6

25 Sep, Falmouth (Cup), Penzance, Won 4-0

27 Sep, Newton Abbot, Penzance,
  Won 53-3

11 Oct, Hayle, Hayle, Lost 0-25

27 Oct, Truro, Penzance, Won 14-6

1 Nov, Penryn, Penryn, Lost 7-10

29 Nov, Falmouth, Falmouth, Lost 4-30

3 Dec, Newquay Hornets, Penzance,
  Won 25-3

6 Dec, Plymouth Albion, Plymouth,
  Lost 3-13

1976

3 Jan, Penryn (Cup), Penzance,
  Won 12-10

10 Jan, Hayle, Penzance, Lost 12-20

24 Jan, Taunton, Taunton, Won 11-0

7 Feb, Launceston, Penzance, Won 19-3

14 Feb, Hayle (Cup), Hayle Drawn 9-9

21 Feb, Devonport Services, Devonport,
  Won 19-3

28 Feb, Camborne, Camborne, Won 10-7

6 Mar, Hayle (Cup), Penzance,
  Won 19-10

10 Mar, St Ives, Penzance, Lost 6-17

13 Mar, Bridgwater & Albion Penzance,
  Won 29-6

20 Mar, Torquay Athletic, Penzance,
  Won 12-3

24 Mar, Redruth (Cup F), Camborne,
  Won 4-3

31 Mar, Penryn, Penryn, Lost 3-6

3 Apr, Barnstaple, Barnstaple, Drawn 6-6

5 Apr, Ebbw Vale, Penzance, Lost 16-21

10 Apr, Wolverhampton, Penzance,
  Won 17-13

12 Apr, Redruth, Penzance, Won 7-0

17 Apr, Saracens, Penzance, Lost 6-13

20 Apr, St Mary's Hospital, Penzance,
  Won 28-14

1 May, Gordon League (Cup), Penzance,
  Lost 9-10

2 Sep, Public School Wanderers,
  Penzance, Lost 0-22

4 Sep, Metropolitan Police, Penzance,
  Won 20-13

11 Sep, Brixham, Penzance, Lost 3-6

2 Oct, Falmouth, Penzance, Won 18-3

16 Oct, Hayle, Penzance, Lost 12-16

30 Oct, Torquay Athletic, Torquay,
  Lost 7-9

6 Nov, Redruth, Redruth, Won 7-0

17 Nov, Newquay Hornets, Penzance,
  Won 15-0

20 Nov, Camborne, Penzance, Drawn 9-9

11 Dec, Falmouth, Falmouth, Lost 9-18

18 Dec, Newquay Hornets, Newquay
  Won 21-3

27 Dec, Truro, Penzance, Won 17-6

28 Dec, St Ives, St Ives, Lost 7-11

1977

1 Jan, Penryn, Penzance, Won 9-6

7 Jan, Kansas City Jayhawks, Penzance,
  Won 19-10

8 Jan, Hayle, Hayle, Lost 3-4

22 Jan, Taunton, Penzance, Won 15-14

29 Jan, St Ives, St Ives, Lost 12-18

5 Feb, Truro, Truro, Won 10-3

12 Feb, Redruth, Penzance, Won 9-0

26 Feb, Camborne, Camborne,
  Won 9-6

5 Mar, Launceston, Launceston,
  Won 25-6

12 Mar, Brixham, Penzance, Won 4-0

19 Mar, Torquay Athletic, Penzance,
  Lost 0-9

26 Mar, St Austell, St Austell, Drawn 0-0

2 Apr, Barnstaple, Penzance, Won 14-8

9 Apr, Ipswich, Penzance, Lost 9-14

11 Apr, St Thomas Hospital, Penzance,
Won 30-9

12 Apr, St Mary's Hospital, Penzance,
Won 16-6

15 Apr, Ebbw Vale, Penzance, Lost 13-18

23 Apr, Plymouth Albion, Penzance,
Lost 4-15

28 Apr, Falmouth, Falmouth, Lost 0-14

3 Sep, Penryn, Penryn, Won 11-8

7 Sep, Redruth, Redruth, Lost 0-16

21 Sep, St Ives, St Ives, Lost 0-19

27 Sep, Falmouth, Penzance, Won 17-6

12 Oct, Liskeard-Looe, Penzance,
Won 44-3

15 Oct, Hayle, Hayle, Won 13-6

29 Oct, Torquay Athletic, Torquay,
Lost 6-42

5 Nov, Redruth, Redruth, Lost 15-21

12 Nov, Launceston, Launceston, Won 22-6

19 Nov, Camborne, Penzance, Lost 9-12

26 Nov, Newquay Hornets, Penzance,
Won 28-12

3 Dec, Brixham, Brixham, Won 15-13

10 Dec, St Austell, Penzance, Drawn 9-9

17 Dec, Falmouth, Falmouth, Lost 0-13

26 Dec, Truro, Penzance, Drawn 7-7

31 Dec, St Ives, St Ives, Lost 0-34

1978

2 Jan, Redruth (Cup), Penzance, Lost 6-14

14 Jan, Hayle, Penzance, Lost 7-16

19 Jan, St Ives, St Ives, Won 4-0,

21 Jan, Newquay Hornets, Newquay,
Won 18-0

28 Jan, Taunton, Torquay, Lost 0-12

25 Feb, Camborne, Camborne, Lost 12-16

4 Mar, Brixham, Penzance, Lost 10-12

8 Mar, Launceston, Penzance, Won 18-6

11 Mar, St.Austell, St.Austell, Won 6-3

18 Mar, Torquay Athletic, Penzance,
Lost 3-9

25 Mar, Saracens, Penzance, Lost 3-21

1 Apr, Barnstaple, Barnstaple, Lost 9-20

10 Apr, Redruth, Penzance, Lost 4-26

11 Nov, Launceston, Launceston,
Won 19-11

9 Dec, St Austell, St Austell, Drawn 0-0

16 Dec, Falmouth, Falmouth, Lost 3-6

26 Dec, Truro, Penzance, Won 13-6

30 Dec, St Ives, Penzance, Won 3-0

1979

13 Jan, Plymouth Albion, Penzance,
Lost 3-14

20 Jan, Launceston, Penzance, Lost 7-10

24 Feb, Camborne, Camborne, Lost 6-22

3 Mar, London, New Zealanders
London, Lost 0-70

10 Mar, Hayle, Hayle, Drawn 3-3

17 Mar, Torquay Athletic, Torquay,
Lost 3-16

21 Mar, St Ives (Cup), St Ives, Lost 0-7

31 Mar, St Austell, Penzance, Lost 3-6

4 Apr, Falmouth, Penzance, Won 10-4

14 Apr, Wasps, Penzance, Lost 4-29

1982

20 Feb, Redruth, Penzance, Won 22-6

6 Mar, Newquay Hornets, Newquay,
Won 16-9

13 Mar, Hayle, Hayle, Won 19-3

27 Mar, Truro, Penzance, Won 6-3

10 Apr, Old Haberdashers, Penzance,
Won 26-9

12 Apr, Maidstone, Penzance, Won 15-13

1986

9 Mar, President's XV, Penzance,
Lost 14-30